D1320590

THE INNOVATORS

By the same authors

GLOBAL STAKES

THE
INNOVATORS
Rediscovering America's Creative Energy

James Botkin
Dan Dimancescu
Ray Stata

1817

HARPER & ROW, PUBLISHERS, New York
Cambridge, Philadelphia, San Francisco,
London, Mexico City, São Paulo, Singapore, Sydney

Grateful acknowledgment is made for permission to reprint "The Declining Middle" by Bob Kuttner, which originally appeared in *The Atlantic Monthly,* July 1983. Reprinted by permission of *The Atlantic Monthly* and the author.

THE INNOVATORS. Copyright © 1984 by James Botkin, Dan Dimancescu, and Ray Stata. All rights reserved. Printed in the United States of America. No part of this book may be used or reproduced in any manner whatsoever without written permission except in the case of brief quotations embodied in critical articles and reviews. For information address Harper & Row, Publishers, Inc., 10 East 53rd Street, New York, N.Y. 10022. Published simultaneously in Canada by Fitzhenry & Whiteside Limited, Toronto.

FIRST EDITION

Designer: C. Linda Dingler

Library of Congress Cataloging in Publication Data
Botkin, James W.
  The innovators.
  Includes bibliographical references and index.
  1. Technological innovations—United States. 2. High
technology—United States. 3. Technology and state—
United States. I. Dimancescu, Dan. II. Stata, Ray.
III. Title.
T1738.B68   1984   338.973   83-48783
ISBN 0-06-015285-0

84 85 86 87 88 10 9 8 7 6 5 4 3 2 1

Contents

Preface

A few guideposts may help the reader through this book. In the course of looking at innovation in America, we discovered that the stereotype of the innovator as inventor is far too limiting. Innovators not only make new products, but equally if not more importantly, they create new production processes and new management styles. They revamp organizations, devise novel policies, and reshape our government and educational systems.

What we present in the pages that follow is not a new theory of innovation. Rather we describe a picture of an emerging America which we have observed in our travels and investigations into businesses here and abroad, and the technological and educational issues that are affecting their performance. We portray this picture through case studies. In chapters 2, 4, and 5, we describe three American companies undergoing rapid transformation. In chapters 8, 9, and 10 we profile three states—Massachusetts, Michigan, and Mississippi—each in a vastly different stage of economic transition. We also describe several educational institutions, especially Carnegie-Mellon University and Worcester Polytechnic Institute, as well as others, in chapter 14.

Internationally, we devote two chapters to Asia because that's where the action is. Europe is being left in the dust of the race between America and Japan *cum* South Korea, Singapore, Hong Kong, Taiwan, and others. In chapters 6 and 7, we talk about American employment prospects, which we think can be bright. We do not, however, deal with job problems in Europe, where the going is far rougher, nor in the bulk of the Third World, where the outlook is so bad that only a concerted effort beyond anything presently conceived can save the situation from deteriorating further.

Readers will find the outlines of our views about America's future described in chapter 1, so it may be helpful to follow the convention of starting at the beginning. It may not be so helpful if, on finishing chapter 1, you do what many people pressed for time do, which is to skip to the conclusions in chapter 16. It may not be obvious how we can start with the economy and conclude with education and proposals for "centers of technological excellence."

But in between, chapters 2 through 15 can be read in almost any order. Each one presents a different perspective on innovation in America, and no one of them is a prerequisite to understanding any other. One critical point, however, is in chapter 3 where we show why computers and their associated electronics are not really "high" technology but "new" technology. The real value of the so-called "high tech" industries is as the new tool makers whose products can revitalize old industries. Throughout the chapters, this central theme will become obvious—that the real action is not just in "high tech" but in the absorption of new technologies into basic industries. Once readers grasp this otherwise rather obvious notion, we think that a whole series of propositions will follow that are neither obvious nor included in present policy. See if you don't agree with us that they should be widely discussed by political office holders and seekers, by business and union leaders, by the country's educators, and by the informed public at large.

Introduction

Early in 1984, we attended a long-awaited media event. On this occasion the fanfare heralded the introduction of Apple's latest innovation, the Macintosh personal computer. Excitement was in the air. Would the underdog bounce back from the mat and return to win the next round? Apple's rivalry with IBM led a business associate sitting with us to hold forth on the virtues of innovation and how "only in America" would one witness such creativity in the marketplace. "From a garage operation to this," he went on, "it couldn't happen anywhere else." His words were cut off by a Parisian colleague, who in no uncertain terms interjected sharply and correctly that the first personal computer had been introduced by an entrepreneur in France in 1973, a full three years ahead of Apple. "That's all well and good," our business associate fired back, "but what good did it do him?" The point was right on. Other countries think big, but Americans deliver.

Something else, however, teased us. The main advertisement for the Mac showed a close-up of the computer screen with the head of a lovely black-haired woman drawn in high-resolution graphics. The surprise was not the exceptional quality of the drawing but the fact that the image depicted a Japanese face. The intent seemed unmistakable. Apple, as American as apple pie, had a product that the Japanese would drool over. This realization, a detail at the time, caused our business associate to modify his words. "Don't feel too badly," he said to the Frenchman sardonically, "only in America do we put the Japanese onto our newest innovations!"

In truth, of course, Steve Jobs and his Apple engineers personify a deeply ingrained American trait that starts with tinkering and results in marketable products. "What we did," says Jobs about the Macintosh, "is go back to our roots of taking great technology and great ideas and figure out how to be clever and pull them down into a mainstream product."[1]

Americans are convinced they're innovative—probably the most innovative people in the world. But that should not blind us to the fact that others are becoming equally adept. A reminder was an article we saw while looking back through an old Japanese business journal: "Car Exports Reach New High," said the headline.[2] Nothing new about that—except that the issue was dated *1962!* "Little" Japan was proudly announcing that 7,781 cars had been exported during the first six months of that year. Of these, a grand total of 1,321 came to the United States. One company, Aichi Machinery, declared its six-month export rate of *one* car. Twenty years later, "little" Japan produced more cars than all of America's domestic producers combined—almost four million more! It had learned to practice the fine art of innovation.

Innovation is a concept as old as time. What does change, though, are the innovators: who they are and where they apply their energies. In America at the present moment, prodded in part by individual desire and in part by competitive pressures, they are active. One result is that change is sweeping through America's old and new industries. Much of it is induced by the rapid evolution of electronic technologies, though this is accompanied by significant changes in management styles and social attitudes as well. Much of it comes, too, from a marketplace that is no longer confined to national borders. The setting is truly global and adjustments must be made to new rules of the economic game.

Pressures come also as new social values confront old institutions. Most Americans are too young to remember the Depression of the 1930s. Only those sixty or older remember it vividly.

Yet its ghost still haunts our economy, and the specter of unemployment looms large in our thinking. So too the second World War. Its aftermath of heavy armaments and military spending has remained and increased, yet less than 30 percent of today's population has direct knowledge of why this is so. And if you're under twenty—like the majority of the world's population—the Eisenhower and Kennedy years of economic growth and undisputed American industrial superiority predate your birth. The result is that younger people's attitudes toward jobs, national security, and international competition are founded on different assumptions and expectations. What worked for the "man in the gray flannel suit" or the union leader with scarred personal memories of battle lines outside U.S. factories no longer holds. As a result, institutions and policies molded decades or generations ago are being forced to adapt.

What brings all this to a critical point in American life is that for the first time in our recent history there is a nagging sense that we have lost our momentum. The Japanese challenge makes this uneasiness tangible. It reminds us, again and again, that we are not best in many areas where we had assumed ourselves unbeatable. Memories of Vietnam and Cambodia remind us, also, that we can blunder extravagantly and tragically in dealing with social and political forces which we do not understand and are not prepared or equipped to influence. The V-8 gas-guzzler and the oil crisis remind us that an economy built on a belief in an infinite energy supply must now be rebuilt on a recognition of finite resources.

Today's innovators are those who understand not only the new constraints affecting us but especially the new opportunities that beckon. Whether production-line or office workers, corporate presidents, governors, or university leaders, they are redirecting their energies to what they hope will be a new generation of prosperity and justice. Success, they understand, will come only to the extent that the new constraints are understood and overcome.

Awareness of an awakening of America's creative energy comes at a time when national policymakers are pondering the merits of various proposals for an "industrial policy." There are many able proponents—Lester Thurow of MIT (Massachusetts Institute of Technology), Robert Reich of Harvard University, Felix Rohatyn in New York City among others.[3] While many people concur with them that through defense programs, import quotas, and tax and other subsidies the United States in fact already has an industrial policy, most Americans question the wisdom of making this explicit because they doubt the ability of federal bureaucracies to improve private-sector development in a global marketplace. They realize that the type of industrial policy attributed to Japan will not work in America. "Industrial policy! those are fightin' words," said one executive we met, and his words reflect the sentiments of many Americans—workers and managers alike. We share this concern, and while we will not burden readers with detailed critiques of present industrial policy proposals, we will offer an alternative course of action that is appropriate to American history and tradition.

America is not alone with its economic problems. In Europe, countries like West Germany, France, and England are struggling to formulate their own versions of government-inspired economic revitalization efforts, but their current short-term prospects are not bright. In 1982, the Common Market countries showed a combined balance-of-payments deficit of $10 billion, whereas seven years earlier they were in balance. In West Germany, the Ruhr steel industries are dying, unemployment rates are 20 percent or higher in textile regions, and much of the electronics is imported. In France, striking steel workers took to the streets to protest massive cutbacks in the steel industry by the French socialist government. "For the first time since the 18th century, the major formative initiatives of an industrial revolution aren't originating in Europe," commented a noted European economist, Michel Alpert. "Europe is in the course of missing out on the third industrial revolution."[4]

Even while we write, plant closings and personal hardships from dying industries are making news in America. At Christmas time in 1983 the United States Steel Corporation announced the closing of three major plants in Chicago, Cleveland, and Johnstown, Pennsylvania, eliminating 15,000 smokestack jobs. Such events reinforce the belief in the inevitable death of the old. In spring of 1984, old strains between management and labor broke out, this time drawing in government policymakers. Extraordinary bonuses paid to top auto executives threatened to open old wounds and retard painstaking progress that had been made in healing troubled relations between autoworkers and management. Events like these reinforce a widespread belief that such basic American industries as auto manufacturing are incapable of shedding old prejudices and rejuvenating themselves for today's competition. The ultimate outcome of the bonus controversy will not be known for some time, but it may eventually force the auto companies to become even more competitive, especially if Washington's trade negotiator, William Brock, carries through with his threat to eliminate quotas on Japanese auto imports.

Another trouble in this big picture of future economic development is the question of ballooning federal deficits caused by a costly weapons agenda and entitlements programs growing out of control. Their existence and escalation belie all the positive rhetoric that brought Republican conservatism into power and threaten to destabilize both the American and world economies.

It is in this context that we felt it important to rethink some of the basic forces at work in our economic future. In our view, the most significant positive trends seem to be emerging not in Washington policy debates, where spending is synonymous with defense, but in the cumulative "bottom-up" impact of several converging factors: the emergence and growth of new industries based on "high" technologies, the accelerating absorption of these technologies into mature economic environments, the recognition that new management philosophies are required for companies to survive in global marketplaces, and a realization that education is taking on strategic importance in the national economy. What is most encouraging is that these trends are being paced by a whole array of innovators—workers as much as managers, academic figures as often as political leaders.

We believe that one of the most visible points where these people and their institutions intersect is in a growing array of "centers of technological innovation"—groupings of companies, universities, and government institutions focused on creating and transferring new knowledge into the economic mainstream. Most of these are largely unknown to the general public. They are places of partnership between universities, industries, and government. They are contemporary manifestations of a truly unique American trait: our creativity and innovative spirit—something we once called "Yankee ingenuity." The net effect is a new source of inspiration and leadership that bodes well for America's future.

1

American Realities

Something new is happening in America. One can see it in the recycled old mill buildings of New England, or in Texan enthusiasm for microelectronic research, or in Detroit's newly equipped auto production lines. A spirit of economic optimism is displacing once-fashionable gloom as many bellwether companies revitalize themselves with the new technological tools of the 1980s. This reality doesn't match another view of the economy that many people still hold. The supposed need to pick winners and losers, the belief that "old" industries should die, proposals that the federal government should orchestrate this process—these ideas do not account for profound changes now taking place. Much of the talk about sunrise versus sunset industries, dying smokestack versus booming high-technology firms, and the need for a national industrial policy is obsolete.

A new reality has taken root. It is outpacing our thinking by making ideas that were novel only yesterday appear old today. But what is more surprising is that much of what we thought was outmoded is rebounding with new-found vigor. Our past holds some unique assets for our future. This dawned on us while traveling between Asia and the United States, contemplating Japan's rapid ascent to technological and economic prominence. In particular, one visit to Nara, Japan's ancient capital, was telling.

The sun was just setting over Yakushiji Temple. Tourists, Japanese and foreign, had left for the day, allowing a calm to return. Quietly a centuries-old past reappeared in the small city's parks and streets. We had been invited on this particular evening for dinner by the director of the research labs of one of Japan's leading electronics firms. Our legs were aching—not just because we were Americans sitting cross-legged at a traditional Japanese dinner—but also because we had spent the entire day walking through a seemingly endless display of new electronics products that had emanated from the company's research labs. The display had been impressive: rooms filled with pocket computers, solar cells, home laser sensors, even machines to translate Japanese into English. And all of these had come from highly automated "laboratory factories." It had been the type of day calculated to scare the wits out of any Americans who, like us, were concerned with Japanese competitiveness.

"Creativity," our dinner host said, "is our number-one priority." His company's business creed reflected it: *sincerity and creativity*. We received a graciously delivered lecture on the importance of both. "That's why we moved to Nara," our host continued, "an ancient city with old Buddhist traditions. We believed that positioning a modern electronics lab next to Yakushiji and other ancient temples would stimulate the maximum of innovation in our researchers." If the display rooms told an accurate story, it looked like he was on the right path.

The next day, however, brought a different story. We met with the seven vice-directors of the Nara labs. Creativity was again the subject. Not its benefits, but the problem of stimulating it. "We're getting too many old engineers," said the second in command. "We're becoming top-heavy with middle-aged middle management. Also, in Japan we have a random assignment system where an innovative person must take a routine job rather than a creative one." While there was a lot of discussion about the need for creativity, there was even more talk about the obstacles to achieving it in Japan. Indeed, they seemed to face a critical crossroads.

Some months later back in America, we found ourselves in Connecticut on our way to the world headquarters of a large but lesser-known U.S. conglomerate. This company manufactures some of the oldest products still around, products whose heyday was the century starting in the mid-1860s, just after the Civil War. These include locks, bottle-making machinery, shoemaking machinery and parts, and other assorted industrial and consumer goods. The common feature of this company's still-profitable product line is incredibly long life cycles. Locks are still made on the same tumbler principle developed in 1869. The shoemaking machinery was invented by the company in 1902. And until recently, their glass-blowing bottle machine looked like the mechanical contraptions in the 1936 Charlie Chaplin film, *Modern Times.*

"If there was ever a staid old American company about to succumb to the Japanese, Koreans, or Taiwanese, this must be it." So we thought as we arrived with our stream of questions about creativity and change. We were wrong. From afar, we had easily concluded, as many others still mistakenly do, that old industries like this one are languishing in America. From within, we discovered just the opposite. Here was a very successful company taking deliberate steps to remain so by transforming itself. New technologies, new management ideas, and new attitudes toward work prevailed. This would have been hard to guess from the firm's president, who said in an understated New England manner: "Well, we thought we ought to brush the rust off the company a bit." To experience what he meant by this, we visited several of the company's operations.

Brush the rust off? A full-scale metamorphosis was in the making. Top management was committed to introduce an array of new technologies to its products and its production lines. Giant pneumatic bottle-making machines were being completely transformed by solid-state electronic devices. Innovative computer-controlled sewing machines were helping shoemakers bring the stitching of cowboy boots back from Mexico to the American Northeast. This place was alive with change. As our investigation continued, we came to appreciate some of the realities of incorporating new technologies into an old-tech environment. Like many Americans, we had assumed that new technology would mean robots taking over the factory production line. That's not the way it was in this company, nor does it help our thinking to perpetuate this misconception about what technological change means to America's older industries. In later chapters we describe what we believe is happening as old, supposedly "sunset" industries wake up to new futures.

This company, like others we saw, has a straightforward approach to change. They simply do it, without all the public relations or the fancy display rooms. Like most Americans, we had been so bombarded with opinions about what's wrong with American industry that we were not prepared to discover a new surge of creative energy where least expected. Who would have thought that bottles, shoes, and locks could reemerge as an attractive growth industry in the 1980s? The conventional wisdom about sunrise and sunset industries and about smokestack versus high-technology firms may not be so wise after all.

The contrast between the sense of confidence in this American firm's resilience and the sense of doubt in the Japanese company's creative capacity signals something new for the 1980s. Both nations may have reached plateaus—one at a low point (the United States), the other at a high point (Japan). When we started our research for this book, this view of a reversing competitive posture did not strike us as realistic. Today it does.

We have spent the past several years on something of an exploratory quest. We examined the spectacular and new in electronics, computers, and other sectors grouped under the catchall label "high tech." We looked closely at the companies that make these products. We looked, also, at the much larger and growing number of companies that use them in their production lines—for instance, robots in welding shops or videodisc-based computer training for insurance agents. In the United States we met not just with corporate managers and workers but with university presidents, deans, and students, with government leaders and officials—both state and federal. We traveled to Europe, to Japan, and to the newly industrializing countries of booming East Asia—most notably Korea and Singapore—to get a firsthand view of the changes in the world economy.

The challenges are formidable. Not only are advanced technologies fundamentally altering the global economy, but they have touched off a redefinition of international comparative advantage. That is, what in the past made the United States strong—natural resources, large but inflexible mass-production systems, and the pressure cooker of quarterly profit statements— no longer provides the competitive edge. What makes East Asia, with or without Japan, the fastest-growing region in the world today is not cheap labor as was once the case but highly skilled human resources, flexible, often automated, manufacturing capacity, and longer-term perspectives.

A number of Asian countries, foremost among them Japan, achieved this new advantage by *targeting*. This means that the government, working hand in hand with industry, identifies certain industries, like semiconductors, and embarks on a strategy of subtle and not-so-subtle subsidies to enable them to dominate a particular slice of the world market. Despite its apparent failure in Europe, the Asian formula for success has spawned a rash of American proposals for an *industrial policy* based on one or another form of targeting. For reasons we will describe, we think the targeting idea will be obsolete by the time Congress can act on it. Yet many people who would agree with this go to another extreme. Those who reject industrial policy as a veil for an intrusive system of targeting often find themselves merely defending the magic of market forces. This "business as usual" view amounts to no more than muddling through in the hope that, as the 1981–82 recession eases and as the energy crisis temporarily subsides, things will simply, magically, "return to normal." We are convinced that this view is as mistaken and unworkable as a "pick the winners" industrial policy.

We offer a simple proposition. America's competitive advantage in the 1980s, 1990s, and beyond will be its capacity to innovate. This is embodied in our history, traditions, and people. It is a spirit ingrained into our national psyche by our very institutions. What America needs now is to rediscover how and why the innovative spirit has worked for us so well in the past and what changes will be required to keep it working in the future. The major caveat is that no one, not even the powerful in Washington, can simply legislate competitive advantage tied to marketplace innovation. Rather, it requires the *collective genius*—the words of an automotive worker we met in Detroit—of business, labor, education, and government exercised in a setting that supports and encourages it. If properly inspired and supported, Americans can tap that genius in the 1980s and 1990s.

From our travels and interviews comes a warning. While the instinct for innovation remains alive and well in America, a host of determined and able economic competitors are trying to outdo us on this important score. They are focusing their own creative energies on technologies, knowledge, and markets once considered home turf to American companies, laboratories, and universities. One of our purposes, therefore, is to show why the business of innovation in both old and new firms, in universities, colleges, schools, and government institutions, should be a top national priority. That's the short of it.

The long of it is more complex. It's not just that the game is being played more competitively, it's that the ground rules are changing. Our country is undergoing a major transition from a labor-based manufacturing, natural-resource economy to one built on technology-based manufacturing, skilled human resources, and an incredible variety of services—some labor-intensive, some automated. The dynamic is not that agriculture, basic industry, or manufacturing will disappear—nor can they be allowed to. It's that the driving force for change will now and increasingly come from new technologies. This does not mean, however, that they are a panacea for the future. Serious questions will have to be resolved concerning jobs and retraining on the one hand and, on the other, concerning the flow of knowledge to revitalize older industries and to stimulate the productivity of the emerging services.

It would be a mistake to believe that this revitalization process is an isolated event or a temporary fad. Rather, it is rooted in economic theory and industrial trends which indicate that we are on the verge of a major new wave of economic development. Joseph Schumpeter, an Austrian economist whose views are coming into vogue to challenge those of Keynes, called this kind of period one of "creative destruction." Schumpeter's picture of how an economy moves from old to new provides powerful insights into some of our contemporary problems of declining productivity, maturing industries, and escalating joblessness. His work lends support to a view of the economy being influenced by what are termed "long waves."

This long-wave theory and its implications intrigued us. Living under the aura of Boston's famed Route 128—"America's Technology Highway," claims a new road sign proudly—we had witnessed firsthand what appears to be the beginning of a new wave. To check our perceptions, we met with some of the country's leading theorists on long-term economic cycles. What we discovered was what you might expect from experts—a lot of disagreement. But on one point almost everyone agrees. We are in a transition period and there's no going back. As Jay Forrester, professor of management at MIT, said: "The 1980s are a bit like the 1930–45 period when it was clear things would be different, but it was not clear in what way."

Periods of transformation typically present the half-empty, half-full dilemma. People who focus on the declining old wave are pessimistic and concerned about loss of jobs. Those who see the rise of the new wave are optimistic, often to the point of euphoria. Our work suggests something different—that the rising wave of technology provides new tools to extend the life of old industries as well as to foster the beginning of new ones. The future holds neither dramatic collapse—unless we stand still—nor a high-technology heaven. What we seek in this book is to redefine the role of something called "high technology" in our economy and show how it can be used in old and new manufacturing and service industries to improve our future.

Critical to this discussion is the emotionally charged hue and cry about jobs. For some, the chief problem is the quantity of jobs and the problem of rising unemployment. Ever since the Bureau of Labor Statistics published its 1982 forecasts that nearly doubled estimates of job openings at the lowest skill levels—a projection subject to serious misinterpretation—public concern about the assumed disappearance of well-paid jobs has risen dramatically. Are we inadvertently creating a dual economy, as some claim, with a few high-paying interesting jobs that enhance human skill and a much larger number of low-paying monotonous jobs that detract from it? This could indeed be the case only if we do not learn from history and if we fail to apply new technological tools with an enlightened understanding of human capacities and values.

The most troubling part of the jobs issue is a widespread tendency to make hard and fast policy decisions based on soft and fast-changing forecasts. The wild fluctuations in the arcane art of job forecasting led us to spend time with manpower experts and with baffling official and unofficial labor statistics. We've watched harried policymakers in industry and education try to derive long-term policies from this or that projection. We've seen commissions formed to create, save, protect, and restructure jobs.

We've come to conclude that a strategy focused on unemployment cannot be successful in the long run—as politically expedient as it may be in the short run. Pressure will always exist for the immediate political payoff. "So many jobs were created this year" may be golden words to a politician on the campaign trail, but it does not help build long-term solutions. We think some straight talk about employment is in order, and we'll try to provide it. As long as we remain uncompetitive in world markets, virtually no job is secure, high-tech or otherwise. It is equally true that if jobs are deskilled to produce uncreative, dissatisfied, and unmotivated workers, we will become even more uncompetitive than we already are.

The worldview of many Americans is still influenced by the Depression. Unemployment is more dreaded than the plague, and until recently government policy has focused on reducing this statistic at almost any cost. But in reality, the late 1980s and the 1990s will be characterized by a labor shortage as post-baby-boom demographic downturns mature. This will be measured not so much in numbers of workers as in terms of skilled, qualified, educated, and productive workers. We must begin to shift our focus to the quality of employment—not the quantity of unemployment—and how to enhance the job system at a time when the number of entry-level workers will shrink by as much as 20 or 30 percent.

The numbers suggest that the transition we are entering is massive. Literally everyone will be affected. Retraining and education will be at a premium. Corporations and their new educational institutes will be as active as schools, colleges, and universities in fulfilling educational objectives. The quicker we can effect the transition, the less pain and cost there will be. What the options are, and what ideas exist to help the most severely affected, are part of our story.

We suggest a new course for America: a far-reaching national strategy that embraces and encourages the innovation process. We will illustrate what we mean by this with policy recommendations that deal with sectors not normally considered "strategic" by Americans. Chief among these is education. We see a new role emerging for institutions of higher education not only as partners in future economic growth but as leaders in a new generation of American life. From our previous research into the future of high technology in America, we are convinced of the need to link new educational priorities to national economic strategy. The rate of reeducating the work force and reequipping our factories and offices sets the upper limit on the diffusion of new technology throughout our economy. It takes decades to replace the old capital stock of an industry with equipment embodying the new technology. It may take even longer to replace old textbooks and update university faculties.

Another strategic area is research and development. America needs to reexamine what type of basic research we do and why its results are often more quickly utilized abroad than at home. We also question our research-and-development (R&D) priorities. Presently our national R&D agenda is heavy on defense and health to the detriment of funding for industrial innovation for economic development. While the United States may be tops in theoretical computer sciences, due largely to the Defense Advanced Research Projects Agency (DARPA), we are no longer the undisputed leader in the manufacture or marketing of computer chips. Even where our universities are ahead, we need to accelerate the rates at which we can transfer knowledge from academia to the marketplace.

Another important consideration is the cost of capital. When interest rates are too high compared with those in other countries, innovation suffers and we are at a serious competitive disadvantage. The higher the cost of capital, the shorter a manager's vision. Investments in productivity-enhancing capital equipment and in risky research projects will go unfunded when the cost of funds becomes excessive. It is no accident that during the 1970s, the United States had the lowest rate of capital investment of any major industrialized nation—only one-third that of Japan and about one-half that in West Germany and France. We argue that a principal responsibility of government is to manage the cost of capital relative to that in competing countries and to influence the allocation of capital between consumption and investment by incentives which encourage entrepreneurial risk-taking by both individuals and corporations. In this regard, restraint in public borrowing—measured in massive and growing federal deficits—is of fundamental concern. As a legacy of one administration to another, it presents highly disruptive and damaging prospects.

But the real challenge lies one step further—where do we look for leadership? To listen to most commentators, the federal government should somehow be accountable for success or failure. While Washington does have a crucial leadership role to play, this will be effective only to the extent that other players—educators, business leaders, state politicians, and labor leaders—understand and accept their responsibilities and roles in making the system work better. Much of the burden will fall on those who manage our industrial enterprise, and for a simple reason. No industrial policy or national strategy formulated in Washington will be successful without their participation. This means changes in their styles of managing a highly skilled professional work force, in their relations with labor, in the corporate culture itself, and in their perception of how best to use new technological tools. For most firms, the time of the old adversarial top-down management is over. The quicker we get to a new spirit of participation the better. The sooner we come to recognize and draw on the rich human potential that resides untapped in our workers and managers the sooner we will become a strong and vital economy. New management styles will be required if we are to progress, and we will report how these are in evidence.

We shall say little about correcting unfair trade practices of others or the strident calls for protectionist policies as solutions to our own problems. That is not to say that our government does not play a vital role in assuring open and fair trade. Rather we believe that for the present the problems we face and the solutions we seek have more to do with ourselves than with the actions of others. "We have met the enemy and it is us," goes the familiar saying. It is what we do as well as what we don't do that will make the most significant difference. Worthy competitors should spur us on, but they are less the cause and more the mirror of our problems. Fighting them by raising tariff walls and other artificial barriers only postpones the solution.

The competitive challenge before us is to lead in the process of renewal—in knowledge, in technology, in capital stock, and in management. This is the comparative advantage which can keep us in front of other nations. At the same time, we have to face a critical question of national priorities—the fundamental conflict between military security and industrial development. We cannot successfully compete with Japan while almost single-handedly providing a security blanket for much of the world. A clearer threat than Soviet missiles is the present danger of rising interest rates, a spiraling interest burden on national debt, and potential defaults on Third World loans and the consequent crisis in the banking system. Yet despite the warnings, the President still refuses to accept that a choice is inevitable between more defense expenditures and greater economic competitiveness. It is not our intention to offer a comprehensive solution to the difficult and complex situation in which the United States now finds itself. Our goal is rather to focus the national policy debate and to raise public awareness of the choices ahead as we see them. By doing so, we hope to contribute toward competitive strategies for a new era of prosperity.

Our first step in writing this book was to go directly to where past problems seemed most dramatic and where new opportunities had the greatest obstacles to overcome: the auto industry in Detroit. What we found offered a new perspective on the rewards and difficulties facing a resurgent American economy in the years ahead.

2

Transformation

In 1973, when Lee A. Iacocca was asked about the competitive advantage of innovation as perceived by Ford, he responded simply, "Give them [American consumers] leather. They can smell it." In Ford's reading of the U.S. market innovation did not pay, styling did. Things are quite different today: technology matters.
> —Abernathy, Clark & Kantrow in *Harvard Business Review*, September/October 1981

The smokestack reference should be banished from our vocabulary as being bad for the health of thinking people and confusing to the public. The industrial revolution which is transforming the U.S. automobile is essentially a high-tech, space-age revolution. . . . We are in an "autotech" industry, not merely automotive.
> —Philip Caldwell, Chairman, Ford Motor Company, *Industry Week*, October 3, 1983

The union has always felt that the hourly employee knew more about making his or her particular part than anyone else. If allowed a voice, that employee who made the part day in and day out could make it better and more economically.
> —Ed Cole, UAW Committeeman interviewed at a Ford Motor Company Plant in Ypsilanti, Michigan

American attention is turning again to Detroit, this time with hope—the hope that a success story is in the making. After years of devastating competition from Japan, the auto companies are rebuilding. It is appropriate to look at this industry as a true test of our adaptability as a society to new consumption standards, to foreign competition, to new technology, and to new production philosophies. Win here and we can win against any economic competitor in the decades ahead.

But winning in Detroit is no easy proposition. It is a bit like asking an American football team to suddenly become proficient in soccer. All the ground rules must change—including attitudes about how best to coach and how best to play. Survival instincts may be forcing a change, but so too are new technologies. This is a huge proposition when one considers that General Motors has 657,000 employees worldwide and Ford more than 375,000. For the automobile industry this means new concepts of management and worker relations on the one hand and learning to tap opportunities brought on by high technology on the other. Of the two, it is the worker who may hold the key to the success or failure of absorbing technology. Without the hourly worker there is no production line—no matter how much high technology is built into it or how many new robots complete their mindless tasks. Thus any solution to the auto industry's competitive dilemma must first consider the human element, the worker "on the line."

At first impression, Ford's Rawsonville plant is like most others involved in the manufacture of basic industrial components. It is one of seventeen assembly and fifty-six manufacturing Ford plants in the United States. Thirty minutes west of Dearborn in Ypsilanti, it had at one time 5,500 people making carburetors, electrical parts, and various other auto components. Employment plunged to 1,900 in the early 1980s. It is now back up to 2,600.

When one looks at Rawsonville, by all appearances one is looking at old industrial America. The space is cavernous—1.6 million square feet, an area equivalent to the floor space of a sixty-story office building. Furnaces melt raw metal; dies shape it; machine tools finish the die casts; and assembly lines turn small and large parts into finished components. Some are as unassuming as windshield-wiper motors, which roll off a semiautomated line at a fast clip. Others are a new generation of electronic fuel-injector systems—devices that control gasoline flow—destined for Escort, Lynx, T-Bird, and Cougar engines. Yet Rawsonville is rapidly becoming Ford's showcase experiment of enlightened relations between management and labor.

"Management used to be authoritarian," said Harper Brock, a United Automobile Workers committeeman. "You were told what to do and you had no right to question it. It was the supervisor on the line who gave you instructions." Sitting at a long table in the plant's conference room, he was the first to speak among a group of twelve workers.* They shared views about work at Ford a few years before. "That's right," pitched in Brenda Lanier, a line worker making electric motors. "After so long being told what to do, employees would just let the line run. People became complacent. All you wanted was to get the paycheck on Friday. I worked on a line making a three-brush machine. It had three brass plates. Many times the brass plate wasn't right but you just went on with it. After a while you're not affected anymore."

For many, working at Ford's Rawsonville plant as an "hourly" in 1983 was not the way it used to be just a few years before. Employees recalled an environment in which many management signals and demands encouraged poor performance and inferior standards of work. Their words dramatized the reasons why Japan was able to make such rapid inroads into the once-impenetrable American auto market. One was the Japanese worker's involvement in quality control, something American management had overlooked after two generations of clipboard-monitored Taylorism. The worker in America was rarely, if ever, seen as a participant in the design of a product, the definition of a task, or the refinement of a production line.

When Frederick Taylor invented a new management system in the early 1900s, a boom in productivity improvements ensued that lasted almost half a century. Labeled by him as "scientific management," his philosophy eventually permeated industrial America. Taylor's ideas evolved rapidly and eventually reduced jobs to minute and mindless tasks. When such efficiency was pushed to extremes, the employee's interests were forgotten. Henry Ford carried the principle to its limits: "The man who puts

*Interview August 26, 1983, with: Ed Cole; Harper Brock; Ray White; Danny Simpson; Denny Royal; Bob Richardson; Marie Payne; C. Thomas Maupin; Jay Palamar; Thomas Hyatt; Brenda Lanier; Helen Teall.

in a bolt does not put on the nut; the man who puts on the nut does not tighten it."[1] This idea would eventually backfire as employees reacted. Ford was hardly alone in feeling the consequences. Throughout American firms in 1974, time lost in labor disputes reached a record high—48 million days. While the causes and motives for such actions varied, at Ford the current president, Donald E. Petersen, acknowledges publicly that the system "thought of the worker as a 'single purpose' machine tool." And he adds, "The worker, in this context, was seldom encouraged to consider better ways to do the job"—nor, he might have added, to help design a better product.[2]

"People on the product line had *no say on quality*," offered Danny Simpson, a machine setter.

From across the table another machine setter, Thomas Hyatt, said: "The only way to express yourself was through the suggestion program. People got discouraged with that. If I did the job as I was told to do it, there just wasn't any way the company could go on forever. The situation was bad for twenty years."

A supervisor, Jay Palamar, remembers the embarrassment of letting inferior products go by. "Employees considered the product as garbage. And the customer accepted it. I would go home feeling I was doing what was expected of me. It got to the point that people working at Ford weren't buying Ford anymore."

For Harper Brock, "It hit home when neighbors came home with foreign cars. That gets to you. That was in the midseventies."

"The bottom line was that it was just a job," added Simpson. "That's all there was to it. I don't mind saying that ten years ago I was in a rut."

Every year millions of pounds of raw metal enter Rawsonville: 8.7 million of steel, 9.5 million of aluminum, 3.8 million of magnet wires. Tens of thousands of units of finished products pour out *daily:* 11,800 windshield-wiper motors and 18,000 other small electric motors, 7,000 carburetors, and similar numbers of engine parts, shafts, plates, rotors, and rods. A flaw in any of these translates into parts that must be reworked or scrapped. In some cases it results in defective cars or trucks bought by consumers and costly warranty repairs for Ford. The problem was not just at this one plant; it became endemic to the entire American auto industry.

Brock again: "We inspected everything. The first-run yield might have been 70 percent good. When things were going well management could afford rebuilding the rejects. I guess people just got used to accepting less than the best." But for the company the cost of throwing away or repairing the parts—once affordable—was debilitating when matched against the far more efficient Japanese production philosophies. Ford—and its peers—had to change if it was to thrive again.

For more than two decades, defective and shoddy work was common throughout the industry—accepted by workers and management alike as the way of doing business. No one liked it, and most often the consumer was the one most inconvenienced. One of them even went to the extreme of burning his Lincoln "lemon" on the lawns facing corporate headquarters. Despite the flaws, the system survived. And then came better-quality products from abroad, jolting the industry out of a self-inflicted ritual of slow death. In a six-year period from 1977 to 1983, the auto companies made major capital investments. At Ford almost $15 billion was spent to redesign products and retool plants. For Rawsonville this meant an investment of nearly $200 million on an expanded floor area and on modernizing production lines with some robots and a lot of retooling.

It was the mushrooming layoffs that hit Ed Cole the hardest. "Since 1978, we went from being a 5,500-employee plant to only 1,900 in 1980. Everybody got worried. We all knew what was needed was *both management and UAW commitment*. Many things didn't go because of the lack of it. But then Don Ephlin [the UAW leader at Ford then] came here and told our local chairman to get rolling. He said, 'Jobs going out of the door don't pay dues!'"

But change came and it had far less to do with machines, computers, or robots than it did with human relations. Half the current workers at Rawsonville are now voluntary participants in a three-year-old program to improve quality and productivity. At

Ford the program is called EI—Employee Involvement—a term coined after considerable soul-searching in joint corporate and union meetings set off by a decline in auto sales. So important was the commitment that it led to experiments in several plants and to a declaration of corporate policy in a form used sparingly in company history. This was a "letter" circulated at the end of 1979—Ford's version of a Vatican encyclical—by Philip Caldwell, then president and now chairman. A separate UAW-Ford Letter of Understanding committed both parties to jointly develop an EI program. The die had been cast on a new approach. Trust and open communication would fuel the process. Loss of either would demolish it. In Detroit those were rare commodities.

"When EI first started, the union and the company were on opposite sides," said Marie Payne, a second-shift production repair worker. "Workers saw this as a game. Workers waited for the union to give the go-ahead. We wanted the assurance that the company would not use us." Now, two years later, she sees a distinct improvement. It excites her. "We're beginning to feel like we're all part of the same company. In the old days it was just competing between management and employees."

And Brenda Lanier, too: "You feel like you're part of something now. By building character in people you end up with quality in parts."

EI is an informal voluntary grouping of employees in working teams. Projects they select cover a wide spectrum from quality and productivity to employee social events or community needs. By company and union fiat, efforts to improve productivity are not measured. The intention is to avoid putting pressure on achieving goals that can be measured only in numerical or dollar terms. When teams meet, the manager/worker label disappears. The goal is to pinpoint a problem and to determine the best solution—and to implement it with management support as fast as possible. After three years of development at Rawsonville, interest is high and a competitive spirit has built up among teams. This is most visible in an array of self-generated team names like Rackum, Stackum and Moveum, Butler's Raiders, Japanese

Eliminators, or the D.C. Hot Shots. Some of the names could have been painted on the sides of World War II bombers.

Workers and their union representatives feel strongly that if anyone knows best how to make a particular part it is the person on the line. If allowed to speak out, the person who labors day in and day out on a given task can best suggest improvements. By 1982, Ford executives and labor leaders were ready to work with new ideas and new management tools. That year they encountered Dr. W. Edwards Deming, consultant and octogenarian guru of Japan's industrial awakening. His work, much of it founded on basic applications of statistical controls, meshed ideally with the separate evolution and rapid maturation of employee-involvement programs in a number of pilot plants. Deming's management tools are founded on a basic dictum: the constant pursuit of quality brings immediate cost advantage.

"Productivity improves with quality," Deming tells his clients. "Folklore has it in America that quality and productivity are incompatible, that you cannot have both. A plant manager will tell you if he pushes quality he falls behind in production. If he pushes production, his quality suffers. That's nonsense," Deming says.

What Deming brought to the process was a technique called statistical process control. It provided workers with a basic analytical measurement that showed variances in quality—and allowed them to trace the source of the change. He was saying, in brief, that problems should be pinpointed at the source and corrected immediately. Simple as it sounds, it just was not done. The old way meant finding problems at the end of the production line, too late to be corrected at the source. For the auto culture, the Deming philosophy was nothing short of heresy. It altered the role of workers on the line by allowing them to participate in the process directly. Yet Ford, GM, and many other companies have embraced it fully.

Helen Teall explained her view of the human energy being put to work. "EI is a team—management and employees. Now if in our team we get stuck on a problem, management will come right down to help. I had a problem with springs from a vendor that were all stuck together in their boxes. It took too much time just to undo them. Management contacted the vendor and got it to supply parts so we could pick them out easily."

For some, like Ray White, machine operator, the fact that weekly attendance at meetings is paid as normal work time is important. It may be the first thing to draw a new volunteer into attending a meeting. "Now I feel like we're getting paid for our ideas. There isn't the mood of battling or bickering with your supervisor. One hour per week we are compensated for our input. I'm proud to do it. We're trying to get back our job security."

To this Thomas Maupin added: "Twenty-six years ago I knew there had to be a better way. But it was all management. The writing was on the wall. It was too long in coming. *There is a collective genius to be found among those on the floor.* It's all wrapped up in employee involvement. If there's a question, they'll come up with an answer."

One has to stop and think for a moment and reflect on what this implies for U.S. corporations in general. Could it have been that these things just were not done in most companies in the past? Could corporate-level managers not have understood the importance of motivating workers and assisting them? One answer can be found in business schools, where an elitist attitude about managing is inculcated in students. High salaries, lots of responsibility, and little contact with workers are the symbols of M.B.A. success. Worse, the M.B.A. expects them as conditions of work—and gets them. Another answer comes from the corporate culture itself. Rewards, status, symbols of achievement induce managers to behave as "managers." Delegating and controlling are more valued than participation and sharing of responsibility.

But here were workers actually talking about enjoying their labor and about participating in making it more productive. That it had happened in only the most random fashion before seemed unbelievably shortsighted. Marie Payne spoke out with her reasons: "All we needed was someone in management to ask our opinion. With unions you had job classification. Now it's *our* job.

To solve it, I might have to go beyond my classification. Of course I could still hold back and work by the rules, but you don't have that feeling anymore. Other employees could call me a 'sucky' but they haven't done that to me. Sometimes they call us 'EIEIOs,'" she said with a hearty laugh.

"Even though I hate to use the phrase 'better quality of life,'" said Thomas Maupin, "I can now say I really enjoy working at Ford. Last couple of years I haven't felt threatened. One person is no better than another. EI eliminates fear in the workplace. Before the attitude was 'you do this or you're fired!' Now *we are given latitude to fail.* In other words people will say, 'Okay, that didn't work, let's try something else.' People are now actually saying 'Good morning.' They're going to try a little harder."

"It's put *a big dent on absenteeism.* It's improved attendance," pitched in Ray White.

Sitting next to him, Danny picked up the point. "EI has meant getting results. For my section many of us stand eight hours a day in front of our machines. The floor is concrete; there's oil on it; some stand on metal gratings. We got our group together and called in vendors to provide floor-mat samples. We were then able to choose two kinds and worked out a plan for the nineteen different machine positions. Before, all this would have been a union grievance subject and maybe resulted in a standard-issue rubber mat. But management worked it out with us."

Examples of worker initiative abound. One team sent a letter of complaint to a vendor about the quality of a part it supplied. The fifteen signatures on the bottom brought immediate results and the part is no longer a problem. Another team brought in a design engineer to see why they were losing market share on the brakes they were producing. "Teams are visiting one another now," said Ed Cole. "One group has a newsletter going asking other teams to visit them and ask questions. One team worked with a production engineer and redesigned the positions on a product line being moved. The result on that was saving time when the move was actually made. There were no complaints after the move."

Company-paid facilitators, both salaried and hourly, are available full-time to help expedite needs and organize meetings. One of their principal tasks is to encourage a team to define specific goals and to focus effort on achieving them. Marie Payne explained her team's consensus. "We made it our goal to reduce warranty returns. Before, many of us didn't know where our parts went. We never knew the importance of our part to the whole line—like motors for wipers."

Danny Simpson: "We had a part with a hole size that didn't always match the screws provided. We got that settled. In the past it would have meant repairs after the product was all put together and tested."

What are some tangible measures of EI's contributions? Manufacturing manager Fred J. Kiener provided some dramatic examples. The D.C. Hot Shots, a fourteen-person team, suggested a way of using plant steam to keep dies at a constant high temperature. This single effort required a company investment of $51,000, but the energy saved in not having to reheat cold dies is estimated at $137,000 annually. In addition, there is less scrap on trial runs, less tooling damage, and start-up time on new dies has been reduced from six hours to one. No one has even tried to measure the full benefit. The Trouble Shooters came up with an idea for freezing a particular part before assembly. A freezer was purchased for $2,000, but annual savings are estimated at $37,000. Those in the Rackum, Stackum and Moveum EI team worked on added protection to be built around propane tanks. Estimated costs for a proposed shelter were pared down by half and much better production was ensured. Internal EI newsletters list dozens and dozens of other ideas contributed and implemented by some of the current sixty-five EI teams.

While strict productivity measures are not kept at Ford, at the Rawsonville plant labor productivity is estimated to be rising at double the rate of improvements in overhead, materials, and transportation. In addition, inventory turnovers have gone from twelve a year a decade ago to nineteen. Repair rates measured in warranty work done on Rawsonville-supplied parts are 46 percent better for 1983-model vehicles over the prior model year— or 4.52 per hundred on cars and 8.8 per hundred on trucks.

"That's much better than data coming from GM or Chrysler," said Fred Kiener, "but still not where Toyota is." The combined rate is still felt by some managers to be only half that needed to keep pace with Japan's annual improvements.

In Kiener's view the EI program is still in its infancy. "We've just scratched the surface. So many things were not solved in the past—mats, leaks, steam, tooling, thousands of problems. We're confident now that we've got things in place to launch EI throughout the plant. If we lose EI, we'll be in trouble."

Corporate and union leaders at Ford believe that Rawsonville is one of the most successful examples of new employee relations in the U.S. auto industry. Some critics suggest that it may be only another example of temporary goodwill and superb corporate PR. Fred Herr, divisional general manager of all electronics operations with responsibilities that include the Rawsonville plant, is an outspoken and enthusiastic corporate advocate of the EI program. He likes to refer to the old system as very simple: "We barked. They reacted." What has caught many managers off guard is that change came fastest from where it was least expected: the workers and their unions. Once committed to experiment, workers set the pace and unions backed them up. Many managers were not prepared. In one plant, a supervisor expressed his reservation in an off-the-cuff remark. "You know something," he said, "this employee involvement shit they're espousing . . . well I kicked ass for twenty years because my job was at stake. You know something, it works!"

The old way meant managing by what the director of the Labor Relations and Planning and Employment Office at Ford, Ernest Savoie, calls management by exception. "This meant watching for an error," he says, "and then diving on it. To change that approach a vast set of cultural rules must be wrestled with." One of the problems is that a new reward system is falling into place, but the rules are not clear. An older system based on easily quantified performance—how many units came off a production line—now includes many more intangible measures. Attitudes about work, grievance rates, EI participation rates are now included in a foreman's, supervisor's, or manager's rating.

"The rating is becoming much more subjective," says Peter Pestillo, vice president for labor relations, who worked closely with the UAW in a joint labor-management effort to conceptualize and introduce EI. He sees the whole EI idea as one that is bubbling up from the shop floor. "The idea belongs to the workers," he says. "This means that a major layer of managers have yet to fully appreciate the implications of EI. But that is changing fast." Ford's U.S. work force includes about 7,000 people with line-supervisory and management responsibilities; another 110,000 are listed as hourly workers.

Some of the side effects of the EI evolution were not easily predictable. "As a union representative," said Harper Brock with a broad smile, "I had high blood pressure. For two years now I haven't taken a pill. There used to be three or four grievances a day; now I have about that many a month." His UAW colleague, Ed Cole, reflected on the real breakthrough that seems to be happening. "When I go into an EI team meeting, I go in as Ed Cole, not as a union man. The company and union EI steering committee jointly agreed never to bring up contractual problems in EI meetings. Anyone can stop me on the floor with an EI problem. The fear is eliminated from actually stopping me to discuss something. We're in the most competitive business in the country. Many can outbid us. That competition will always be there. It will last. Ford is smarter."

In a closing remark, Brenda Lanier summed up her expectations of the long-term potential for EI. "I don't think we'll ever go back. The company cannot be a company without us. EI and jobs mean families and lives."

Whether she is right is another matter. A lengthy history of management inexperience or disinterest in employee participation and sharing in decision-making offers little comfort to those who may be counting on sustaining the spirit evident at the Rawsonville plant. While many key managers are keenly supportive, the managerial culture at companies like Ford has yet to come fully "on board." One of the major stumbling blocks is to persuade middle managers of its benefits. Many talk about a decade-long period of reeducating managers and workers. Is ten years too long?

Workers are one key to successfully rebuilding Ford; new technology is another. How quickly the auto makers can transform themselves with computer-based factories of the future is a critical issue for America precisely because this industry, a symbol of both strength and weakness in our culture, is intimately interwoven with everything that is American. More than $80 billion will be spent between 1978 and 1985 by the Big Three to rebuild their competitive strength. The business press suggests that an equal amount will have to be spent in the ensuing five years for the industry to return to a truly dominant worldwide position.[3] GM spends over $2 billion a year just on research and development of new tools and product designs; its rival, Ford, $1.7 billion.

Such spending is enormous by any standard. But the sheer power and simplicity of such numbers does not imply any shortcuts to success for an industry making a product that has as many as 100,000 distinct nuts, bolts, microchips, wires, motors, and other components gathered from all parts of the world. If the Rawsonville story highlights the role and changing status of the employee in an automobile factory, a visit to what is considered the *world's* most modern car-engine plant—in Ford words, "the highest technology equipment and tooling in the industry worldwide"—highlights the new role of modern computer-monitored machinery.

The Dearborn Engine Plant is the embodiment of Ford's technology investment in the future. One of the goals for Ford—and its competitors in Detroit—is to move rapidly toward the flexible factory of the future. In its idealized form, this would allow the company, said one manager, "to think in terms of cost-effective production runs of *one*"—a single car customized to a single buyer's specifications. To get to such a point means absorbing a vast array of computer technologies, robotics, production knowledge, and new product designs so that a unique car can be produced simply by punching in specifications on a terminal. Getting that far will probably never happen; getting even partway is not easy. At Ford, the first steps have been taken to introduce elements of what is commonly called the factory of the future.

It could not happen in a place more symbolic than the immense production complex known as the Rouge, in Dearborn, where founder Henry Ford kept offices until after World War II. One has to see the complex to understand and feel the vision that brought American industrial power to its apogee in the 1930s and 1940s. Huge ships deposit coal, limestone, and ores in enormous stockpiles—5 million tons per year at peak capacity—at one end. At the other end, shiny new Mustangs roll off production lines. Seventeen thousand people labor here, only a fifth or a sixth of the work force during the Rouge's most active years. Nowhere else in America is there a plant that has all the production steps located in one place. One way to think of it is as a living museum—one foot in the past, one foot in the present.

The past is a steel operation with absurdly inefficient production processes more than a generation old and with wage rates so high one wonders how Ford has survived this long. Ironically, in 1982 a group of Japanese companies headed by the steel giant Nippon Kokan K. K. offered to buy a majority interest in the mills. Because of union intransigence on wage rates, the negotiations were eventually dropped. Ford threatened to close the mills outright in order to get labor to make wage concessions. The potential loss of 4,300 jobs led the union in September 1983 to accept a reduction of $4.50 per hour. Two months later, Chairman Philip Caldwell appeared at the mill to formally thank the employees—an act considered unusual in Detroit—and to announce a dramatic decision. Ford would not only keep the mills going but would invest $50 million to reline the blast furnace and another $200 million to build a continuous caster—the latest technology in steel production. "We're the only auto company which makes its own steel," he told plant employees. "We could have taken the easy—and safe—course and quit. We needed the help, understanding, cooperation, and support of our union and our work force. And we got it. The UAW, the leaders of Local 600, the salaried and hourly people stepped up to a difficult task.

Sacrifices were made all around. We bit the bullet. The mill survived." This act represented an almost full turnaround in Caldwell's battle to belie the old image of smokestack America.

The working symbol of this change is only a few hundred yards away from the aging mill complex. It is the Dearborn Engine Plant. For many years it was the site of a wartime Pratt & Whitney aircraft facility built in 1941 and purchased six years later by Ford. For the next thirty years, until 1978, the Dearborn Engine Plant produced the now infamous gas-guzzling V-8 engines. But after a $600-million expansion program that doubled the factory floor to the size of forty-one football fields (2.2 million square feet), the plant produces one million small four-cylinder Escort and Lynx engines a year. Electronics and computers are the central new ingredients. The aim is to produce flawless engines by frequent automated testing during various stages of assembly—a Japanese-inspired approach contrasting sharply with the older method of testing the engine only when it rolled off the line with whatever defects might have been built into it.

At the front office, tech-talk is common. The company is into CAM (computer-aided manufacture), computer monitored "hot tests," automated engine-production lines, driverless minitrucks delivering inventory to the line, or WC^3G—in-house shorthand for Worldwide CAD/CAM Coordinating Group, a team working to create corporate standards for computer use. Secretaries praise the newly installed word processors and corporate electronic mail system.

In the cavernous and spotless factory, an electric golf cart carries visitors past cast-iron engine blocks manufactured at a rate of 154 per hour. Automated machinery completes the machine-tooling tasks in sound-proof casings. A new generation of tools have longer productive lives; old tools could machine 25,000 pieces, the new ones do 287,000 in the same time. Tooling that used to cost about five cents per block now costs one tenth that amount. The golf cart travels more than half a mile to complete the length of the assembly line. Of more than a thousand specific assembly points, 135 are fully automated. Farther away is an immense parts storage bay with forty-foot-high automated loading equipment ferrying in and out of 5,200 storage "cells."

One important feature of the automated line illustrates the impact of computer-controlled tools and testing equipment. There are thirty-nine hot-test locations. A hot test simulates actual operating conditions on an engine, allowing defects or other problems to be diagnosed. These tests, once done by manual control and only for a standardized set of conditions such as a given simulated load or a given speed, are now computerized. Tests can be programmed to simulate a car climbing a steep grade, pulling a trailer, or operating at high altitudes or at varying rates of speed. One hundred and twenty readings are recorded per engine, a total of 240,000 per day. They provide an immense data base of engine characteristics that can be analyzed for statistical process control—a Deming innovation. Any variation in standards is apparent, and patterns can be quickly determined to trace back to machine failure, human error, or other problems.

If Deming took American ideas to Japan, might not their impact on our own industries also hold immense potential? In Japan they were nurtured over several decades into a sophisticated system of management of which the quality circle is only the most visible manifestation. One example is the Japanese steel and shipbuilding company, NKK, with 34,000 employees, a winner of the highly coveted Japanese Deming award. Eighty percent of the workers participate in quality circles. They have generated a total of 160,000 suggestions, of which 80 percent were adopted at an estimated saving of more than $200 million to the company. Some think that Ford's future—and those of other U.S. firms—may depend on its ability to be as innovative in its own plants.

At the Dearborn Engine Plant, because the test stations are dispersed along the production line, detection of defects comes early. Here, too, statistical measures of any defect provide immediate information necessary to correct the problem—a blunted drill, flaws in a metal alloy, or an operational defect in a carburetor seal. One result is a much higher chance of producing a perfect engine at the end of the line. This is a critical and early payoff of an investment in moving toward the factory of the future. Quality measures are 50 percent better now than in 1980. Productivity measures are equally promising. Compared to the period between 1976 and 1980 when Ford manpower efficiencies grew at a rate of 5.4 percent per year in all its engine operations, the Dearborn plant is improving efficiencies at a rate of 13.6 percent per year. This is 1.6 percentage points higher than the 12 percent improvement objective set by Japanese companies.

Thirty-year-old Robert Yee oversees the plant's computer and electronics operations. In a factory employing 1,400 hourly and 345 salaried workers, Bob is one of only fifty engineers. Under him are the plant's six other electrical and computer-science experts. "I'd like to see upper management think of technology as a resource," he explains. "We need many more interfaces between us and the rest of the divisions. Without them we will have problems." One of these is a shortage of people who can repair computer-controlled equipment. There are 700 of these machines on the production line, and most electricians are not fully trained to either diagnose or repair the equipment in place. "We are seeing quick advances in high technology," says plant engineering manager John Shaw, "but the skills of the workers are not always keeping pace. This puts a big burden on our engineering staff to provide assistance in maintaining the equipment. We're striving to bridge this gap."

A very different problem comes from the legacy of an antiquated steel plant existing side by side with a plant containing the latest manufacturing technology—all under the same corporate and union umbrella. At the Rouge complex, the highest wages are paid at the steel mill. Annual earnings of $40–50,000 for the simplest tasks are common; one hourly worker earns $79,000 plus generous benefits. Even the most skilled workers trained for state-of-the-art technology in the engine plant are easily lured away by a "promotion" to the steel plant. This means a tremendous amount of waste. "We can train people," said Shaw, "and lose them." One solution may come from the earnings settlement negotiated with the union and with the announced incorporation of the Rouge plant into a separate legal entity.

Dearborn, Michigan, is suburban, wealthy, and clean. Long

ago Henry Ford bought a vast acreage of flat land here that is now the site of various complexes of company buildings he never saw. Acres of lawn surround the twelve-story glass building that houses Ford's world headquarters. On the top floor, the company chairman, president, and senior officers have plush offices. What is significant is not that this is corporate America as one might remember it in William Whyte's classic *Organization Man,* or that Silicon Valley's corporate founders, CEOs, and workers would be ill at ease here without the open floor layouts common to most of their offices. Rather it is in the repeated concern senior executives express about their industry's public image. The word "smokestack" is out; "high tech" or "auto tech" is in. Ford Chairman Philip Caldwell speaks of his industry and firm as "technology-forcing." By this he means prodding suppliers to meet new technological standards. "We have more electronic computing power in a 1984 model than an Apple computer," one executive says. "We're the first engine-control system to use sixteen-bit microprocessors," another states. Or, "We're the largest computer electronics manufacturer in the world." Yet clearly within sight of Chairman Caldwell's office's are at least sixty auto-industry smokestacks—almost half of them just a few miles away at the huge Ford Rouge plant with its array of antiquated steel mills. But they too will be subjected to a life-saving technological face-lift.

The dichotomy of living with one foot in a legacy forged by founder Henry Ford and another in the opportunities to be grasped in the new high technologies becomes apparent. Seen through one set of corporate eyes, the Ford Motor Company is as high-tech as Hewlett-Packard or Intel Corporation. From another perspective, the company still functions with outdated operational habits common to an earlier generation of innovative and winning industries.

Varied and conflicting forces push and pull Ford. The energy crises of the early 1970s and concurrent federal auto-emission and fuel-economy standards were vital catalysts. In Congress, strong views prevailed. In 1975 Senator Henry Jackson said: "There is a growing and increasingly widespread conviction that the fuel shortage is a deliberate, conscious contrivance of the major integrated petroleum companies to destroy the independent marketers, to increase gasoline prices, and to obtain repeal of environmental legislation." From such views emerged the Energy Policy and Conservation Act in late 1975. Fuel-economy standards were firmly established for the auto industry to meet in 1978, 1979, and 1980. They pushed the industry into high gear. At Ford this meant quick measures to reduce car weight and to bring electronics into the engine in order to improve fuel-consumption rates. "Earlier, in 1971," says Dale Compton, vice-president of research engineering and research staff, "you would have had a nine-to-one vote in our technology committee against electronics. Up until 1975, most here still saw conventional technology as the solution."

Only in 1976 was an electronics division created. Its successes would come step by step in spite of what Executive Vice-President Thomas C. Page calls "a primary obstacle of getting people to change attitudes. For so long this was mainly a mechanically oriented industry. We've begun to convert the mechanical engineers only by a steady flow of PR, sales, and marketing to demonstrate our new electronic systems." After Ford reluctantly let itself be pushed by outside forces into modernizing, it found itself—much to its dismay—unable to prod the high-tech electronics firms into catering to its needs. Perhaps because Ford, like others in Detroit, had for so long dictated terms to suppliers, it was surprised to find that some suppliers didn't want to bother with relatively small orders from "smokestack" America. "The semiconductor industry," as Page puts it, "was not ready for the auto. It was almost a shotgun marriage." Ford needed special chip design and production for its engine controls. The semiconductor industry couldn't be bothered.

Unable to rationalize building its own manufacturing operation, Ford tried a different tactic. Why not design its own chips and then get them manufactured by a supplier? Here, too, the Detroit image didn't help. "At first, we couldn't get any of those young chip designers to even think of moving here," said Page. According to him, there are only 1,200 qualified chip designers in the United States—and maybe 2,000 in the whole world. "They are in such demand that they can live almost anywhere," he added. Unfazed, the company set up a subsidiary in 1982 called Ford Microelectronics, Inc., and located it in Colorado Springs. It managed to lure ten designers and supplied them with a fifty-person staff under the direction of a thirty-two-year-old. The group will soon grow to 120. The intention is to create an "interface" between Detroit's mechanical and electrical engineers, who can call on the designers to custom-make a chip, and the producers in Silicon Valley and elsewhere, who haven't the time to waste with old-line engineers. The irony now is that senior managers see their entire corporate strategy—founded on making the Ford car an "electronic" marvel—almost hostage to these few electrical and computer engineers in distant Colorado.

To speed up the evolution within Ford, an informal steering committee was created to cross the boundaries of organizational charts and ensure contact between the people who understand the new technologies and those who develop cars—two corporate tiers away from the electronics division. To Page and the head of his electronics division, Frederick Herr, "what is needed is a human investment, not a horrendous capital investment. We need people who can apply these things. The ideal would be an electrical engineer with vehicle experience. But there just isn't a school around in which to learn this."

Ford is introducing an electronically controlled load-leveling system in its cars. One of the stumbling blocks was a lack of sufficient electrical engineers to design it. This resulted in a long delay in getting the idea to be understood and accepted within the company. Process technologies, meaning the actual ways in which the car is built, are also of major concern. Fred Herr would like to get to a point "when manufacturing processes will themselves push the development of new products." A more flexible line of computer-controlled tools could in time allow the product to be tailored to specific markets with only minor production adjustment costs. Here again, though, the lament is familiar. "At present our problems are manpower and money," says Herr. Of 10,000 who work in his division's U.S. operations,

70 percent are hourly workers. In the division's main engineering building are only 600 engineers. But of these, 400 are electrical and computer scientists. This is 350 more than six years earlier.

Louis R. Ross, executive vice-president for technical staffs, has a corner office on the twelfth floor. His newly created title, directly under the corporate president, gives him authority over three previously separate vital operations: environment and safety; purchase, supply, and manufacturing staff; and research and engineering staff. One of the major changes to occur at Ford, he believes, was a reorganization that decentralized R&D. Now there will be divisional labs in addition to a central engineering lab. Ironically, just the reverse is happening in many Japanese companies. There, longer-term pure-research tasks are being consolidated into centrally run laboratories.

"Petersen," says Ross, referring to Ford's president, "has innovation as an objective. Too much regimentation will stifle it. So he is allowing a lot of 'skunk' works. These are independently initiated efforts allowed to spend anywhere between 5 and 25 percent of allocated R&D." The key to getting innovation, says Ross, "is whether management creates the environment to achieve it. Tech people get quickly dissatisfied if not listened to."

An illustration: Word had been passed down to Rawsonville managers and workers that an outside supplier might be considered for delivery of a new generation of carburetors. This would have meant large staff and employee cutbacks. In a move that earlier corporate rules would have inhibited, the plant production engineers were allowed to contract with the University of Michigan to develop a more effective fuel-handling system. A $500,000 grant produced quick results in the form of a highly innovative small fuel system that promises to keep business at Rawsonville.

An awareness that change will affect all aspects of the corporation's well-being—including its suppliers, dealers, and service departments in the field—worries planners. This concern is putting new stress on the need to reconsider the importance of education as a strategic tool. Executive Vice-President Thomas C. Page is outspoken on this aspect of the company's future. "The task of reorienting and strengthening much of our engineering organization around the world," he says, "is enormous and will require continuing intensive effort. An equivalent retraining effort will be required in a number of our manufacturing locations and in dealerships that service the vehicles." When the numbers of people affected are not just in the thousands, or ten of thousands, but in the hundreds of thousands, one begins to grasp the scale of the challenge. Peter Pestillo worries about it too. "Now that EI is in place, our next priority for hourly workers is to institute a corporate education policy." The stage was set in an agreement with the UAW forged in the 1982 collective bargaining agreement—a landmark agreement in which the EI concept was cemented into place and a commitment made to education. The goal is straightforward: "Employees—active and displaced—will be helped to adjust to and use changing technologies, learn new production skills, sharpen old skills, and pursue career-development opportunities either inside or outside the company." Five cents for every hour worked by employees is contributed to an education fund that supports the program of a newly established UAW-Ford National Development and Training Center.

To grasp the implications of change at Ford one has to envision the sum total of these small and large initiatives. Concern for education, a new fuel system, floor mats, reorganized corporate charts, electronic sensors, new labor contracts, relined blast furnaces—the task is immense, and it still leaves a lot of kinks to be straightened out. At Ford—perhaps as at GM or Chrysler—the disparate and far-flung corporate parts don't always sum to the advantage of the whole or to the fullest benefit of the consumer. For example, during the summer of 1983 several late-model cars were displayed on the glass-sheathed ground floor of Ford's world headquarters. One was the Sierra, a European bestseller. In the U.S. market it could easily have displaced Japanese imports—but Ford had not transferred its styling and manufacturing capability to North America. In a lengthy article on Ford, *Forbes* magazine asked the same question: "Why not just import the Sierra?" It offered the following answer. Not only was it rear-wheel drive, but "the UAW would have a fit if Ford imported the Sierra in quantity."[4]

Another car on display was the Telstar, a Ford car marketed in Australia and Japan. Its lines and interior comfort matched the best of Japanese cars. Its development—much to the surprise of anyone who thinks of Japan as Detroit's nemesis—was the result of joint research by Ford Australia and the Toyo Kogyo company, the Japanese maker of Mazda cars which is 25 percent owned by Ford. Like the Sierra, neither was the Telstar marketed in North America. In 1984, though, a half-billion-dollar investment to build a Telstar factory in Mexico was announced by Ford. Part of its production would be aimed at the U.S. market. The complexity of such arrangements begin to boggle the mind. An Australian/Japanese jointly developed car being produced in Japan under one set of names, and in Mexico under another, by two different companies, one partially owned by the other. Complex? Yes. The cars on display demonstrated, in part, the dilemma of an immense corporation with a legacy of autonomous corporate operations in various world regions and global sales of $37 billion a year. The standards achieved for one market were not seen as valid in another. That, indeed, may account for the success wrought by Japan. It set a high qualitative standard for its own market and then exported the standard. Others were then forced to meet it or lose the competitive race.

Rebuilding competitive strength means something very tangible to Louis Ross. "To achieve it we will need the complete cooperation of the work force. There is no doubt in my mind that more has happened in the last two or three years than in the prior twenty-five years I've spent at Ford."

Several months later, the big three—Ford included—announced its whopping management bonuses. Offering lavish rewards to managers while asking workers to restrain wages does not bode well for what some hope might be a "new" vision in Detroit. But even with the hope of better times to come on the horizon, the prospects are dim for those now out of work or accepting lesser-paying jobs. For most of them the "right" to return to a better-paying Ford job may never be exercised. The company is currently down to half its peak employment levels of hourly workers and expects only modest increases at best. Of those remaining, Ford will require new skills and more time in training programs. Of its suppliers, it will require stringent commitments to quality.

Much has been said about the auto industry—and undoubtedly much more is yet to come. The big question is whether it can improve the quality and manufacture of its products to be able to confront and beat foreign competition. Few would challenge the fact that a major effort to transform the industry is going on. If you are jaded by years of auto ads hyping chrome and over-powered engines, or by high recall rates and Nader revelations, you may appraise the changes occurring in Detroit with great reservation. Even a more positive view leaves one awed by the immense obstacles between trying and actually achieving an enduring top-to-bottom change. In between is a vast array of uncertainties. So diffuse is the anticipated transformation that few corporate leaders fully comprehend it. "We're on new ground," says one executive. "There are no models of how to do what needs to be done." What they have made clear, though, is a willingness to invest enormous amounts of resources to relearn the business of making cars. It is that will to experiment that is charging the atmosphere with new-found energy and enthusiasm.

Above all, union initiative is pivotal. Its leadership decided to grasp the EI concept, for example, and push it forward. This explains in great part the effectiveness of the program and the enthusiasm one encounters from workers and managers. For each the symbol of this cooperative spirit is the innovative agreement struck in 1982. Terms were decided in thirteen days almost six months ahead of time and without a single strike. This had never happened in the industry before.

To consider the full implication of the Ford story one has almost to stand back and take a deep breath. Does it really signal something significantly new about America's productive power? Or is it just a case of new bottles for old wine? While one might be skeptical about declarations of corporate goodwill and new-found ethical zeal, one can judge whether or not the transformation at Ford goes beyond externals. A profound change does seem to be in the making—driven as much by self-interest as by recognition of new forces at work in the world economy and the culture. The response to Japanese competitive pressure is genuine—after all, survival is at stake. The belief in the need for a new relationship between manager and worker rings true—fragile as it is and difficult to sustain.

In completing this account of transformation, we should take note that the federal government is missing as an agent of change. True, the government has influenced the amount of competitive pressure through import quotas, tax policies, and emissions regulations, which condition the business environment. Still, a metamorphosis is in progress with no new industrial policy, development bank, or central planning board. The changes stem from a vision which empowers and challenges workers to deliver their full potential, which draws on new technologies to boost productivity, and which enlists new quality management concepts to build products better and cheaper. Without organization leadership and vision responding to market opportunities and competitive challenges, revitalization has little chance to succeed.

Central to the Ford story is a question yet to be answered. Is the transformation under way merely a step—a big one at that—toward catching up with Japanese concepts of car design and production? Or is it a far more fundamental and truly innovative attempt to outrun the Japanese by introducing brand-new concepts of car quality and production-line management? Analysts of the auto industry are far from agreed on a single clear answer. At GM, corporate managers talk about building a car in sections and then plugging them together. Is this more or less innovative than Ford's belief that it is more innovative to engineer new designs and performance features into its cars?

Where most observers do agree, however, is that new technologies have come to pervade all parts of companies such as

Ford. Of these electronics, the ones most talked about are breathing new life into the company—and into a multitude of other business enterprises throughout the United States. The effect this is having on the economy as a whole is the subject to which we turn next.

3

High-Tech Tools

Man is a tool-making animal.
　　　　—Benjamin Franklin

High tech, the term denoting computers, electronics, and other new technologies, has captured the American imagination. What has not yet fully permeated public consciousness is that the high-tech industry is entering a new phase. As it does, our view of what it is and how it can shape America's future will also change. Until now, the prevailing view has been that all this electronic wizardry represented a new industry that by itself had the power to usher in a new "information age" American economy. The Ford case shows otherwise. It indicates that the real payoff from high technology can be in so-called mature industries.

But our mental image of computers is slow to change. People think of them more as stand-alone devices and seldom as something that, for example, improves the performance of a car. When *Time* magazine dubbed the computer "Man of the Year" in 1981, it reinforced this image of a new hero on a lone rescue mission. The contrast between the auto and the computer was complete—whereas the car had been the American mark of status in the 1950s, the personal computer replaced it as the symbol of success of the 1980s. More and more, however, people are coming to understand that this separate but equal view of computers is a flawed picture of reality.

The question is not a choice between old and new; it's whether new technology can sufficiently revitalize our basic industries—from manufacturing to services—to reinstill competitive vitality. It is in this restructuring process that computers will have a major, but by no means exclusive, role to play. This is why it is false to pose "high tech" as an alternative to "smokestack America" or to picture the two in a win-or-lose struggle for resources. While it is true that some older industries, especially those dependent on unskilled labor, will inevitably change or go under, it is also true that many electronics firms themselves are caught in a shakeout period. Most of this has little to do with an either/or confrontation between basic and high-tech firms. Rather, we see marriage in their future.

High-tech industries are best envisioned as toolmakers. Computers, robots, word processors, communications equipment, and other products boost the productivity of all types of people—of workers and managers, in manufacturing and service industries, and in hospitals, universities, and even government agencies. Their impact is pervasive and at every level. It is visible in a constant stream of new developments, some of which are end products but most of which are embedded in other products and processes.

What is high tech? The term means different things to different people. To some it's a grab bag of different industries; to many it's the latest gadgets; and others see it as an exclusive club of experts. For what it's worth, the U.S. Department of Commerce identifies high-technology industries as the following: agricultural and industrial chemicals; aircraft and parts; communications equipment and components; drugs and medicine; electrical industrial apparatus; engines and turbines; data-processing machines; optical and medical instruments; plastic materials and synthetics; professional, scientific, and measuring instruments; and radio and TV receiving equipment. Experts do not agree, however, that this list is definitive. Many argue, for example, that radio and television receiving equipment, industrial chemicals, and engines are now mature industries. In a later chapter, we'll examine why it is so hard to classify high-tech firms using industrial categories and SIC (Standard Industrial Classifications) which were established in an earlier era.

What most people do agree on is that high-tech growth is explosive. The great race for high-tech employment and tax revenue stems from the truly boggling projections of sales for some of these industries. Electronic computers are one example. The U.S. market for data-processing systems and related equipment is growing from about $33 billion in 1982 to $74 billion in 1985; during the same period software will jump from $1.7 billion to $7.5 billion, about 400 percent; the demand for domestic communications equipment will almost double from $5.7 billion to $10 billion.[1] Peripheral components such as the revolutionary Winchester hard-disc drives will sell at a predicted rate of nearly $2 billion by 1985; they did not exist as a product prior to 1980.[2]

The best way to define what makes an industry high tech is to note its chief feature—the advanced educational level of its employees. In contemporary technology-intensive firms, an unusually high proportion of employees have college or advanced degrees in engineering and science. In electronics and computer firms, one-third of the work force have college or postgraduate educations. Many are electrical engineers and computer scientists. Another third have technical degrees from community colleges or technical institutes. The reason for this is simple. Accelerating development causes a continuous stream of new products and applications which require a large number of talented people to design, manufacture, sell, and service them. In contrast, an industry matures as its underlying technology stabilizes, resulting in more standardized products and applications and less opportunity for innovation and novel ideas.

A good example is Intel, one of the major semiconductor manufacturers. "Like it or not," says one of its top officers, "Intel is run by Ph.D.'s. Of our top management team, one man's got a doctorate in physics, another in chemical engineering, our QA [quality assurance] manager and three division managers the same, and we've got some fifty more Ph.D.'s scattered around the company. What's great is that these guys have a basic interest in technology as a critical part of the management process."

In contrast, in a mature firm only 5 or 6 percent of the employees are likely to have college or higher degrees, a similarly small proportion will have technical degrees, and a large percentage will have no special skills. The auto industry is an example. Ford's electronics division has 16,000 employees, 80 percent of whom are hourly workers. Fewer than 5 percent are engineers. At the semiautomated Dearborn engine plant, where 1,800 people work, there are only fifty engineers. Of these, seven are electrical or computer-science engineers—and this in a factory heavily dependent on computers. As Daniel Yankelovich, the widely known social forecaster, puts it, it was in such environments that management operated "on the assumption of a large pool of semiskilled workers, not very well educated, responsible to authority, and working in blue-collar manufacturing jobs, with very low discretion and control over their performance."[3]

Another distinguishing feature of a high-tech industry is its high level of R&D spending. As a percent of sales, these companies tend to spend two to three times as much as mature firms, or generally about 7–12 percent of sales. Cray Research, the maker of huge superfast computers which sell for $10 million apiece, leads the list by committing about 15 percent of its sales revenues to R&D. On a per-capita basis GM spends only a sixth of what Cray does, even though it makes the greatest commitment to R&D in absolute terms—$2.175 billion a year, of which 80 percent is spent on development.

A recent report to a congressional subcommittee said: "The technological driving force of the postwar period was the internal combustion engine, and its most stunning application—the rugged and affordable automobile. . . . The technological driving force of the next period of economic expansion will be the semiconductor and its most stunning application—the microcomputer."[4] That may be so, and many statistics can be cited to support the truth of these assertions. But one cannot draw the conclusion from statements like these that computer firms can thrive without industries to use their products.

The broader picture has another dimension. The methods for making cars, both now and even more radically in the future, are becoming highly computerized. As we saw in the case of Ford, auto manufacturers today are among the biggest users of electronic products like robots and computer-aided design and manufacturing equipment. The auto companies are also busy incorporating microcomputers and other electronic products in engine controls and other extended automobile functions. One of the four largest semiconductor manufacturers in the world, Delco, supplies its computer components exclusively for auto applications.

Of course, electronics is not the only new technology that may impact the future of the automobile. Ceramics for auto engines has gotten a lot of attention in Japan. The United States is now developing a plastic engine—a prototype was put into a racing car in 1984—in response to the burgeoning new market for ceramic engines in Japan. Other developments are a graphite-reinforced epoxy chassis (no steel, no aluminum), a replaceable battery pack fifty times more powerful than today, and four electric motors driving wiremesh wheels (no internal-combustion engine, no synthetic rubber). These radical innovations, based on new materials rather than on computerization, have profound implications for industries like steel, aluminum, and rubber. Will the American automobile disappear? No, not any more than agriculture ceased after the first industrial revolution. And just as the methods of farming were revolutionized by industrial machinery and new fertilizers, so will the means of producing cars be transformed by new technologies. Yet for the foreseeable future, the automobile will remain indispensable.

Misconceptions surrounding high tech are legion. One of the most enduring is that it is still mysterious and best left to experts and other "high priests of technology." The name itself is misleading. The real distinction should not be made between "high" and "low" but rather between "new" and "old." In the 1920s and 1930s, electrical generators and petrochemical refineries were state-of-the-art activities. While these did not carry the label "high tech," they probably would have if the term had been in use at the time. Today, telecommunications is considered high tech, even though ten years ago telephones were considered a mature industry. New technology was also misunderstood back in the 1800s when Alexander Bell invented the telephone. Few people in Bell's time grasped the full significance of his work. The inventor was on sabbatical from a teaching post at Boston University when he developed his ideas, but the school did not view his activities favorably. Bell had to quit his university position in order to complete his invention.

James Utterback, professor at MIT and historian of industrial innovation, says that "thirty years from now semiconductors will probably be considered old hat. Something else will come along that makes today's so-called high technology just another mature product. This is not to deny the importance of, say telecommunications and computers—which I think are head and shoulders above everything else in importance today—but simply to say that innovation is a dynamic process. What's new today is old tomorrow. So it is with high tech."[5]

High technology is likely to be with us for a long time. A recent investment analysis shows that the U.S. capital base is shifting. In 1982 nearly a third of all capital investment went into electrical machinery, computers, communications, and instruments, and for the first time the nation's high technology capital stock exceeded total basic industrial capital investments.[6] The percentage has continued its rapid climb with a strong surge of investment in high-tech equipment. One cloud on this bright horizon is a forecast of continued high interest rates—due in large part to ballooning federal deficits to pay for defense expenditures. Whether American firms can afford to sustain the needed investments will have a lot to do with the cost of capital.

Richard Nolan and David Norton, chairman and president respectively of a leading data processing consulting firm, calculate that the computing budgets for *Fortune* 500 companies will increase by a factor of seven in the coming decade while the price/performance ratio of computers will increase thirteen times. The result will be a hundred times more computing power per company by the early 1990s.[7]

Other forces will also impact high tech. Concern about jobs is one of them. Peter Drucker, an outspoken and well-known management economist, projects that by the year 2000 manufacturing will occupy only 6 percent of the labor force, down from its present 25 percent, just as agriculture dropped from 45 percent of the labor force in the 1880s to 25 percent fifty years ago and to only 3 percent today.[8] If this trend holds, as we think likely, then the gut issue of jobs will draw technology's future into front and center stage of the political debates. High tech: Job creator or job killer? Salvation or curse? Trying to answer these questions reminds us of the old English story about the two expert economists on Threadneedle Street: "Only two people know the answer to the question, and they disagree."

If most people are still confused about what this field really is, there is even more confusion about the employment effects it will have. A recent poll indicated the public's total ambivalence about the impact computers will have on jobs. One-third believed that the increased use of technology would create jobs, one-third were convinced it would destroy jobs, and the remaining one-third said they didn't know.[9]

One reason for this confusion is that the largest impact of the new technologies will remain hidden. For years to come, most present-day products and services will retain the same essential functions they now possess. What will change, and what will be less visible, will be how they are designed, produced, and delivered to the user. The automobile, for example, is an integral if not permanent feature of American life, as is the vast infrastructure of highways, gasoline stations, showrooms, and repair shops. It will still take years before cars appear radically different. They will continue to have four wheels, a steering wheel, bumpers, and windshield wipers. But it would be a very dim view of American ingenuity to imagine that our auto industry cannot and will not respond to the challenge of its competitors.

If our concern is international competition, it is obvious why we should worry about productivity in the auto industry. But what about services? Japanese, Korean, or Philippine workers, regardless of their diligence and pay scales, can hardly take jobs away from our hospitals, schools, banks, and hamburger stands. Aren't these safe havens for American workers?

All people in the economy are interdependent on each other for world competitiveness and higher living standards. For example, it is estimated that an average car produced by General Motors carries a $500 cost for the health-care insurance of auto workers. Blue Cross/Blue Shield, which provides it, is the biggest single supplier to GM with annual sales of $2.2 billion. "Our health-care costs will double in five years," says GM Chairman and CEO Roger B. Smith, "unless something is done to change them." More productive hospitals and insurance companies lower the indirect cost and make our cars more competitive in international trade. The more auto workers pay for health services or education for their children, the more they will demand in wages. And with higher costs and fewer cars sold, there will be fewer jobs in service industries. The productivity of government workers enters in as well. Inefficient government services require higher taxes to pay for them, which again are passed along either in the prices of our goods and services or in lower living standards.

Every segment of our economy must become more competitive if we are to maintain or raise our standard of living. Contrary to popular belief, the need for competitiveness may be even greater for our service sector than in manufacturing since it absorbs such a large percentage of the work force—63 percent for government, retail trade, and other services versus only 25 percent for manufacturing. Moreover, some kinds of services, especially in the financial-services industry and in data processing, are increasingly "traded" internationally. As we will show in more detail, high-tech products will play an important role in revitalizing not only autos but service industries like insurance, where major structural changes are already occurring.

There is, of course, precedent for upheavals caused by structural change. In our agriculture a hundred years ago, for example, employment in tilling the soil declined dramatically. But the decline was not so steep if we think of agriculture not just as tilling the soil but as making farm machinery, creating fertilizers, and processing and distributing food. Vast numbers are employed in all these related parts of what is now called agribusiness. A century ago, sons of farm workers shifted to making tractors and fertilizer and began to experiment with new agricultural techniques at the emerging land-grant colleges. And sons and daughters of auto workers will likewise go on to build and operate machine-vision systems, computer-aided manufacturing equipment, and robots. In this perspective, the primary issue is not whether employment to support our transportation system will decline; the issue is how the nature of the jobs will change. The question is how fast and under what conditions we can move from assembling cars to assembling robots, from inspecting parts to inspecting machine-vision systems.

Cities, states, and regions from coast to coast—many of them battered by the recession and with high unemployment rates—have turned to high tech as an economic panacea. Cornfields sprout billboards boasting of future industrial parks, politicians make speeches about vast growth opportunities in computers. In Pennsylvania, the Department of Commerce announces in media ads that "advanced technology has a friend in Pennsylvania." This theme is repeated in nearly every state in the union. Of course the movement is also international. Silicon Valley in California is imitated in name by "Silicon Glen" in Scotland, "Silicon Mountain" in Korea, "Silicon Island" in Kyushu, Japan, and "Silicon Fjord" in Norway.

Lack of understanding of high tech does not stop the politicians in many states from vying for its business. At last count, some twenty-seven states had established special programs to attract electronics industries. Tennessee plans a "technology corridor" from Oak Ridge to Knoxville. Georgia established a special center to encourage start-up firms. Michigan has a new Industrial Technology Institute and another for biotechnology. Maine, with its eye on Boston's Route 128 companies, is searching for a new economic growth strategy. Missouri and Utah are also interested. Even mundane consumer products as varied as garments, furniture, and audio sets are acquiring new looks. A recent article in a national magazine explained the architectural style of a new hotel and the sign placed prominently in front: "The decorative grooves along the new sign's base have a certain high-tech quality." [10] High tech has indeed literally become a sign of the times.

But it is not reasonable for every state in the union to start up its own computer industry, any more than that the United States should have fifty auto companies, one per state. What is reasonable is for states to build on their local economies by modifying and absorbing new technology into their present and planned industries.

How important is high tech as an overall force in the economy? Even when the facts are known, interpretations differ radically. For example, the size of the computer and electronics industries is often compared to that of the automobile industry. High-tech electronics firms have sales of about $170 billion a year and employ about three million people. Sales of the four leading auto manufacturers total about $110 billion, and they employ just under 800,000 people; another one million are employed in supplier firms. Yet old attitudes are slow to change. A leading management authority at the Harvard Business School had this to say about high tech: "I don't really think of the electronics sector as critical because it is just too small. Look, even if you increased employment by 25 percent you'd hardly make a dent on the unemployment rate." Yet to him the automobile industry, because of its "size," is fundamental to the economy. One reason that people still misjudge high technology is not only because it is new but because its products are often hidden or embedded in old products. While everyone has learned by now what a car is and how it relates to steel, highways, and even housing, there is far less understanding about the significance of high tech for other industries or for our future.

America's high-technology firms are presently its most bullish economic performers. Pushing their high rates of growth is demand from all segments of the economy. According to the U.S. Department of Commerce, between 1970 and 1980 the most sophisticated R&D industries grew at twice the rate of the combined industrial output; prices of their products grew at only one-third the rate of inflation; and their productivity grew six times faster than the average for all U.S. businesses.[11] Next to agricultural products, they are our best performers as export commodities.

But for all its robustness, it is no secret that computer, semiconductor, and communications manufacturers face stiff competition from abroad. As we will show in later chapters, there is intense competition to determine who will be the toolmaker to the world. This comes not just from Japan, but from a whole dynamic of international competitiveness that originates in Asia. Because modern computers were first developed in the United States and because of the seeming invincibility of companies like IBM and concentrations of innovation in Silicon Valley and Route 128, it is hard to imagine that this industry could become second best. But it could.

When William Shockley and his team invented the transistor in 1953, a new industry was born—and with it, a new mystique that is part reality and part myth. The reality is hard science and places like Bell Laboratories, which nurtured the new ideas and gave birth to the new industry. Reality also is the inventor's departure from Bell to set up his own Shockley Transistor Company. And the entrepreneurial chain did not stop there. The family tree of companies that were formed as spin-offs from Bell and Shockley Transistor has spread deep roots in the economy and in the American psyche. We have an entrepreneurial culture, and the history of the development of the semiconductor industry and its computer offspring demonstrates it in all its splendor. That is today's reality.

The myth is that this process will go on forever, even if unsupported, undernourished, and assaulted from talented competitors abroad. The key to staying ahead, both in the development of new tools and their absorption into mature industries, lies in our capacity to innovate—that is, in our ability to create, develop, market, and use new products and processes. We'll have more to say about innovation and the need to not take it for granted. But to get a practical and empirical view of innovation as a process, we decided to look at how two "traditional" companies are coping with the new tools. One is in manufacturing, one in services. Both have plunged unreservedly into the new technologies.

4

A "Mild" Revolution

The ultimate responsibility for the overall business strategy of any company rests with the chief executive officer. It is he who approves the final strategy that commits the company to a course of action. In other words, the buck stops at my door. I accept this.

> —T. Mitchell Ford, Chairman, Emhart Corporation

Traditional manufacturing engineering will eventually disappear at Emhart. The product designer will soon have a direct input into manufacturing. In the future it will be knowledge-people running the overall show.

> —John Rydz, Vice-President for Technology, Emhart Corporation

Some unlikely companies have taken the lead in what some people are calling a second industrial revolution. A Harvard professor of business, Wickham Skinner, sees production and process engineering as the bright new fields after more than fifteen years of being "old hat." Who would have thought that making tractors was a "leading-edge" technology? Yet the press headlines the Iowa-based Deere and Company's introduction of sophisticated production-line technologies in the town of Waterloo—of all places. General Electric boasts a brand new automated locomotive plant. Western Electric introduces electronic links between designer and production-line machines. For all of these companies computers are the driving force of the new era. These companies are far from alone, and the process they are going through is far from simple. An appreciation of the complexities of the transformation can be gained from a closer look into the way one company turned to the future.

The pedigree of the Emhart Corporation goes back a long way. During the 1950s it acquired what is now the conglomerate's oldest operation, a Swedish glass-container-machinery plant in Sundsvall which opened its doors in 1754. Two centuries ago, glassmaking was an art. It became a craft with the invention in 1902 of new processes by two graduates of Edison's laboratories. Since then, the machinery sold by Emhart's glass division has retained essentially the same mechanical operating principles. Pneumatic controls activate levers and tubes that form glass containers. Now new technologies, such as microelectronics, are providing an opportunity to rebuild both products and processes that remained unchanged for a hundred years.

With roots that go back some 225 years, the Emhart family tree includes familiar industrial names like United Shoe Machinery Corporation (USM) and others like Kwikset and Bostik that are less well known but that have also been around for a long time. Four out of ten sales dollars at Emhart come from three very mature core businesses: glassmaking machinery, hardware, and footwear, including materials and shoemaking machinery. These are basic products in stable markets. Shoes, glass containers, fastening components, and hardware are widely used and will be for a long time. The pin-tumbler locks sold today are essentially unchanged since their invention in 1869. One reason they last so long is the nature of the market. As the president tells it, "We've been building our business for more than a century. We're an old-line, New England company that makes unsexy products, but products that satisfy some very basic human needs. At Columbia University, for example, as far as we know every door has one of our locks. The convenience of having a single master key to open all of these is very important. This is a very basic reason why our clients stay clients." The master-key concept is the basis of the company's marketing success in this line of business. Another reason, as one executive put it, "is that doors are still popular. And our locks have kept up with change."

Unlike many old companies, Emhart remains very successful. In 1983, it had revenues of over $1.7 billion worldwide, with net earnings of $84 million. The company had grown into a far-flung world enterprise with 29,000 employees in the United States and twenty-nine other countries. It ranked two hundred and first among the *Fortune* 500 companies in sales, and ninety-third in payback to shareholders over a ten-year span. Its product lines led in almost every category.

Machinery that makes footwear is one of Emhart's most successful businesses. In 1976 Emhart acquired USM, whose prime product, first invented in the 1890s, was so successful that in the 1930s *Fortune* magazine labeled USM a "perfect" company. But changing social and political conditions caught up with success, and in 1957 the company was broken up after out-of-court settlements under the antitrust laws. That legal action helped divert management's attention away from continued improvements of its shoemaking machines. These, and shoe materials, are now manufactured in a dozen countries and at the Beverly, Massachusetts, headquarters plant, located in a building dating back to 1903. Today, Emhart's shoe machines are still built much the way they were a generation ago—using the craftsmanship of experienced machine toolists to run small lots and, where applicable, the occasional computer-controlled machinery.

More than anything else, what made this conglomerate's basic industries so successful was decades of well-maintained customer contacts and superior customer service. With a highly reputable array of products and a finely tuned marketing operation, Emhart was what business analysts call a stable, mature business. It was financially healthy and generated lots of cash. At least up until a few years ago, sales were easy. As one executive put it, "You could invite the president of a key client company to play golf for a day and then discuss business with his VP for purchasing. It all happened over drinks." But with a suddenness that caught many off guard, "We found ourselves one day with the same president accompanied not just by his purchasing VP but by his new technology advisers. They would start asking questions about new technology we just couldn't answer."

Something had to change, and it did. During the last few years, Emhart went to work modernizing its divisions. By 1983 it was getting harder and harder to recognize the old Emhart, so rapid were some of the changes. From being a holding company less than ten years earlier, it became a thriving multinational. Strategic planning and new productivity measures were introduced. As a result of a companywide audit of its competitive strengths, products and processes were targeted for upgrading with new technology. Turning the tide did not come easily.

Although every case has its own particulars, the Emhart story mirrors many of the challenges facing mature American industries today. How Emhart responded to those challenges holds lessons for many other old companies. Emhart has committed itself fully to integrating state-of-the-art technologies to *prevent* obsolescence in many of its operations. In some parts of the company results are radical, in others, modest. But for Emhart, as for many companies, the governing dictum is: "There is nothing permanent except change." What is most remarkable about Emhart is that it was able to set this change in motion without the immediate threat of foreign competition or the specter of bankruptcy. How it was able to do so is a tribute to several of its far-sighted managers.

In going from old to new, Emhart followed its own "typically deliberate Yankee fashion," as one observer put it. Even though by the middle 1970s many people within the company sensed that the company had to absorb new technologies, the problem was not taken on as a corporate priority until the late 1970s. Until then, an older generation of corporate managers controlled operations. But the company chairman, Mike Ford, had been exposed to an array of technologies as a member of the board of United Technologies, and he saw the time coming fast for Emhart to shift gears. By 1979, he was ready to make his first move, setting profound changes into motion. With a wit and self-effacing modesty reminiscent of the famed Senator Sam Ervin's comment, "I'm nothing but an ol' country lawyer," Ford likes to say, "We've done what we've done instinctively since 1979. We're a very stodgy place . . . nobody here but us chickens."

It was the winter of 1979. The people sitting together at lunch often ate in the employees' cafeteria. The company president was proud of his tradition of mixing management with employees at meal time. On this day, T. Mitchell Ford sat with a few of his key executives. Everyone knew the company chairman as "Mike." Also at the table was Wally Abel, then sixty-two years old, an inventor, innovator, and technological genius who had been brought under the Emhart umbrella through its acquisition of United Shoe Machinery Corporation.

In the wake of serious problems in a subsidiary operation, Ford had asked Abel to look at all the technologies in the Emhart group. Apparently, the subsidiary in question had adopted a new molding process that proved faulty to the point of near disaster. Plastic autobody parts were rolling off a new plastic-injection production line so pockmarked that hours of expensive hand labor were required to make them acceptable. Expensive deliveries by commercial jets to distant auto plants were required to meet production deadlines. Emhart lost millions. Management responsibilities were reshuffled. Now, over their cafeteria lunch, Ford, who had decided to alter priorities at Emhart, wanted Abel's judgment as to the company's future prospects.

"I just sat there and didn't say anything," Abel recalls. "He asked me, 'Wally, what do you think?'" Abel's normally infectious optimism and constant curiosity didn't show. He was much too serious on this day.

Abel remembers Ford asking again. "Finally I looked at him. 'Mike,' I said, 'Emhart's going *down the tubes!*' I really meant it. We could coast for three to five years on what we had. But in seven years we would be down the tubes." The hyperbole in his words was paradoxical. On one hand Emhart was eminently successful—on paper. Yet from another perspective, its investment in new ideas, it was falling behind. Focused on this point, Abel's urgings converged with those of Ford, who had now completed

the critically important first step on his own agenda for the future—consolidating his acquisitions and reorganizing the company. "It was clear to me that Wally saw me taking the company
to ruin. But for two years I had wrestled with the results of a
merger that turned us from a $350 million company into a $1
billion corporation overnight. We had lived through that and by
the end of 1979 we were ready." Within four years, a strategic
plan for technology had been developed and an action plan to
implement it instituted—two further steps in moving the corporate culture from the "old" to the "new."

By 1983, the effect was evident. The new vice-president for
technology, John Rydz, calls it a case of corporate entrepreneurship. "Many people believe that a single individual can bring
change in a big corporate setting. They are wrong. There is no
way to solo it. The corporate entrepreneur has to orchestrate
what ultimately has to be a team effort." One example, the
"$100-million gob," illustrates the change. Although seemingly
modest technologically, it would have spectacular financial implications.

Glassmakers have long wrestled with the problem of making a
bottle of uniform thickness and strength. Until recently most
molten glass technology did not allow glass to cool evenly, a
problem that forced bottle makers to compensate with extra glass
at weak spots. More even cooling would mean less glass and
faster, cheaper production. Hence the challenge of controlling
the glass from its molten gob shape to a final formed bottle. The
innovation occurred in the division producing machinery that
makes glass bottles. Its success could be traced to a new managerial attitude and the application of an array of new technologies developed in other industries.

At work, most glassmaking machines are noisy, hissing, mechanical contraptions. From such machines come gobs of molten
glass from which single bottles are formed. In addition to being
outmoded and painfully noisy, the machinery has other problems
as well. One is competition from other machinery manufacturers;
more serious, however, is competition from cheaper non-glass
containers. Glass-bottle makers shipped 6 percent less product in

1982 than the year before in the $5-billion-a-year industry. In brief, Emhart found itself challenged by a market calling for higher quality at less cost.

Innovation in this case meant more than just random improvements here and there. It meant some fundamental changes. In 1980, the glass-machinery division went to work. One thrust was to focus on a single critical feature in its product, the mold that forms the initial gob of glass. In an unexpectedly short time, a breakthrough occurred. New aerospace and computer technology, combined with a management commitment to change, brought forth a new product at once both mundane and spectacular. To the technicians, the new gob mold is formally known as the "1:2 vertical blow mold triple overlap with added reheat machine for quad gob." To corporate financiers, however, it's a life-saving new component with a market potential of over $100 million. Significantly, this may be the first of a whole series of complementary innovations with similar market potential.

For companies like Emhart, future success boils down to just such innovations. These can be achieved by redirecting two complementary paths: product innovations (a better mousetrap) or production efficiencies (a cheaper mousetrap). For many firms the new technologies—already invented and marketed by high-technology corporations—make the choice possible by updating an overaged capital base and upgrading a low-skilled work force.

To understand Emhart's achievement, we focused on three aspects of how it is coming to terms with the new technologies. At the corporate level, we looked at reorganization at the top and at the key individuals who prepared the groundwork for change. At the operations level, we investigated the case of glassmaking machinery and what lay behind the successful "gob." And to get a feel for what innovation means on the factory floor, we learned about another old product, shoemaking machinery. Each tells a different story in technological innovation.

In 1979, Mike Ford—having put in place the mechanics of running a worldwide operating company—turned his attention to blending two traditions. He had to adapt an Emhart product line that was little affected by laboratory research to a long-standing history at USM of encouraging research and development. One of the first steps he took was to create the corporate-level title of vice-president for research and development. This signaled new intentions to top management. Wally Abel was appointed the new vice-president, an acknowledgment of his contributions at USM, where he had come to be known as the evangelist of change. In Ford he saw an open and receptive CEO and an opportunity to make tangible contributions without being impeded by bureaucratic hurdles. To his job he brought the belief that new technologies were less matters of choice than of necessity.

In 1939 he had graduated from Worcester Polytechnic Institute with a bachelor's degree in mechanical engineering. From there he walked straight into the United Shoe Machinery plant in Beverly, Massachusetts, and into its research department—and never left. Twenty-two years later, in 1961, he was appointed its director of research.

In the wake of the 1976 acquisition of USM by Emhart, a decision had been made to abandon the central research operation in favor of a highly decentralized corporate structure. For someone of Abel's zeal, turning over R&D responsibility to each group was tantamount to self-destruction. The new title assigned to him came after a management reorganization in which Mike Ford came out the winner for a more highly centralized organization. In his new role, Abel was called on to *recommend* overall R&D policies and objectives. The president and board would retain control over the interpretation of these recommendations. The immediate task, however, was to "preach the technology message" throughout Emhart—which Abel did. No opportunity was lost in becoming the company's technology champion.

Soon afterward, at Abel's instigation, a second position was created with the title "director of productivity." The person chosen to fill the new assignment came with a unique track record of success as a new kind of executive. He was an entrepreneur and innovator skilled at working within a corporation. This implied taking risks and sharing successes far differently than the more common view of an entrepreneur as a loner striking out to build a growing enterprise from the ground up. John Rydz is a tall, heavy-set man with a friendly but determined manner. A graduate of MIT, he arrived almost perfectly tailored to the challenge ahead of him. Years before, he had turned a failing low-tech product—the Singer sewing machine—into an unbeatable winner by adapting microelectronics into its operation. Before that, as vice-president of Diebold Incorporated in Ohio, he had made a company building bank safes into a dominant force in the manufacturing and marketing of remote electronic bank tellers and computerized security systems for financial institutions.

He was the right person at the right time. The job evolved quickly. In August 1982, two years after his hiring and a short time before Abel's retirement, he received the new title of vice-president of technology. Simple as it sounds, the term meant a lot. R&D was dropped from the title as being misleading. "The issue was application of ideas with an emphasis on the immediate," says Rydz, "as well as the long-range. This means combining not just R&D but also design and process engineering as well as manufacturing. 'Technology' is the term that encompasses all that." A more important yet subtle change came in the revised job description inherited from Abel. Rather than merely recommending objectives to the president, Rydz was given responsibility for assisting in the "the *means* for achieving these objectives." In short, a strategy and the mechanics for implementing it were being introduced throughout Emhart. In the complex world of corporate culture a truly fundamental change was being signaled from the top down. To someone unfamiliar with corporate behavior all this may seem far too arcane to be important. But when one considers that a work force of almost 30,000 people in thirty countries would be affected, a single mistaken or miscommunicated step could prove disastrous. Many are the companies unable to articulate a strategic vision or lacking the leadership to execute one that may be well articulated.

"Working with operating units," says Rydz, "requires a highly competent corporate technology staff, as well as a will and desire to help operating groups to implement new technology." The job of the corporate innovator is neither to monitor nor to police operating units, in his view. Rather, the function is to act as a catalyst by identifying technologies that can help operating units achieve strategic goals and to suggest ways of implementing change.

After two years on the job, John Rydz has helped induce a new attitude and a strategy for technology. What he achieved was an understanding that the essence of change would be found in new technology. According to Ford, "We're psychologically ready now as a company to assimilate new technologies as part of a series of innovations and changes needed. We think that the culture of the firm has changed." The facts seem to bear him out. Patent applications were up 30 percent during the prior year, and a new awards system is in place both in the divisions and at the corporate level. Four or five technological innovation "Oscars" are now presented each year. Such steps might seem trivial, but they work. "We want innovative people," says Rydz. "It's the key to continued success."

Rydz also instituted a small staff of specialists whose job is to monitor twenty advanced technologies and to translate them into threats or opportunities for Emhart. He calls this team his "salesmen—marketeers of the new technologies throughout the corporation." In an effort to link the corporate pieces into a coherent view of the opportunities ahead, a quarterly technological review is circulated throughout the firm's worldwide operations.

Communication of a corporate strategy is part of the team's assignment. One form this takes is three-dimensional cubes drawn on Rydz's personal computer. Each cube represents a product group. At the bottom are several horizontal layers—a sandwich of corporate technological resources. For one product group this includes the following layers: microelectronics hardware and software; sensors and new microhydraulics; machine diagnostics and mechanism analysis; computer-aided vision. On the side of the cube each horizontal layer has an accompanying label of external resources: consultants and vendors; universities and vendors; universities; universities and consultants. The message is clear. The corporation will provide support in each of these areas, and the group is urged to make use of external talent to add depth to its own resources. Above these horizontal layers are vertical blocks, each representing a product line in the group. The message: each product can use one or all of the resources listed below it.

Monitoring this evolution is a newly constituted technology committee, formed in October 1982 and made up of four board members with strong personal experience with new technologies. Meeting four times a year, they review trends and the corporate position relative to them, consider technical goals and their consistency with the corporate strategy, and ensure that all required steps are being taken to implement technology programs.

Changing the corporate structure is essential if a firm is to make the passage from old to new. Such transitions require unique talents of those who make it their business to effect change. These innovators can have widely divergent skills depending upon which stage of change a firm finds itself in. This is no better illustrated than in the personalities and styles of Wally Abel and John Rydz. One knew how to raise warning signals, the other how to implement change.

To understand Abel and the philosophy he nurtured for almost half a century, one has to look back to his earliest days at USM. "Good ideas are priceless," he says. "I learned this from John Homan, who was in the department early on. He'd get ten cents out of his pocket and bet you a dime on something you didn't think could be done. We'd be in there weekends and nights. He just motivated the hell out of us. We just don't do that anymore with dull dreary jobs." The war years turned the research division into an almost self-sufficient profit center of eager inventors. Abel and his youthful colleagues worked on mechanical computer controls for antiaircraft guns—not knowing that electronic breakthroughs were already being made at Sperry. They worked on rocket-propelled aerial torpedoes. While this didn't do much for United Shoe's product line, it did lead management to ask Abel to redesign and modernize the research department.

"That whole experience had given us jobs we couldn't believe they trusted us with. We were so young. There we were, a bunch of guys in a shoe-machinery company telling the army, air force, and navy what they were doing wrong!" With a knack for mechanical things and for anticipating the future, he quickly moved a generation ahead of his time. "Control of a machine was the most important thing. How to speed it up and not lose control. What's the fastest and smallest thing that could be used? I kept coming back to an 'electron.' I knew early on that we should be heading toward that. I didn't know then that we'd call it a 'chip.'"

Two decades later, Abel retired. At a ceremony in his honor, his successor, John Rydz, paid tribute to the legacy he had inherited and described his own approach to managing technology. "The management of technology is like an Olympic race. The technology manager is given the baton and he runs his lap, passing the baton to his successor." The race on this sports field of course never ends. Each technology manager in turn runs his "lap" and passes on the baton—as long as the corporation exists. "Since it is a race that never ends," said Rydz, "there is no single individual winner. Winning comes by staying out front during your own particular lap. For one manager, a look over the shoulder might reveal robots and automation coming up at him. For the next it might be microelectronics." Of Abel, his successor said: "He gave us a good lead and passed the baton on smoothly."

An incident that happened years earlier at USM illustrates Abel's constant pressure for change. Electronics were not well understood at USM in the midsixties. The research department experimented with putting shoe-stitching instructions onto magnetic tape. "That was a time when our machines had rudimentary paper-tape controls. What we were trying to do would have meant a paper tape literally a mile long. Somehow word got out about the mile-long tape and nobody believed that magnetic tape would ever work." Persisting through the criticism, however, Abel got a few trial stitching machines into the field. Tests seemed to corroborate all the worst expectations. Dirt got onto the tapes and they gave out the wrong signals. "The marketing guys told us that even with the kinks worked out, we'd sell only five machines—total worldwide." The prevailing view argued that such innovations were unnecessary. The solution, traditionalists in the industry argued, was to get Washington to stiffen import restrictions. "My attitude about that," said Abel, "was to shove it. That was the absolutely worst position they could take."

Now perfected, 2,000 USM computer-controlled stitchers have been sold. An indirect effect of this innovation has been to bring one part of the shoe business back to America. U.S. makers of fancy cowboy boots, who once subcontracted for complex sewing of designs in Mexico, now do it at home—cheaper. Complex patterns are sketched on computer-assisted design terminals at USM headquarters, and sewing is done in shoe companies equipped with computer-controlled USM sewing machines. Stitches on thick leather are run at a rate of 2,500 a minute—a speed and perfection unmatched by any other leather-sewing machine in the world. Automation of this segment of the business affects the production of about 15 million pairs of boots per year, or about 5 percent of the shoe manufacturing volume in the United States. It doesn't provide Americans with a lot of jobs, but it's more production than what it was in the past.

Through the efforts of Wally Abel, the evangelist, and John Rydz, the consummate manager, several more crucial pieces were added to the corporate structure. A Center for Technological Innovation was created and located at the United Shoe site in Beverly, Massachusetts. It coventures projects with any of the corporate divisions working on new technology applications. The costs are shared by the participating divisions. The Tech Center serves, in effect, as a research and development resource for any division. In this manner, state-of-the-art technologies can be monitored and applied in CAD/CAM, microelectronics, or new materials research and distributed throughout the corporation's divisions.

All of the corporate changes and the new emphasis on innovation had to work their way down to the operating divisions. We learned how this process occurred by following developments in glassmaking machinery, the division where the $100-million gob success had occurred. To find it, we drove fifteen or twenty miles north of Hartford to a small Connecticut Valley town. The recently built headquarters are in a modern complex on the knoll of a rounded hill. Farms still surround the neatly landscaped industrial park. The man to see was Bob Douglas, the new director of R&D. He had come to Emhart in 1981.

What faced him then was no easy task. Ten years before, he had been at Emhart but had left to take a job at GE's Nuclear Division and later its Corporate Research Center. When he returned to Emhart after a decade, he remarked jokingly, "It felt like I had been gone a week and a half. Nothing had changed." That stagnation was now Douglas's problem. Emhart's profitable but aging machinery could not compete with the cost effectiveness of plastics and new technologies for long. In Europe, some concerned clients were taking Emhart representatives to see their production lines. Electronic monitors provided instant information on how much machine capacity was being used. If it was 89 percent, they wanted to push it to 91 percent. Emhart was not ready for this kind of fine-tuning.

"The glass and metal people know their days are numbered," says Dr. Laszlo Bonis, chairman of the Composite Container Corporation in Massachusetts. "In five years, you'll hardly be able to find glass or metal in the supermarket." Bottlers know this, and many hedge their bets by having glass and plastic lines side by side. "They didn't care which one it was," says Douglas. "What caught me off guard was that the customer wasn't going to push us to innovate in glass. They'd switch if necessary. We had to do it ourselves if we wanted to keep our product alive. To keep the product alive it had to provide the glass manufacturer, our clients, with the means to compete. We had to work on the productivity of our machines, which in turn would allow our customers to drive their own costs down." More than half a century of carefully nurtured contacts and an excellent service record didn't help; performance and new technology did. New technology and innovation were to become the keys to improving productivity. Douglas's strategy was to do it incrementally, one innovation at a time. The payoff, if the strategy worked, would be large. His initial markets consisted of several thousand huge multimillion-dollar glass-bottle production lines operating throughout the world—many with Emhart machinery.

Cost savings were a critical competitive factor here. The packaging we see on supermarket shelves often costs the producer five times more than the food or beverage it contains. Consumers are in effect paying most of their money for costly packaging. Thus the glass-machinery division's new R&D manager, Douglas, had a very direct challenge: cut costs by producing more bottles a minute with reduced energy and labor inputs, yet ensure the highest possible quality. And above all, make sure that glass bottles are not replaced by containers made of other materials.

For Bob Douglas the question was how to do it. His first move was to get division management to agree not to look for a quick fix but rather to focus on long-term technological changes. The second step was to envision a totally new glass-container production line, fully computer-controlled, which could be developed incrementally. This would allow the customer to buy one affordable new improvement at a time and thus to survive. Emhart would come out with new sales as development yielded new products.

Interestingly, much of Emhart's creative activity was in its European divisions, but lack of a coherent strategy prevented the corporation from putting their ideas into practice. Douglas described the problem as he saw it: "You had most of the innovations coming out of our European operations. But only a few innovations made the trans-Atlantic voyage. Bit by bit the company found itself with incompatible noninterchangeable parts. Innovation had been focused on solving specific customer needs and not on creating a uniform and competitive overall product."

What Douglas had inherited were groups on two sides of the Atlantic, one not coordinating with the other. He reorganized these into several groups. In England one team focused on process physics and computer modeling with an emphasis on thermodynamics; another in the United States tackled electronics and controls; the Swiss center worked jointly with its American counterpart in product-support R&D and applications engineering.

Product engineers would acquire developments from the first two of these groups and translate them into actual product designs. "With this organization in place and roles defined, we could now tackle a product line basically untouched for fifty years," said Douglas.

To illustrate how Emhart had turned to existing technology to change an old product, Douglas described the gob-making innovation—or axial cooling, as he calls it—mentioned earlier in the chapter. To the uninitiated the process, when described in words, takes on an imagery of molten lava magically transformed into endless streams of familiar Coke bottles. In the expert's language the molten lava becomes a uniform flow of constant-temperature glass in a twenty-foot channel. This molten glass—with temperatures measured in thousands of degrees—is metered by a feeder that extrudes it as an undulating stream. Scissors then shear it into gobs. So far, it all sounds very modern and mechanical. But then comes an element of human craft harking back generations. A "bottle maker" looks at the shape and color of the gobs being sheared. Relying on experience—and occasionally on a notebook filled with sketches of varied gob types—the skilled artisan makes manual adjustments to the controls. When everything looks right, he authorizes the production run. "These bottle makers are skilled craftsmen," says Douglas. "Their methods were developed for machinery that is now seen as too slow and not sufficiently productive. One of my tasks is to quantify and automate this aspect of the craft."

The R&D on this single task took only one and a half years, most of it in the British labs. Results were staggering. The new molding technology, one step in the long process of making bottles, can be plugged into existing machines. It sells for $50,000. Just this one add-on component could translate into sales of 2,000 units within three to five years—or half the installed lines worldwide. The gross revenue potential of this one innovation is on the order of $100 million.

In the past, improvements were largely results of trial and error. No systematic process was involved, and costly interruptions of production lines were often required. One challenge for the future would be to conceive a totally new machine with improvements programmed one step at a time using any and all of the new high technologies. A key concern would be to minimize the financial risk and downtime for clients. Getting this done would not only be costly to Emhart but an error could prove fatal—to careers as well as to the competitiveness of the whole product line.

This brief look into Douglas's axial cooling innovations is not concerned with the issue of large and risky capital investment or with the uncertain return from expensive pure research. The gob innovations were achieved, in fact, at relatively low cost. The point, rather, is to show what corporate leadership and sound management can do to stimulate innovation. Many companies have all the required ingredients for success: the people, the technologies, the capital. But they can still fail if they cannot apply the proper leadership and organizational skill. For Bob Douglas, "a formal structure imposed on a problem just doesn't work. A rigid organization doesn't encourage innovation. Every invention needs the dedicated push of the scientists/inventors and the engineers who must reduce it to a practical product. With an R&D staff dispersed worldwide, informal communication on a person-to-person basis is most effective and fastest. It's what helps tie all the pieces together. This becomes even more important when you try to move a product idea out of the lab. Everybody needs to be involved—sales, service, quality control, manufacturing, engineering. They need to identify with the new product." Douglas insists on frequent meetings to discuss different stages in the development of a product. The procedures he describes have a unique quality—they are fluid. To freeze them into a series of boxes connected with arrows on a chart would miss the reality that every product will have its own personality and particular blend of key actors. What is formal, however, is the deliberate sequence in planning a product by first defining a problem and then identifying a solution that is shared with marketeers and selected customers. "As we get into design," adds Douglas, "I look for key actors to throw rocks at an idea. We ask ourselves whether an idea is indeed produceable; with others we discuss the engineering features needed to make it operational; and yet others to review the marketability and service reliability."

"We don't do research here," says Douglas. "Rather, a majority of our work is development and another large share is engineering applications. As far as research is concerned I encourage my managers to allocate some money to try new things. The process is very informal."

Accompanying changes in the product were changes in the makeup of the glass-machinery division's engineering staff. In 1980 fewer than 10 percent were electrical engineers; by 1985, 30 percent will have electrical or computer-science degrees. Now the whole division is focused on rethinking the entire production line. Microprocessor technologies are being adapted to alter what Douglas describes as "an archaic series of production islands" into an integrated computer-monitored and -controlled process.

What promised to be a major product evolution in one division contrasted sharply with efforts in another division to modernize the production environment. To see the effect of the new corporate strategy on the factory floor, we visited United Shoe Machinery, a much more traditional-looking manufacturing operation, in its hometown, Beverly, Massachusetts. "The Shoe," as it is called locally, goes back almost a hundred years to its founding in the 1880s.

When Emhart bought USM, it acquired a slice of old American industrial history. By 1899, it was the first company in the United States to create a formal research division, which at its peak during World War II employed about 900 engineers and scientists. Early in its history, USM became the world leader in shoemaking equipment, which it leased out to clients with the back-up of full service, supplies, and financing. This novel idea of equipment leasing and service support—used extensively today by companies such as IBM—brought the firm to the fore in the early 1900s, a time when "mechanical inventions were falling off the wall," as the current USM vice president for R&D, John Meuse, puts it.

USM also figures prominently in the checkered history of antitrust cases. So successful had the company become, it turned into the world's major supplier of shoemaking machinery and associated products. But as government and public attitudes toward corporate power changed, it was ultimately forced to split into two companies by a final antitrust court ruling in 1957. The legal procedures had spanned almost twenty-five years. These efforts and others instituted against IBM and AT&T would provide openings for foreign companies unfettered by similar antitrust constraints. At USM, the drain on management was immense. As a result of the ruling, the company was obliged to sell about 60,000 of its leased shoemaking machines, which resulted in a huge cash reserve. This windfall was used by USM to diversify into a range of businesses from automotive plastics, mentioned earlier, to minicomputer components, while maintaining a significant share of the world market for shoemaking machinery. Later it would find itself devoting its top-management energy to a futile effort to prevent an Emhart takeover. In the process less and less time was devoted to improving its product line of machines sold to shoemakers worldwide.

To understand USM, one has to think of the shoe industry in two parts. One includes the shoemakers themselves, USM's clients. The other is the maker of shoemaking machines and the supplier of materials; USM is the world leader. The actual making of shoes is a complicated and competitive business. To manufacture one shoe requires over a hundred steps carried out on a selection of a hundred or more machines. Many of these machines are highly complex mechanical marvels, little impacted by electronic technologies, and still labor-intensive since each production step must be managed by human hands. The shoes these machines produce come in dozens of widths and shapes, and hundreds of color and styling variations. Any and all of these can be affected by the fickleness of fashion and seasonal changes.

To make matters worse, competition among shoemakers around the world is intense. American makers have been mostly on the losing end. One reason is that the industry remains relatively labor-intensive and moves to where labor is cheapest. From 1977 to 1983, U.S. employment in leather footwear dropped 20 percent, from 156,000 to 125,000. At the end of this period, about 300 million pairs of shoes were produced annually, down from 600 million in 1966. Imports are about 50 percent larger than America's total annual production. Most come from Taiwan, South Korea, Italy, Brazil, Hong Kong, and Spain—twenty times more than in 1960.

Early in the 1970s, at Wally Abel's initiative, USM set out to identify tactical and strategic priorities for the U.S. shoe industry. In a private report submitted to the Department of Commerce, it concluded that U.S. shoemakers could remain competitive only if the time between style design and production could be shortened dramatically and if productivity could be increased massively—by rates on the order of 300 to 800 percent. Obviously these were magnitudes far greater than that normally expected from evolutionary manufacturing changes.

Despite all the energy focused on updating shoe machinery with new technologies, it is not evident that costly new technologies are the answer to what one might think of as a "new" machine. While customers are calling for machinery allowing maximum flexibility to accommodate rapid changes in style, the probability of ever seeing a fully automated shoe production line is remote. Instead, a manufacturer is most likely to accumulate a series of improved free-standing machines, each performing one of about seventy-five to a hundred different semiautomated tasks at best. It turns out that it's not so easy to put microelectronics into machines like "nailers," "tackers," "pulling and toe lasting," "fitting stitcher," or even "computer-controlled stitchers." Because leather is difficult to work with, basic sewing is more efficiently done on hand-run machines unless it involves complicated patterns. The fantastically successful automated sewing machine helped keep the cowboy-boot business in America and away from cheap-labor competition in Mexico. But to date, this marriage of computer to shoe machine is the exception.

The challenge for USM is that a shoemaking machine can be made almost anywhere. What you need are basic machine tools, skilled machinists, and a well-run management system. Italians, for example, are strong competitors, offering similar machines at lower cost. Shoe machines are made in very small quantities and are manufactured from a large number of parts. This makes sophisticated automation difficult.

For managers such as Neil Bouchard, vice-president of sourcing—a title that includes overseeing all manufacturing at USM—the task ahead leads in two broad directions. One is to introduce new computer-controlled or automated tools selectively on his shop floor, such as in the Beverly plant, where they can increase productivity in making large numbers of specific parts. The other is to focus on what he suggests "are indirect costs that represent between 60 and 80 percent of the hourly manufacturing costs and determine if they are truly cost-effective." Bouchard mentions studies indicating a 20 percent higher productivity rate at Beverly per worker than in Italy—which helps compensate for wage differentials. "The real problem is the indirect costs," he says, "made up of managers, costly services such as computers, paper work, and other administrative activities." All of this translates into a product that is similar in quality to a competitive Italian machine but far more costly. During the next five years, innovation at the Beverly plant may mean a brand new management structure which prunes out inefficiencies and passes down many responsibilities to the shop floor. "On this we are just beginning," he commented.

Meanwhile, the Beverly plant—"The Shoe"—is being modernized. The tactic in this case is to move ahead only on those technological improvements proven to be cost-effective. Unlike companies such as Ford where production is measured in millions of units, at USM production is completed in very small runs. Shop floor assignments can shift from one production line to another. As a result, it is difficult to justify costly automated equipment. Any purchase of new technology must be carefully reviewed, and consideration must be given to how well it will fit into a plant that has gone through several technological revolutions in its time.

The shop floors at the plant are in a huge four-story turn-of-the-century prefab concrete structure. When it was built in 1903, it was the largest building of this kind in the world. Eighty years later, external appearances have not changed much. Inside, one looks in on a quarter-mile-long vista of well-ordered rows of machine tools. Seemingly unchanged from a generation or two back, the machines grinding away represent the end of an era. The old, interrupted here and there by the intrusion of trendier computer-controlled tools, live in a heritage of man-monitored hydraulically operated machines preceded by pneumatic and mechanical ones. Bit by bit, Wally Abel had added the latest technologies to the plant. "He is just unsinkable," recalled John Meuse. "He would keep telling us, 'The problem is that you just don't know where you want to be.' And he would push us a step further."

Changes from such proddings are visible. There are several massive brand-new computer-controlled machine tools built in Japan, a new computer-run quality-control station, an improved painting and baking line, and to date a lone robot used to weld rough metal into cabinet frames. It operates in a screened-off area, almost like a rare animal in a zoo. The workers say it looks like a cross between a seagull and a rooster. It is controlled by a young welder named Peter Bulger. He has the appearance of an old-time blacksmith, muscular, good-looking, sweaty from the heat, wearing a small leather apron.

Labor statisticians count Bulger as a welder. To his union he's a welder; to management he's a welder; to his friends he's a welder. But because he runs a robot, Bulger is no ordinary welder. "They don't have a real name for me yet," says Bulger. Probably he is no ordinary "robotics-programmer-welder" either. Without saying so explicitly, he has a vision of a new way, a new mood, a new turnaround. Contact with robotics has opened his eyes. He knows what's happening in Japan; he's aware of cost constraints; he sees the problems of redefining job skills. The misconceptions about robots irk Bulger. "They say robots replace tedious, monotonous jobs. That really puts me down. If I had thought welding was monotonous, I'd never have become a welder." Nothing has occurred to reduce his skill as a welder. To him the robot is a new tool improving his productivity.

Finding more welders qualified to work the robot is not so

much the problem. No jobs were lost when his robot came on line, but then fewer new people may be hired because Bulger's productivity has increased substantially. To the plant managers robots must be introduced incrementally. For Bulger it could happen a lot faster. "A lot of other people, even young ones, aren't interested in robots," he says. "They just want to keep doing it the old way. We could make this thing do great work. And we could make it make money."

Below on another shop floor lined for almost a quarter of a mile with machine tools is a new computer-controlled high-precision testing room. Metal parts are tested for the minutest flaws. On a summer day, the outside air is humid and hot. Inside the small room, air-conditioning keeps the computers at the right temperature. The operator—who a short time before was in greasy overalls on the shop floor—wears a white shirt and tie. His co-workers now view him differently, perhaps envious of his new station. Educating other workers to become programmers able to operate the testing equipment is underway. Some workers wouldn't dream of becoming computer programmers. They would much rather enjoy their machine-tooling craft. Managerial time is spread thin and no one is available to oversee the training. Someone talks about bringing in college-trained programmers even though it might be cheaper and more effective to concentrate on training knowledgeable shop-floor employees.

Nearby, in a vast three-story covered courtyard, are two new computer-controlled machining centers—made in Japan—sitting idle for the moment. Scheduling them to work at peak capacity for two 10-hour shifts is difficult and requires experimentation. In the interim expensive downtime rankles the managers. Looking out on the cavernous shop floor, one realizes that the "old" is not about to disappear. An expert machine toolist cannot be eliminated. There is too much to understand about the cooling of tools, oil, setting up tasks that cannot be programmed into the best electronically controlled device. What the "new" means here is a slow and steady introduction of better tools wherever they can be cost-effective. And the "new," if anything, means that the management of the Beverly plant may be the key to its future. "We've got to make our administrative services far more cost-effective," stressed Neil Bouchard. While the Beverly plant is only one of many producing USM shoemaking machines worldwide, it is a test of American resilience. If it remains unproductive, work will shift to USM plants elsewhere. Survival probably means production of a narrower and more specialized product line in which technology provides a competitive edge. It also means leaner, more effective management. New rules must be learned to deal with product-line automation, job-classification adaptations, and flexible manufacturing systems. USM has made a start at its Beverly plant. The jury is still out on how fast it can proceed.

Seen from afar, the view of Emhart we have described is compelling for several important reasons. The most obvious is the corporate recognition that its survival is intimately wedded to the proper introduction of high-technology tools. What became evident at the glass-machinery operation was that much of this technology would result from ideas flowing back and forth across national borders, as we discovered with Bob Douglas's research teams in the United States, Switzerland, and England. The internationalization of technological innovation is becoming a way of life in an age of highly specialized and sophisticated technical expertise.

This chapter tells us, too, that new technology alone cannot provide a company with a new lease on life. Part of the equation is human, and it requires a new cadre of engineers steeped in the latest knowledge who can sustain innovative changes over the long term. This means a firm commitment from upper management but most emphatically from the chief executive and the board of directors. Part of their responsibility is to share a vision of the future with their employees and to create the proper environment to thrive. As the firm's senior public relations officer, John Budd, Jr., puts it: "Credibility of this message is vital. Our strategy is to repeat and to reiterate the importance of technology. Gradually this worms its way into the corporate culture in a way that head-office fiats or manifestos never can." Freer lines of communication and formal recognition of ideas that contribute to corporate well-being, such as Emhart's annual awards, are vital catalysts. And finally there comes another conclusion, less well understood in many firms. To complete the transformation of an old company culture into a new one, attitudes and skills throughout the work force must evolve.

A new generation of technology cannot be introduced without a work force skilled at controlling and maintaining sophisticated equipment. Peter Bulger, an educated and motivated individual, exemplifies a key of success or failure at Emhart—and in "old" corporate America. For Emhart, change means focusing on the retraining of almost 10,000 of its current employees or about one-third of its present work force. Mike Ford knows that they will have to adapt "to new ways of work, to the new things we make, and to our changing position in the marketplace." That task is Mike Ford's next priority at Emhart. He has given it strategic prominence. This makes explicit a belief that his company's future competitiveness will rely in great part on the education and skills of its work force.

While Emhart is a good example of how manufacturing businesses can and should change—some heavy industries and other producers of consumer products—they now account for a vital but slowly shrinking portion of employment in the United States. Today one out of four working Americans is employed by firms of this sort. More than twice that number, however, are in firms grouped under the general label of services—banks, food operations, hospitals, schools, insurance companies. To get a feel for changes affecting this massive and diffuse service sector, we visited one of the nation's largest insurance companies caught up in what is known as the financial-services revolution in which insurers, bankers, and brokers are competing for one another's business. The problems and opportunities facing the Ætna Life and Casualty Company provide interesting parallels and contrasts to Emhart.

5

Systems, Systems, Systems

The resource that will most clearly distinguish us from others over time is our people—their education, training, motivation, and resourcefulness. This will determine our success as a nation, as a corporation, and as individuals.
—John Filer, Chairman, Ætna Life and Casualty

Our day-to-day lives are surrounded by what the statisticians call the "service sector." Newspapers, television, radio, banks, offices, schools, restaurants, shops, hairdressers and innumerable other businesses and institutions account for the 72 percent of the nation's jobs that are categorized as services.

A predominant characteristic of all these jobs is that they are labor intensive. Office paperwork, food service in a restaurant, laundry services all require enormous amounts of hand labor. When it comes to office work, it is estimated that productivity rose only 4 percent from 1960 to 1970, while factory productivity jumped twenty times more during the same period.[1] One explanation is that the investment in machines was ten times higher for industrial workers than for office workers. When it comes to office paperwork, stories of inefficiency are legion. Many of these are related to what we now familiarly describe as "bureaucracy." Many people picture this as acres upon acres of desks where documents are shuffled and rubber-stamped. This image turns out to be accurate in many cases—but it is less and less true in many others. Technology has been making significant inroads in those businesses whose primary product is information and whose primary medium is paper. Ætna Life and Casualty is one of these.

In a company like Ætna, it seems out of place to talk about "new" technology. Ætna has used computers for a long time.

The first IBM commercial computer, the "650," with its revolving drum and 2,000 vacuum tubes, ran some of its earliest programs here in the 1950s. Even as far back as 1917, punched cards were in use. The company had machines such as sorters, tabulators, and collators that were leased from the Computing, Tabulating, and Recording Company, the predecessor of IBM. Ætna's first data-processing department was until 1954 called the Hollerith department, a name harking back to the inventor of the first punched-card machine in 1890. In 1954, Irv Sitkin, now vice-president for corporate administration, helped program the 650 as one of Ætna's first two computer-staff people—"trainee #2," they called him. In 1965, Ætna received the first shipment of the famous and highly successful 360 line of IBM computers, which Ætna people helped to debug. "They called us Poughkeepsie East," recalls Sitkin, referring to the fact that IBM's Poughkeepsie staff spent a lot of time getting their hardware and new operating system to work at Ætna. In those days, Ætna even helped design IBM's path-breaking though not yet intelligent terminal, the 2741 model II.

Yet even in this technologically sophisticated environment, something new is going on. "The new changes are immense," says Bob Phillips, corporate vice-president for personnel. Only ten years ago, 60 percent of Ætna jobs were clerical and 40 percent technical. Now the formula is changed and there are nearly as many technology jobs as clerical ones. "Increasing complexity plays a part in this shift," notes Phillips, "but the numbers come from the technology." The Ætna Life and Casualty Company has been among the first to create a completely electronic "paperless office." "When we want to close a deal with a big client, we do it in the 'paperless office,'" said another officer. And as technology has become even bigger, this company has had the foresight to abandon the infamous mechanistic approaches to work associated with Taylorism. This approach is still in evidence in other insurance companies such as Blue Cross/Blue Shield, as reported by Bob Kuttner in a recent article in the *Atlantic*.[2]

At least three revolutions are going on simultaneously at Ætna. One is that technology has exploded from centralized data-processing machines to decentralized microcomputers, satellite networks, and a new management tool—computer-based education. Another is the education revolution. The ability to deliver instruction about new products and services is viewed as a new and important strategic advantage by Ætna managers. A new corporate institute for education, directed by a former Harvard faculty member, has been launched. These two revolutions in the technology system and in the company's education system are giving birth to a third—a jobs revolution. The profile of the work force of this still-labor-intensive company is changing so rapidly that academic theory and the perceptions of the general public are not able to keep pace. All three of these revolutions are happening at a time when the business environment is evolving rapidly from insurance to a widening spectrum of financial services that may encompass banking, real estate, and stocks and bonds. As a large, well-established insurance company, it is no easy matter for Ætna to shift gears. How this bellwether company responds to these forces has a lot to say about what is likely to happen in a large portion of the vast services sector of the U.S. economy. The financial-services industry alone employs almost 2 million Americans.

Across from a huge neo-Georgian headquarters building near downtown Hartford, a new structure of glass and brick is taking shape. It is the Ætna Institute for Corporate Education, to be housed in a 390,000-square-foot edifice with state-of-the-art electronic learning aids, hotel facilities, and classrooms. "It is significant," notes Institute president Badi Foster, "that even during bad economic times, the company continues to invest in education."

Rapid changes in the marketplace coupled with developments in new technology were making some jobs obsolete. This worried both the company chairman, John Filer, and its president, Bill Bailey. During the autumn of 1983, a number of people had been declared "surplus," not just in low-level positions but at high corporate levels as well. "Jobs go obsolete in this business just like any other," says Bob Phillips, head of corporate personnel. And in this business, like any other, it's traumatic to be told the work you've been doing won't have to be done in the future. Professionals who are older and more experienced present a special challenge. "It's easier to retrain and place the file clerks than the officers," says the Ætna recruiting head, Kevin Price, whose job includes reassigning the surplus pool.

But unlike most other businesses, including competitors like John Hancock and Prudential, Ætna developed a policy called "Ætna jobs for Ætna people." As the going gets rougher and the competition increases—as it has with a vengeance in the last year or two—the company has instituted a hiring freeze. It has opted to retain—and retrain—its work force. This policy accentuates the company's growing commitment to education.

When the company first decided to build an educational institute in 1980, it had no "grand plan" in mind. Chairman John Filer recalls how the idea evolved. "There was no single stroke of genius. A group of some fifteen or so executives noted we'd run out of space for training." The building was first referred to as the Training Facility and its initial purpose was to consolidate and coordinate the various routine training programs common to any *Fortune* 500 corporation. But typical of Ætna tradition, which eschews grand plans (the company has no written mission statement or booklet that articulates its overall goals and philosophy), good ideas not only grow organically but are seeded slightly before their time. "It's fortuitous," says Sitkin. No one explicitly coupled the need for education with the personal-computer revolution. No one foresaw the value of an education institute to backstop "Ætna jobs for Ætna people." Nor did many, except perhaps the officers at the very top, fully understand the importance of hiring someone whose background was in education rather than insurance. What Badi Foster represents is not just job training but educational leadership.

"If we hire a computer professional to run our data-processing systems," states Filer, "we need to get an educator who can do the same for our 'human systems.'"

Although Foster, president of the Ætna Institute, looks like a normal corporate executive, he's not routinely seen as one. A

Princeton Ph.D. and formerly of Harvard University's Graduate School of Education, he is seen as an educator with ties to the world of higher education. Significantly, he represents another world too. Born on the south side of Chicago and having lived and studied in shanty towns in the Third World, Foster also personified Chairman Filer's interest in "community involvement" as it pertained to service to the unemployed and underemployed. When the company decided to remain in Hartford, it needed a symbol of community participation as well as educational leadership. It got both in Badi Foster. The image was strengthened with the addition of David Rippey, Foster's chief aide who is doing a doctorate at Harvard and is deeply involved in community participation as well as relations with local universities.

"I don't know what we would have done without Badi," says Lucia Quigg, responsible for what Ætna calls food management, a new name for cafeteria services. One of the first moves was to provide educational opportunities to a group of workers at the lowest level of the organization, people who some trainers had earlier written off as "untrainable." Catherine Jenkins, an educator with a degree from Harvard's School of Education, had struggled against what she terms an "Upstairs-Downstairs" bias against kitchen workers. Her program was extremely successful, and one of the reasons was that she and her staff made the effort to work in the kitchen itself before designing an education program. Few people in upper management or even at the supervisory level—at first—had ever thought of responding to employees' needs in this way. "These were the lost folk," she said. "Few thought that education had any meaning down there at level B." Whether it's downstairs at the cafeteria or upstairs in the corporate penthouse offices, the Institute plays an important part in the New Ætna game.

Ed Jowdy, a sharp businessman with a hard nose for the bottom line, directs Ætna's massive computer-training program ADPEP, the Ætna Data Processing Education Program. He explains the new strategy this way. "Over time, education has become a prime means to enable the company to stay ahead of competition. When senior management said let's build a building, they also meant let's hire an educator to run it." Actually, while Foster will shape the policy of the new education, Ed Jowdy will run the building. He is responsible for administration and utilization of the fifty-two classrooms and the 271 bedrooms. He already is responsible for thirty-five ADPEP instructors and thirteen more in his computer-based-education section. His ADPEP operation alone, folded into the Ætna Institute for Corporate Education, provides data-processing courses to over 6,000 people per year.

Few know for sure what the overall Ætna budget is for education. "Whatever the number people think it might be, it's probably too low—it doesn't capture the whole thing," notes Bob Phillips, to whom Badi Foster reports. And whatever the number is, currently estimated at about $35 million in annual operating expenses in addition to the $44 million needed for construction costs, it would rank Ætna education on a scale far higher, for example, than Foster's previous employer, the Harvard Graduate School of Education. By way of another comparison, the budget for Connecticut's Department of Higher Education for 1985 is projected to be $270 million. But even this amount is insufficient to keep a public system up to date. For example, at the University of Connecticut, only one computer terminal will be available for every fifty students. The ratio at Ætna Institute will be one to one.

While the Ætna Institute for Corporate Education may be critical to Ætna's future survival, the universities, colleges, and community and junior colleges in Connecticut hold a key to the survival of the Institute itself. When Ætna first announced its plans, most of the state's schools saw a direct threat. The University of Hartford and local community colleges, for example, derive income essential for their operations from adult education. Since Ætna employees were a prime source of students, they feared losing them.

To date, none of these fears have materialized, thanks in large measure to Foster's initiative in establishing what is known as the JAC, or Joint Advisory Committee. The JAC is composed of the presidents and provosts of twenty-two Connecticut colleges and universities as well as the top officers of Ætna. What they have jointly arranged is a surprisingly diverse array of exchange programs, faculty fellowships, internships, and sharing of resources. Jim Tatro, who coordinates the JAC meetings, notes: "The JAC has produced a spirit of collaboration and a mechanism for making outside higher education resources available to Ætna."

The technology revolution in Ætna is massive. "Pervasive" is the word used most often by corporate officers and the rank and file work force to describe it. Offices without computer terminals do exist, but they're hard to find. In 1984, there was one terminal for every three employees—and this includes all of Ætna's 40,000-person work force. Irv Sitkin cautions people to remember not "that we're one of the biggest users of technology but one of the best." Despite his caution, Ætna's computer and communications systems *are* big. We heard statements like these from many people: "We're IBM's biggest client." "Except for the phone company, we have more miles of cable than anyone." "We're second only to the Social Security Administration in the number of checks we write—by computer, of course." It doesn't matter that some of these statements may be technically inaccurate. What matters is that there is a nearly universal belief at the company that they're more or less true, a typical phenomenon of "corporate culture by anecdote." Ætna owns part of a satellite system (it is a joint sponsor of Satellite Business Systems Inc. with IBM and Comsat) and now that portable microcomputers are here, many expect Ætna to become even more technology-intensive than it already is. What was not expected, however, was the degree to which technology would impact the education process, and the extent to which Ætna is rapidly emerging as a leader in computer-based education.

They call it "the experiment." Mal Snyder, head of creative services in the corporate communications department, refers to the experiment as "the most significant advances we have made in technology—the newest competitive management tools yet." Lana Wertz, director of the educational technology unit for the Ætna Institute, explains that "the experiment" is really five gambles to strike it rich in the field of educational technology. And those involved are determined to succeed. "Dry holes are not appreciated at Ætna," according to one of the experimenters. The five programs include a "made for television" three-hour series on attitudinal training (a corporate soap opera of sorts); an interactive laser-driven videodisc program on financial analysis which is a first in the nation; a tele-education series that uses the SBS satellite network to bounce the classroom 23,500 miles up and 23,500 miles down to earth (signs around the company remind employees that it takes only 0.3 seconds to communicate with other parts of the company); an ambitious computer-based education department to teach people about computers by computer; and a "corporate information center" whose goal is to hook up self-paced learning stations to every Ætna field office as well as to some 500 professional data bases and other learning resources.

Dick Jackson was one of the principal designers of the videoconferencing facilities which are used for tele-education. The problem was not just the massive travel schedules needed to keep company personnel in touch with one another. The biggest headache was the difficulty of bringing thousands of people in from the field to upgrade their knowledge. "Let's say you and I were the same age and sex and hired on the same day. You worked in the San Francisco office, and I started at the home office. After eight years, I would have had fifteen to twenty courses on the latest in insurance, technology, and financial services. You would on average have had only one or two. Everything else being equal, who do you think would get the next promotion?"

"We spent $250,000 just trying to reach 1,400 people for training," explains Lana Wertz, responsible for educational technology. "Now we were asked to reach 7,000. We had to turn to tele-education." The plan is to take some of the best classroom instruction and to make it available either live or by videotape to anyone in the company who can get to one of the videoconferencing facilities. So far, there are rooms in Hartford, Middletown, Windsor, Chicago, and Washington. With some exceptions, they are virtually identical. They can all be operated by the person responsible for the meeting or a designee—without any technical experts present. A class of students can take a course in a forty-five-minute time slot, or two time slots back to back. It's not unlike the academic scheduling, except that courses start right on time. And they end on time, if only because someone is usually knocking on the door to start his or her own session on time. "That's what the executives love," notes Jackson. "They can schedule their time over the satellite and know that people will stick to the schedule."

What has made the tele-education system cost-effective is a new communications computer called the CODEC which compresses 90 million bits of transmitted data by 6000 percent. The cost is more than halved. The CODEC is produced and marketed by Japan's NEC Corporation and costs $160,000 per unit. California-based CLI (Compression Laboratories, Inc.) has now also gotten into the game. Ætna has an NEC machine side by side with a CLI model. "The American unit is presently cheaper," notes one of the operators, "but you can sure see the difference in quality where the Japanese still excel."

NEC Corporation frequently sends its Japanese staff to study Ætna's tele-education facilities. They copied one perfectly and reproduced it in their U.S. sales office. Except for one thing. The Japanese managed to arrange all their camera and communications equipment onto a single "blackboard." They installed casters on it so it could be wheeled from one location to another. Now they've got a movable supersystem of their own.

Not everyone likes videoconferencing or its sister activity, tele-education. Jackson relates how his staff resorted to cleverness to get people to try the new medium. Once they held a dinner meeting via satellite. A group of twenty in Chicago met for dinner with another group in Hartford. "We had the same meal, roast beef, on each end of the satellite hookup. The group in Chicago got wine, but due to a quirk in company policy, the group in Hartford had to have ginger ale." At first Jackson thought it was a bust. "People said it was corny. 'Thanks,' they said. 'It wasn't so great.' But next month, you know what happened: 'Hey,' they said, 'let's try that teleconferencing again.'" They've been users ever since.

Tele-education is especially important to Ed Jowdy's ADPEP program, where he is faced with having to train 6,000 people every year on technical matters for data processing (DP). "We're experimenting everywhere," he explains. As computer functions become decentralized, he has to contend not just with the DP experts who design and maintain the systems but with the "end users" who are increasingly getting into areas previously reserved for experts. ADPEP's cost per student day has risen from $37 per day in 1975 to $49 in 1983. After the cost of the new Ætna Institute is factored in, that figure will jump to $77. This will put more pressure on the company to find cost-effective ways to reach more employees with even more effective education in order to lower the unit cost.

"We're engineering a transformation here," says Jowdy. People are literally lining up for new courses, whether via satellite or more likely still in classrooms or computer-based instruction. The computer-based educational unit had five courses in 1979, twenty-one two years later, and forty-two in 1983 involving 20,000 connect hours of instruction for computer-based education. Three thousand field terminals provide employees with access to learning resources at 300 sites across the country. "Who's going to lead this company in the future? A large part of the leadership will be educational," says Jowdy.

Probably the most innovative and controversial part of "the experiment" is the interactive videodisc program. Peggy Mick in creative services calls it the most advanced in the nation. It's what educators in academe have been thinking of doing for years but were unable to do because of lack of funds and administrative support. Ætna's five-module financial-training package consists of a Sony videodisc hooked up to an IBM personal computer. This $10,000 learning station starts with a narrator in full color and motion explaining a concept like the time value of money. The new twist is that when the viewer touches the screen the narrator stops and a computer menu appears. Want to hear it again? Want to try an exercise on what the narrator was explaining? Want to skip to a more detailed explanation? The new videodisc system allows all of the above.

For generations grown up on television and growing up on computers, this is the ultimate educational device. It allows learning at one's own pace in an exciting and intellectually challenging way. "It's fun to use," said Lana Wertz. "It has the potential to democratize education." While it looks like a familiar old television, it has the power of a computer. The creative services division of corporate communications sees great potential in the new device. As if to underscore its giant steps beyond conventional programmed instruction, Snyder noted the change in image this has brought to his department: "We don't lend overhead projectors anymore." But he also emphasized the bottom line. "We provide the tools for our people to market their products and services. Everything we do is oriented toward helping them do their jobs better. In the final analysis, our educational services have to be profitable to the company."

Not everyone is sanguine about the profit potential of the interactive videodisc. While the hardware costs are plummeting, the number of hours required to produce one hour of instruction is still excessive. The experience of Ætna's computer-based-education department suggests that standard education by computer may require 100 to 300 hours of preparation and development to get one hour of instructional material. Ed Jowdy estimates that when interactive video is added, the additional filming and programming is multiplied by a factor of ten. To Irv Sitkin, interactive videodisc is still in its infancy. "It's still a toy, but a toy worth experimenting with."

Sitkin is constantly searching for new opportunities to exploit technology in all aspects of Ætna's business, including education. One difficulty is the necessity of finding or developing educational approaches that make sense in the Ætna environment. Six or eight years ago, he experimented with Control Data's PLATO program, which had impressed him when it could teach in one hour a biology experiment that he had needed eight weeks to complete as a genetics student at Cornell. But an obstacle was the expensive terminals and network that were required. "I carry my office under my hat," says Sitkin, "and I want terminals readily available wherever my office is. The Ætna Institute for

Corporate Education is the gateway for this function. It will have the most important impact of any tool we've created thus far."

Since the cost of producing interactive video is so high, a number of companies have been exploring a collaborative arrangement. Each company would share in the cost of creating some of the basic hardware and software needed to drive the system. If such collaboration is developed, it probably will not center on a university. More likely, it will channel its funds to a small independent start-up firm. One such company, Interactive Training Systems, was spun off by former faculty members of the Harvard Graduate School of Education. Another important effort is underway at the Digital Equipment Corporation, where the Interactive Video Information System (IVIS) has been developed and marketed. This pattern is in marked contrast to the Emhart case described in an earlier chapter where a major research effort, in that case robotics, was undertaken on a collaborative basis with Worcester Polytechnic Institute.

Many people think, mistakenly we believe, that while technology enriches a few high-level jobs it debases and trivializes low-level ones. The phrase that captures this idea is "the missing middle," a reference to the notion that technology might eliminate well-paying middle-level jobs. Experience at Ætna suggests just the contrary. Instead of a missing middle, at Ætna the bottom has been dropped. What we found was that over the past ten years the lowest job classifications have disappeared and new ones have been created higher up. The lesson, we believe, is that coupling education to technological change has produced a powerful force for upgrading the skills of Ætna employees.

Carol Rady, head of human resources for the employee benefits division, describes the changing job profile in the group insurance benefits claims-processing offices. With 13.1 million people covered and $7.2 billion in premiums at the end of 1982, the accounting is enormous. Nightly, 100,000 or more checks and claim explanations are mailed out. Claims processing is routine—it's boring with or without a computer. In the days before computers, it consisted of vast rooms of file cabinets and large numbers of file clerks, people who gathered the relevant folder when a client's claim was submitted. A file clerk had a job-classification code of 18—almost the lowest number in the Ætna coding system. Today, there are few file clerks, and almost no field employees in class 18. "We took the bottom out," says Rady.

What does the claims-processing office look like today? There are five job levels. First come a few microfilmers, job code 18–19. Their function is to use micrographics and optical scanners to enter basic data about a claim into the local computer system. Next come the people who process the claims, job code 21–23. These people, 80 percent of them salaried women employees, operate a computer terminal to help them decide whether a claim should be paid or not paid. Then comes a newly created job—customer service representatives, job code 24. Their assignment is to handle client queries and complaints, to explain why a claim was not paid or only partly paid depending on the coverage. Then come claim representatives, people who go to an employer's premises to discuss insurance policies and claims—job code 26. Above them are trainers/auditors (job code 26–28) and supervisors (job codes 28–32).

Before computers, many of the jobs were class 18 file clerks. After computers, most of the jobs are class 21–23 processors and a completely new category, class 24 customer service representatives. Rady summarizes the net effects this way: "Clerks are almost gone, processors are classed higher, service reps are growing like wildfire, claims reps always existed and still do, trainers/auditors have more complex jobs, and the supers have stayed about the same." The number of clerks is declining at the rate of 15 percent per year, while customer service reps are growing at more than 10 percent annually.

But the story doesn't stop here. The real issue is pay. "We have never lowered pay. We raised it for processors and customer service reps," according to Rady. A typical entry-level processor earns at least $9,360 in Lubbock, Texas, to a minimum of $12,000 in Boston, New York, or San Francisco. The maximum is near $20,000. On top is a 38 percent benefits package. None of their work is on an hourly basis, nor is any of it part-time. The big change at Ætna is that it has gone to a thirty-two-hour work week for processors but has maintained the same pay—and interestingly, the processors have maintained the same volume of output. This move, known as the "resource management" program at Ætna, has produced an unintended side effect. Now there is pressure from other employees who still work the full thirty-seven and a half hours per week to lower the shorter-work-week pay scale. "Are we now overpaying new people?" wonders Rady.

Another major issue in claims processing is how much control the computer exerts over the users' work. "We were concerned about people's attitudes toward an environment that lends itself to oppressive mismanagement," noted Jim Devlin, head of the new Center for Management Effectiveness in the Ætna Institute. "Claims processing is a work environment where this can occur." In the mid 1970s, two things happened at Ætna to cope with this issue. First was the introduction of the "modulars," as the company calls them. Rather than have vast claims-processing operations fragmented by functions, groups of sixty to eighty employees are responsible for all the needs of an assigned list of clients. This allows employees to see the full process and how their work contributes to the final delivery of service. This has required more education and training so that all employees have familiarity with the five or six functions necessary to claims processing. Many of the modulars have names—the Pepsi Unit, the Boeing Unit—reminiscent of the Ford Motor Company's employee involvement teams. "Have we licked the problem?" asks Rady. "No, but there's constant experimentation to see how we can make the job more satisfying and help people move up to the next job classification level."

About the same time that the modular system began, another complementary change was instituted. Jim Devlin recounts how much of the company used to be on a work-measurement system—"a sort of *do it to 'em* mentality rather than a *do it with 'em* approach." While a shift in management style had started as early as the 1950s at Ætna, it was in 1975 that the claims-processing departments announced, "We don't want the report card any-

more. We're throwing out that mechanistic wage-incentive idea."
For several years, only rudimentary measurements were taken of
employee performance. Soon, however, employees took it upon
themselves, with Devlin's help, to design their own measurement
systems and the incentive and bonus payments that accompanied
them. Now instead of measuring only how fast a person processes
how many claims, performance is based on a weighted average of
the number of resolved claims, the quality of service, the time-
liness of response, and, as of 1984, an indicator of cost-con-
tainment. The net result is that the old concept of "efficiency"
has been replaced, on the employees' initiative, to "effectiveness." To an outsider the words suggest a purely semantic
game. To insiders the effects are apparent. "Since January 1,
1983, we've had an 8 percent gain in productivity," notes Devlin,
"and we've given 5,000 employees the power to determine their
own bonuses."

There are other indications of management's preference for
effectiveness instead of efficiency. One is the "employee involvement" program, a counterpart in the financial-services business
to the EI program at Ford Motor Company. "If you involve employees, you'll get productivity improvement," says Devlin. "We
use action teams, quality circles, nominal group techniques.
These are the vehicles for employee involvement." This change
in thinking is not unique to Ætna. Devlin is a member of the
Productivity and Improvement Committee of LOMA, an association of insurance companies. Eighteen firms are represented on
this committee. In 1980, they abandoned their original committee
name, which had been Work Measurement. In 1983, they
changed their orientation by reporting not to the association's
financial officer but to human resources.

The human resources orientation is critical. To get efficiency,
you instill fear. To get effectiveness, you provide education. Jim
Devlin's work has encompassed this full transition. Although he
started in mechanistic measurement in the 1950s, as of 1984 his
operation will become part of the Ætna Institute for Corporate
Education and will be renamed the Center for Management
Effectiveness. What's the payoff in the long run? "When the job

markets loosen up, people are going to work for companies that treat them like human beings," he commented. "Those in financial services that still measure people keystroke by keystroke are going to run into trouble."

Katherine Simmons, who develops the pay and benefits programs at Ætna, reflected on the impact technology has had in her experience at the company. "I don't know what we'd do without computers. How else would you keep pay scales equitable when you're talking about 7,000 different types of jobs and 40,000 employees?"

"Our objective," says Ætna's chairman John Filer, "is to provide a good job—40,000 of them at present—to each individual employee." From his work on a panel Jobs for the 80s sponsored by the United Nations Association's Joint Economic Council, Filer sees a broad social movement developing to improve one of the things America does badly—planning and managing human resources. "The time's coming, probably within ten years, when an employer won't be able to terminate a career employee without just cause. Society is not going to sit still for firing people just because the nature of their job has changed. The recent legislation in the U.S. Congress on age discrimination is symptomatic of this trend."

What lies ahead for Ætna and its new emphasis on education? "*Credibility* is our chief test," said Ed Jowdy, referring to the future of the Ætna Institute. "We have to demonstrate tangible accomplishments that further the company's aims. Can we foster innovation over a long period of time—can we create the mechanisms that help manage change and even make it more rapid?"

Those "mechanisms," as Jowdy called them, are not just the new Ætna Institute. Its success or failure depends on a whole set of interrelated forces. Ætna was fortunate that it went heavily into education at a time when technological change accelerated. It was equally fortunate, or unusually far-sighted, to hire an innovative educator as the Institute's president. But none of these moves will work without continued support from top management that provides the open atmosphere and confidence that the company cares for its employees. "Ætna jobs for Ætna people" is an important part of this commitment. So is the willingness to retrain and upgrade employees from the lowest job classifications on up. In all of our visits to Ætna and our discussions with people at every level, one message was clear. Those at the lowest level see technology not as a threat but as an opportunity. When they perceive that they can move up, and when they have the chance to learn the new tools, the system works. When any one of these links in the chain is broken, employee morale, and with it quality service, breaks down.

Ætna Life and Casualty is a company that works hard at cultivating feelings of loyalty. It was rattled when many employees balked at moving with their division seventeen miles away to a new regional office. It had considered leaving Hartford altogether but now has made a commitment to stay and has added an assurance to maintain and improve job quality. But is the company unique? Does it represent a forerunner of the emerging service economy, or is it the exception? The crucial issue for Americans is jobs. While Ætna's experience is a cause for optimism about future job prospects, it is only part of the story. Another part, reflected in the press and in the rhetoric of public officials seeking election, is more pessimistic about employment prospects for the nation. While it is not our intention to try to resolve the ongoing debate whether high technology creates or destroys jobs, whether it demeans or enhances human skill and satisfaction, we will present some of the data and cases that we think are indispensable for informed discussion. Chief among these are the statistical minefield of job projections, and the option to either manage or mismanage technology.

6

Jobs: More or Less?

Nobody who makes projections about job supply and demand has a perfect crystal ball. Anyone who did would be playing the stock market instead.
　　　　　—Betty Vetter, Executive Director, Scientific Manpower Commission

Robots: Will they enter our future as burglars or as friends? We all know that the world of work is changing, but for better or for worse? Daniel Yankelovich, in a recent report, found that nearly half of those surveyed said their jobs had been impacted by technology, and three-quarters of these said the impact had been positive.[1] Our own experiences at Ford, Emhart, and Ætna confirmed this sense of optimism. In contrast, a more pessimistic scenario comes from the official statistics and those who report them. They tell us the future lies not in a shift toward technology-oriented jobs but in more of today's common ones—more secretaries, more fast-food workers, more truck drivers, and more janitors. The chasm between the statistically generated pessimism and the experience-based optimism reflected in our field work is striking. What's going on?

In 1982, the Bureau of Labor Statistics projected 700,000 new jobs for secretaries by 1990, 500,000 for nurses' aides and orderlies, another 500,000 for janitors, and large numbers for truck drivers and fast-food workers. These numbers helped fuel a backlash that was already in evidence against exaggerated claims and overpromises made in the name of high tech. Now the media tell us that high tech is no solution to the nation's unemployment problem. Some scholars say that technology is creating more low-paying than high-paying jobs; the net result, they project, will be a "missing middle" as America becomes stratified into a nation of haves and have-nots. Unions tell us that technology firms are exporting jobs to Asia and deskilling the ones left at home. Robots and office automation are said to threaten our job satisfaction as well as our jobs.

But just as the high-tech claims made in the late 1970s were exaggerated, so are the pessimistic forecasts of the early 1980s unrealistic. While ample evidence can easily be gathered to support and fuel the fears of change, the reality is another story. One fact is clear: No one is advocating that we jettison high technology. But what is its proper role, and what is the most likely job outlook for a technology-intensive future?

To get a picture of the future employment outlook is no easy task. The statistical base for even counting present jobs much less projecting future ones is at best confusing and at worst misleading. In short, it's both a jumble and a jungle of numbers. In studying jobs, one thing we learned was that searching for tomorrow's answers in yesterday's data is not the path to follow. There are many reasons why this is so. First, the basic statistical categories reflect an older industrial era. The U.S. Government's SICs are good examples of industrial terminology that no longer fits present realities. Employment categories in agriculture, forestry, and fisheries as well as mining, construction, and manufacturing still predominate; computers are buried in "nonelectrical machinery" while semiconductors reside in "electrical equipment and supplies," a category that also includes household appliances. But the SIC problem, while irksome for researchers, is less serious than the difficult business of projecting future job growth and openings.

The major source of employment statistics is the Bureau of Labor Statistics (BLS), which conducts an employers' survey every two years. Most of the media quote the BLS figures, and they are widely used by public officials and high-school and college career counselors. A second source of data is the decennial census, which counts what employees say they do. The BLS and census figures seldom agree. For over half the jobs in the United

States, the 1980 census data differed from the BLS numbers by more than 20 percent, indicating that the two do not concur on where we are. When we get to future projections, the situation becomes even worse. Let's take a look, for example at the occupation that the BLS projects will experience the greatest growth in the next decade—secretary.

In 1982, the BLS published a list of the fastest-growing occupations. Although it has been publishing these projections for years, the 1982 figures generated an uncommon amount of interest. Every major newspaper and newsmagazine, as well as many public-policy analysts, seized on the numbers to make a point: that the largest number of new jobs would not be in high-technology fields but in the low-skilled and low-paid service sector. Bob Kuttner in his *Atlantic* article, "The Declining Middle," reflected the growing malaise. His interpretation of the figures showed America heading toward a dual economy with lots of low-paying service jobs and many fewer high-paying jobs in the much-vaunted high-tech fields. Henry Levin and Russell Rumberger of Stanford University used the figures to show that we are overeducating our workers, and that certainly no widespread effort for high-tech education would be justified based on these numbers. What were the numbers, and where did they come from?[2] Do they justify long-term policy prescriptions, or do they fluctuate radically from year to year?

Secretarial jobs, for example, according to the 1982 BLS report, will experience the greatest increase between 1980 and 1990. Seven hundred thousand new secretarial jobs will be created in that decade. That's a lot of jobs. Such high projections are not new. A decade ago, in 1972, the BLS estimated that there were some 3,047,000 secretaries and stenographers employed nationwide. The BLS said then that four million would be employed by 1980 and five million by 1985. What actually happened? The number of secretaries in 1980 turned out to be 2,750,000—a drop of more than a quarter of a million rather than an increase of one million. Should we succeed in adding the currently projected 700,000 new secretarial jobs, this would merely bring us back to the level reached in 1975.

Even if the BLS forecasts had been right, do they tell us anything about how a secretary's job is changing? As is true with many familiar job classifications such as "secretary," technology is already having a substantial impact. In an age of word processors, electronic filing systems, and voice or electronic mail, how will the secretarial function change? Should they still be called secretaries? Will word processors and optical-scanning input devices eliminate what are now called stenographers and typists?

Everyone instinctively suspects what the problematical BLS forecasts demonstrate: Making projections is a risky business. But even worse is the tendency for the press and policymakers to accept the projections uncritically and base long-term policy on them. Ronald Kutscher, associate commissioner of the BLS, has correctly criticized such incautious misinterpretations. "Economists and others involved in forecasting economic activity understand the uncertain nature of projections. However, others, including those who are primary users of the information, may not. . . . Despite BLS's experience with and concern about the subject, we still are not sure our users understand the uncertainty attached to our projected data."[3]

Certainly we could have cited cases where the BLS was right on the mark. Elementary-school teachers are a case in point. In 1970 the BLS predicted 1.3 million elementary teachers by the end of the decade, and by 1980 there were indeed 1.3 million of them. Perhaps being on the mark is easier here because there is a direct relationship between the known number of elementary-school-age children and the consequent number of teachers required. But often the projections in what seem to be the most predictable fields are off. In 1972 the BLS projected that there would be 615,000 auto mechanics by 1980; the 1980 census counted over one million. The number of building custodians was projected at 1.4 million; ten years later the BLS found 2.8 million instead.

When it comes to projecting employment in the fast-changing technology field, we have an even more serious problem. Let's take a look at the statistical minefield relevant to high tech.

The changes at Ford, Emhart, and Ætna show us that large numbers of jobs are affected by the new technologies. But the BLS statistics have no adequate way to reflect this fact. Only four or five job categories seem to refer to high tech. Those most often cited are computer operators, programmers, systems analysts, and a catchall "data processing mechanics," a title that few people even in the data-processing industry would recognize. What is the BLS forecast for these so-called high-tech jobs?

In 1970, when the country was bullish on computers, the BLS made lavish forecasts that proved too high. For example, it said we'd have 425,000 systems analysts by 1980. In fact, both the census and BLS estimates show we reached less than half that number. But then again, what is a systems analyst? As we move from the centralized mainframes of the 1960s to distributed mini-computers and now the personal computers of the 1980s and 1990s, the role of systems analysts has changed dramatically. Many people who use computers today with spread sheets and high-level languages serve as their own systems analysts and computer operators as well.

The BLS also overprojected the numbers of computer operators and programmers, it seems, at least according to its own estimates of 1980 actuals. But the census data show otherwise. They show that the high forecasts turned out about right. But census data to the contrary, the BLS is taking no chances. Its forecasts for 1990 show computer operators increasing at a low annual rate of 5.2 percent and programmers at an even lower 4 percent per year. The comparable figures from the census, based on actual 1970–80 performance, were 13.6 percent and 7 percent respectively. If we used these rates as a basis for making forecasts, the media would not only be telling us that high tech is growing super fast (high-tech jobs already rank among the fastest growing, even using the low rates) but that it would be near the top of the list in the creation of new positions.

Clearly the data have to be treated with extreme caution. Check the following case for just how cautious you have to be. In its data on occupations producing the most new jobs, the BLS lists fast-food workers, waiters and waitresses, and kitchen helpers as three separate occupations among the top twenty projected for high growth. Together, they are forecast to create nearly one million new jobs in this decade. In terms of annual job openings, the numbers are staggering—800,000 for waiters and waitresses alone. This seems unbelieveably high until you learn that a "job opening" occurs every time a job turns over. In the fast-food business, which employs many young high-school students, this may be once a month or more. Nonetheless, the impression is that there will be lots of jobs in the fast-food business.

At the same time, McDonald's, symbol of the fast-food age, is fast becoming the symbol of the automation age. Not only does the restaurant chain already use a computerized ordering service, but management is considering using robots to cook the hamburgers. Again, this should come as no surprise. Horn and Hardart introduced "automats" to dispense food back in the 1930s. The surprise is that people continue to imagine that industries like the highly competitive, cost-conscious fast-food business will not exploit new technology to substantially increase their labor productivity.

In the wake of the controversies over the 1982 forecasts, the BLS scrapped its old computer model and acquired a new one. As announced in the November 1983 *Monthly Labor Review,* "Following the last round of projections, it was determined that the BLS macro model was inadequate for further projections. . . . The decision was made to look to the private sector for a macro model that would satisfy the needs of Bureau economists. . . . The Bureau now uses the Chase [Econometrics Associates] model to develop its projections." Perhaps the new model will be better. For computer specialists it yields slightly higher growth rates. For secretaries it shows a drop in employment— only 3.2 million in 1995 versus the old model's prediction of 3.4 million in 1990.

A different type of projection that provides a good fix on the overall employment picture comes from demographics, which are far easier to predict than job numbers. As the "baby boom" gives way to the "baby bust," fewer new people will be entering the labor force. The number of American eighteen-year-olds is projected to fall from about 4.1 million in 1980 to 3.6 million in 1985 and 3.4 million in 1990. The net result will be a decreased rate of growth in the number of new labor-force entrants from the 2.5 percent annual growth in the latter half of the 1970s to 1.7 percent between 1980 and 1985, 1.2 percent from 1985 to 1990, and 0.8 percent from 1990 to 2005. And this trend takes into account the continually rising labor-force participation of younger women as well as continuing immigration.

America, still suffering from the Depression syndrome, is preoccupied with unemployment and how we are going to find jobs for all who want to work. Actually, the real problem in the 1990s may be a shortage of workers, especially when you add qualifiers like educated, skilled, and knowledgeable. In some states like Massachusetts, the decline in eighteen-year-olds is projected at higher than 30 percent. The impact of these demographic changes has yet to penetrate our thinking and affect our policies for the future. To compensate for such a large decline will require a shift of emphasis to new labor-saving technologies and to programs to induce more women and minorities to enter higher-skilled occupations.

There is another, frequently overlooked dimension to this story. The general fear is that technology will displace workers. Indeed it may, although the Ætna case demonstrates how displacement need not lead to unemployment. But the other side of the coin is that technology can also save jobs that would otherwise be lost to foreign competition. That is, if new technology allows a factory to stay open and compete internationally, then a significant number of jobs are preserved. Indeed, the dynamic may be dramatic. Contrary to popular perceptions, we are beginning to see the first cases where technology is repatriating jobs that were until now moving abroad.

A lot of attention has been given to what is called the export of jobs. What has been neglected, however, is the emerging tendency to repatriate jobs. This is happening in cases where high-tech equipment reduces costs to the point that proximity to the market becomes a greater competitive advantage than cheap foreign labor.

For example, Motorola, one of the largest American makers of semiconductors, is repatriating jobs. "By further mechanizing assembly," says *Electronics* magazine, "[it] plans to offset high U.S. labor costs while cutting turnaround cycles."[4] The American payoff in this case is a new plant in Chandler, Arizona, with a work force to grow to 1,500, and the closing of plants in Asia. "We consider it at least a break-even proposition to do assembly and testing here rather than offshore," a company official stated. The economics are clear. In 1970, the cost of the labor to assemble an integrated circuit manually was three times higher in the United States than in Hong Kong. By 1980, with the use of automated equipment, the labor cost was virtually identical in America and Asia.[5] A similar story is true of Delco radios manufactured in a highly automated U.S. plant for GM cars. Once imported from foreign manufacturing centers, the radios are now made in America. While it is too early to estimate how large the aggregate repatriation of jobs might become as a result of automation, the signals of a positive job gain are strong. On the one hand, automated factories and their small job gains for the United States translate into factory closings and large job losses for Third World countries. The overall world impact is more difficult to assess. On the other hand, higher-paid Americans will be able to import more, increasing their demand for Third World goods. Productivity gains through automation is not a zero-sum game. The end result is increased wealth and higher living standards for everyone, although it may be slow in coming.

Japanese manufacturers of semiconductor chips, who have captured large portions of the commercial market for 64K and now the new 256K chips, have long based their competitive strength on automation of production at home. The major advantage this provides is better quality and better control over scheduling and inventories. Japanese executives often remark how easily American manufacturers were lured by the short-term payoff of moving production to cheap-labor centers and postponing an investment in domestic automation. The problem with offshore production, in their view, is that the quality of the product is not as good as that of equivalent products produced by automated machinery.

Hideo Yoshizaki, a former high-ranking MITI official who now heads Texas Instruments Japan, noted that "American chip manufacturers prefer to use Third World countries. Inertia prevents them from using automated technology at home." His explanation says a lot about American labor and the need for retraining: "Quality of labor is the major problem for the U.S. production line. In Japan, for example, if an automated machine breaks down, the operator can fix it. The reason is that in America the most important person is the chip designer, then the process engineer, and the lowest is the production line person. We do not have that problem."

Despite the continuing lure of cheap labor, other automated assembly plants are beginning to emerge in the United States. The dominant reason may well be quality. North American Philips Corporation is finding this out by moving back to the United States from Mexico. Soldering, once done manually in Mexico, is now fully automated. Defects that ran at seventy to eighty per 10,000 when done by hand are now down to three per 10,000. "That's a major reason we're moving production," said a senior vice president, Robert Lukingbeal. "It means we can spend far less money on troubleshooting and repairs before goods leave the plant."

Another case where high tech is bringing jobs back to the United States is the shoe industry. An Italian shoemaking-machinery company, competitor to United Shoe described in an earlier chapter, provides equipment with the slogan: "We give you the tools to make shoes at a lower price." Unital Inc. recently purchased such machinery and opened its doors in the old New England whaling port of New Bedford. Andre Sheinman is a partner in the new venture with Georgio Morelli of Italy, a hundred-year-old concern that exports shoes worldwide. When the plant opened in 1983, it was hailed by political leaders as an indication that the shoe industry was coming back to New England. The company hopes to employ a hundred people when the plant is fully operational. The reason it is able to compete with Italian imports is new technology. "With new technology," said Sheinman, "Unital can make very precise components at a reasonable cost. Americans in the shoe industry are killing themselves because they didn't go with technological progress."

Shoe production has been declining drastically in the United States over the last twenty years. The figures show that domestic production, and the associated jobs, fell by half between 1960 and 1982. Imports that were only 4 percent of American consumption in 1960 now account for 60 percent. Most come from Taiwan, Korea, Brazil, and increasingly from the People's Republic of China.

What mix of factors allowed Unital to go against the import tide? The reasons are not self-evident. First, according to Sheinman, is that an American shoe company close to the U.S. market can anticipate changes in styles that typically require long lead times for shoe exporters. Being close to the market is a real advantage in the shoe industry. Also, a domestic shoe manufacturer can ensure a more stable supply of shoes to retail outlets. The question of low-cost labor, however, goes against the common wisdom. Unital will produce shoes formerly imported from Italy. Italy no longer has a comparative labor-cost advantage over the United States in certain types of medium- and high-quality shoes. According to Sheinman, "The Italian labor cost, with associated government benefits added, is higher than in the United States." Also, he noted with a twist of irony, a U.S. firm can lay off workers according to seniority during a market turndown. An Italian firm must operate without layoffs or shut down the plant entirely.

Robots have come to symbolize our worst fears—either the dehumanization of work or the displacement of workers. Robots are a highly visible though not the major element of flexible automated systems and computer-integrated manufacturing. In the decade 1971–1980, the total U.S. investment in robots was only $248 million, a minuscule hundredth of one percent of the total capital investment for that period. The investment in computers, by contrast, was 140 times greater in the same period.[6] "And yet," says analyst Laura Conigliaro, "we are talking about an industry which has generated enough publicity in virtually every newspaper of any size in the U.S. during the last year and a half [1981 and 1982] to fill several large looseleaf notebooks."[7] How serious is the robot threat to jobs?

The Robotics Institute of America defines five kinds of robots. The first four are the ones that make headlines in the media. They are computer-controlled and can be reprogrammed with minimum effort to perform different tasks as needed. At work, these machines tend to be fairly clumsy-looking; most work fairly slowly but put in a longer workday than a human being can. Many are frozen to one position on a shop floor and are used most frequently to perform welding, loading and unloading, foundry work, and painting tasks. There are fifteen thousand of them in Japan, about one-third that number in the United States, and one-eighth to one-tenth in West Germany and France respectively. A fifth kind, nonreprogrammable machines, that automatically pick up, transport, and place objects, are too simple to be referred to as robots. Of these there are great numbers: 55,000 in Japan, 40,000 in the United States, 38,000 in France, 10,000 in West Germany.

While just a few years ago robot manufacturers could be counted on one hand, by 1983 there were about seventy American and foreign companies promoting sales in the United States. Many small start-ups and some big companies have come into the game, such as IBM, Westinghouse, Bendix, United Technologies, and General Electric. By 1990, according to the Institute and other analysts, American industry will be buying robots at a rate of 30,000 per year. The total number accumulated will range from 75,000 to 150,000, depending on whose numbers are used. One of the key limiting factors is the high cost of installation and a long period of learning how to make effective use of them.

What about jobs? Two academics at Carnegie-Mellon University, Robert Ayres and Steven Miller, looked at what they termed theoretical limits. By 1990, they could foresee a displacement of four million workers out of a manufacturing labor pool of about twenty million. They reach such high numbers by making the *theoretical* assumption that all possible jobs that could be replaced with robots will in fact be replaced.

A more realistic estimate is made by H. Allan Hunt and Timothy L. Hunt, two researchers at the Upjohn Institute for Employment Research whose data are extrapolated from Michigan's experience in the auto industry. They reported in 1983: "We estimate that robots in the U.S. will eliminate between 100,000 and 200,000 jobs by 1990, with roughly one-fourth that number in the auto industry. . . . In terms of job creation, we see 32,000 to 64,000 jobs in the United States." These will be in the manufacture, engineering, supply, and use of robots. "The largest single occupational group of jobs created by robotics will be robotics technicians—those persons with the training or experience to test, program, install, troubleshoot, or maintain industrial robots."[8] The limiting factor on growth, they believe, is the shortage of engineers. And they note the important fact that the jobs lost will most likely be those least skilled; and those created will be for workers with significant technical education. They call this the most remarkable feature of the impact of robotics and label it the "skill-twist."

Wassily Leontief, Nobel prize winner in economics, has made one of the best studies to date on the impact of automation on employment. Once known for his pessimism about the U.S. job outlook, his conclusions after a recent detailed study are that "the labor-saving effects of computer-based automation over the next twenty years will not be so dramatic as to result in significant unemployment provided that the economy is able to realize a smooth transition from the old to the new technologies." His optimistic conclusions, however, like our own, require "the availability of workers with the training and skills that match the work that needs to be done." If adequate training is not available, he warns, some three quarters of a million managers are likely to lose their jobs "and over 5 million clerical workers would be potentially unemployed in 1990." At the same time, there would be an equal number of unfilled positions in other occupations.[9]

While it is by no means clear what the ultimate outcome will be, the prospects for the United States are basically positive. But the game could be changed by a wild card—international competition. The outlook is not good for Europe, where the high-tech industry is weak and the employment systems rigid. Nor is it favorable in most Third World countries, which are rapidly losing their conventional comparative advantage of cheap labor. And even in Japan, the traditional lifelong employment system is under severe pressure. This means that international competition for jobs is going to increase dramatically.

Some industries, like autos, must automate to survive international competition. Turning the factory into highly computerized flexible manufacturing systems will preserve a number of jobs at the same time that it changes and probably displaces other jobs. Other industries, represented by Motorola's IC assembly plant and the Unital Shoe Company, are using the new technologies to bring industries back to the United States, thereby reducing jobs abroad but creating different jobs in America. Still other industries are simply automating, either in response to domestic competition or to lower the price to consumers, McDonald's being a case in point. In some cases, enlightened management action may be able to influence this process. But in large numbers of cases where international competition is a threat, the only option open is to preserve jobs through new technologies. A common thread to this trend will be the need to upgrade skills in order to have a work force that can not only understand the dynamics of an automated production environment but also diagnose and maintain sophisticated, electronically controlled equipment.

One of the most critical job categories is electrical engineering and computer science (EE/CS). There are presently about 300,000 electrical engineers working today, and projections for the future range from virtually no-growth to a doubling by the end of the century. Here again forecasts of future needs give rise to a continuing debate as to whether we will have too few or too many engineers. Since engineering schools are now operating at peak capacity, educational leaders have a particular interest in knowing whether today's strong demand will last, or whether the surge in enrollments will soon saturate the market. In Massachusetts, for example, the output of bachelor-level electrical engineers alone has increased by 60 percent since 1980. Some would argue that's enough and that the crisis in engineering education is over.

We disagree. Not only will there be a continuing need for EE/CS professionals who design, manufacture, and sell high technology products, but also the demand will accelerate for people who select, apply, and maintain these new tools, especially in old industries. Again in Massachusetts and other states, while the output of EE's has grown dramatically to 1984, further growth will be limited as engineering schools have capped enrollments in an effort to upgrade quality in overcrowded classrooms and laboratories. While no one knows for sure what the future demand will actually be, our case studies from Ford, Emhart, and Ætna indicate rapidly rising opportunities limited in large part by a limited supply of well-trained people. This means that the growth of the high-tech industry, and equally important the diffusion of new technology into mature manufacturing and service industries, will be gated by the quality and quantity of engineering graduates. Also, people with engineering training will be needed to conduct research, to teach continuing education, to update material for textbooks and interactive television, and for military as well as business applications. We return to these important issues and their implications for education in a later chapter.

7

Jobs: Better or Worse?

What will ultimately happen in terms of overall employment will depend not only on technology but on factors like international competition, demographics, and rates of economic growth that lie beyond our direct control. But within our control is the answer to an equally significant question—whether corporations will manage or mismanage technology. Many fear they will mismanage it, and that technology will be used to dehumanize jobs. This need not be so, but the knee-jerk reaction is that technology leads to deskilling rather than reskilling.

"Most high tech jobs do not demand high skills or pay high wages," according to an op-ed writer in the *New York Times*.[1] "Most high tech jobs are 'incredibly mind stunting, mind dulling,'" he reports, quoting labor authority Arthur Shostack. Surely there are cases to which these statements apply. But our investigation shows another story. Yankelovich in his recent report, *Putting the Work Ethic to Work,* shows that "of American jobholders who say that they have experienced significant technological changes on their jobs in the last five years, nearly three-quarters (74 percent) say that the changes have made their work more interesting, and more than half (55 percent) say that technological changes have given them greater independence."

The present is not yet characterized by deskilling, nor need the future be so. While we will cite several cases of deskilling, our message is that such cases can and should be reversed. One of the surest ways to become uncompetitive is through deskilling and demotivating the work force. And one of the best cases for abandoning the obsolete Taylorism style of management can be made around the new technologies. Let's look at several cases where technology has reportedly been mismanaged.

Ellen Cassedy and Karen Nussbaum, coauthors of *9 to 5* and founders of clerical workers' union 925, ask, "Will the office of the future be like the factory of the past?" If it is, not only will we revert to the same destructive adversarial system between management and unionized labor, but this time around we will lose our ability to compete internationally. Cassedy and Nussbaum describe such debasing: "Computer technology makes it possible to break jobs down into very small tasks and to keep close track of how quickly employees complete those duties—by the day, by the hour, and even by the minute. In a company in which employees handle phone calls from customers, a computer can measure the average delay in answering the number of calls each clerk handles per day. A video display terminal can record the number of keystrokes per minute and the number of lines processed per day. And one major insurance company measures the output of its office workers in 6½-minute units—almost 74 measurements a day! 'That machine feels like a foreman breathing down my neck,' one woman complained."[2] Like any tool, high technology can be used either to enhance human skill or to devalue it. Which of these will characterize our future depends on management and worker action here at home, not on Asian policies abroad.

Bob Kuttner cites the disturbing case of Blue Cross/Blue Shield as a way not to use technology:

At Blue Cross Blue Shield, the work force grew 46 percent, to 88,000, between 1970 and 1982. As in most insurance companies, the main activity of Blue Cross Blue Shield is collecting premiums and paying claims. Computerization and remote data transmission have made these tasks more routine and have allowed them to be performed almost anywhere.

According to Theron R. Bradley, who oversees employee training for

Blue Cross Blue Shield of Massachusetts, computerization has not had the same effect on everyone who works for the company. For professionals like him, it has provided new possibilities. . . . At the same time, the computer has had a different effect on Blue Cross Blue Shield's large clerical force. Bradley says, "In the past, the lowest six levels of our clerical structure looked like an inverted pyramid. [Now, by contrast, we] have a lot more routine jobs at the bottom, and a few more complex jobs at the top, where you need someone to analyze hundreds of pages of data."

Blue Cross Blue Shield's largest job category is that of claims examiner. . . . A claim takes about a minute to process, and a good clerk can dispatch 300 a day; the computer keeps track of productivity. On average, the clerks are paid between $4.50 and $5.75 an hour, but wages are adjusted every two months to reflect each clerk's output. Blue Shield provides a fifteen-minute paid lunch break and a week of vacation after one year. It provides no health insurance.[3]

The *Wall Street Journal* picked up the same story and amplified it. "Automation is being used to increase control over employees and to create a situation of constant pressure for productivity. The computer keeps track of how much work is done and prints out a production report for each employee every week. The report shows the time a job should have taken along with the actual time it took. A productivity score is calculated to the second decimal point."[4]

Extrapolating from this case creates a problem—it is more characteristic of the past than the future. Such descriptions are reminiscent of turn-of-the-century textile mills, and no longer apply to any but a handful of companies. Management is concerned with excess levels, not the disappearance, of middle management. We checked at the Ætna Life and Casualty Company, and found no missing middle but a shrinking bottom, pictured in figure 1.

Between 1975 and 1984, Ætna increased its middle management from 39 percent to 46 percent of its work force while clerical staff fell from 57 percent to 49 percent. And this is no isolated case. Wassily Leontief's model shows for the entire U.S. economy a dramatic decline in clerical jobs and an equally sharp

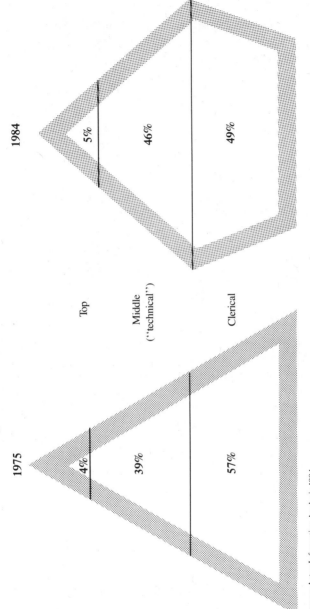

Figure 1. Percent of Aetna Work Force by Skill Level

1984

1975

Top

Middle
("technical")

Clerical

5%

46%

49%

4%

39%

57%

SOURCE: Aetna Information Analysis 1984

rise in professional positions by the year 2000.[5] The details are as follows: Under the scenario with the highest absorption of technology, professionals would comprise 19.8 percent of the year 2000 labor force, clericals would fall to 11.4 percent from 17.8 percent in 1978.

Technology can be used to upgrade work, sometimes even making old and time-honored professions difficult to recognize. The garment industry provides an interesting instance of how, for example, the age-old and respectable occupation of tailor is becoming redefined by technology. Dr. Louis Robinson, IBM's director of university relations, cites the following case:

Each morning on Seventh Avenue in New York City in the heart of the garment district, an employee comes to work, puts on his white work coat, and steps up to his work table. On that table he unrolls the bolt of cloth he is to work on this morning. After he has smoothed the cloth out on the table, he examines it to see if there are any imperfections in the cloth. Hovering over this table is a device that looks a little bit like the movable x-ray machine that you see in your doctor's office.

In fact, it is very much like that because it has in it a flashlight bulb that casts a cross-hair down on the cloth. Now the tailor, in examining the cloth, sees an imperfection in the cloth. He turns a few dials, and this machine, which is cantilevered over the table, moves automatically until the cross-hair shines directly onto the imperfection. Then he presses a button on the side of the machine, and the computing machine that is connected to this device memorizes the geometric locations of that imperfection. Then he sees another imperfection, and he turns the dial until the cross-hairs shine down on that imperfection. He presses the button, and the machine memorizes the location of that imperfection. When he feels he has identified all of the imperfections in the cloth, he looks at the order form he has, and he sees he's being asked to cut, say, a man's size 40, regular suit. He keys that information into the system.

All the rules and formulas and algorithms for taking the standard man's suit pattern and adjusting it to whatever the order is resides in the memory of the machine, so it calculates what the pattern ought to be. Then the computing machine lays the pattern out on that cloth, guaranteeing that the pattern never intersects any of the known imperfections in the cloth that the tailor has already identified to the machine and allowing for the proper matching on the cloth. The system ensures that the minimum length of the bolt of cloth is used in the process. When that is done, the tailor presses a button, and a laser beam comes out of that device and it cuts the cloth.

Now, when that gentleman goes home at night, and someone asks him what he does for a living, he says, "I'm a tailor."[6]

Robinson's example of course contrasts sharply with the grim reality of many garment, apparel, and textile operations to be found in the United States. An article from *Ms.* magazine, "Life on the Global Assembly Line," paints a different picture:

Walk down 149th St. in South Bronx and see one sign after another—se necesita operadoras (operators wanted). . . . A visit to Damak Sportswear in the Bronx revealed a typical neighborhood garment operation. Thirteen Puerto Rican women were bent over sewing machines in a poorly lit room. The shop, on the third floor of an old tenement building with wooden stairs and floors, lacked fire alarms and a sprinkler system.[7]

As the two cases illustrate, there are contradictory trends in the textile and apparel industry. On the one hand, many firms are being challenged by imports, while others are pressed by domestic competition and government policy. On the other hand, firms that have modernized are doing well. This is especially true of those that have adopted new technology such as in carpets or new synthetic products that replace cotton and wool. For example, U.S. exports of rugs and carpets grew twice as fast as the import rate, from $10 million in 1965 to $320 million by 1980, the first year in which exports exceeded imports in total value. During the same period, synthetics became the favored raw material for woven products. Use of U.S. man-made fibers skyrocketed from seven billion pounds to seventeen billion pounds; cotton declined from four billion to 2.7 billion during the same period.

At the same time, there has been a huge rise in the imports of garments in which the labor content is high. One illustration is men's suits. Imports rose from $14 million in 1965 to $427 million in 1980. During the equivalent period, U.S. exports also rose, but from a modest base of about $3.7 million to $39.5 million.

Like the shoe industry, garment and apparel work remain labor-intensive and in trouble. At present, the industry provides jobs for over 1.6 million Americans. One out of every eight workers in manufacturing, more than basic steel and autos combined, still works in this industry.[8] For every one hundred garments made in the United States, seventy are imported and sold here. Unemployment is well above the national average—15.4 percent in the apparel industry in 1982 compared with the national unemployment rate of 9.7 percent. This bleak employment picture falls hardest on women, minorities, and recent immigrants who take up the majority of the jobs. Hong Kong, South Korea, Taiwan, and China are responsible for 70 percent of the apparel imports into the United States. The People's Republic of China is the greatest producer of textiles in the world today. According to author Theodore White, writing in *Time,* (September 26, 1983, page 39), the Chinese have

the largest cotton industry in the world today, 18 billion square yards annually (6.6 billion in the United States in 1981). . . . The largest cotton mill in all China sits in Chengdu, in Sichuan. It makes a profit producing for the China market. Its workers get paid perhaps $25 a month in take-home pay. The China market absorbs all the flower-printed cloth that comes off the print mills, but the factory management is under considerable pressure to pursue Western markets and make dollar profits, which are the great prize. Can American textile workers possibly compete? Six dollars a day against an average North Carolina wage of $250 a week less deductions? In Shanghai, the net cost of the labor that goes into the making of a man's suit is $2. New York's garment industry—or Philadelphia's, or Chicago's—cannot compete with that.

The only way Americans can compete in this environment is through new technology. But technology is slow to come to traditional garment manufacture. We spoke with Carl Proper, education director of the International Ladies Garment Workers Union, who detailed some of the dilemmas of technology in textiles. He described Dominic Domenico's new plant built in Lynn, Massachusetts, three or four years ago to produce female apparel. Some technology was introduced, allowing people to maintain their jobs and produce more. However, there were no automated sewing machines. Lasers don't apply to women's garments because the production runs are too short and the equipment too expensive. The products are never quite the same, making most of the garment industry job-shop operations. Two-thirds of them employ fifty people or less, and they do not have the capital resources to buy new technology. According to Proper, "You can only modernize to a certain extent. You can talk about getting into high tech with textiles, but we have a hell of a lot of people with low education that want to work hard."

Technology can be used to improve jobs. *Fortune* magazine recently carried a story on how AT&T used technology to upgrade the image and self-respect of its technicians.

Faced with becoming a competitor in a deregulated communications business, AT&T is already changing the role of some of its workers. The technician's job has in fact become more sophisticated. He still has to know how to solder wire or bring a line into a building, but he may also have to reprogram a computer-controlled office switchboard. The CWA [Communications Workers of America] generally likes the new approach, so long as workers and the union get to participate in shaping the changes.

Like most telephone installers and repairmen—known these days as "systems technicians"—Paul Laincz, 32, used to go to work in jeans, his waist encumbered with a sagging belt loaded with tools. Now he makes his calls for Pacific Telephone in Sunnyvale, California, in slacks, shirt, and tie, and with his tools stowed in a briefcase. Instead of a van, he drives a company sedan. He used to be assigned jobs at random, working off a list handed to him by his supervisor, with each job closely timed. Now Laincz works only with five corporate clients and he decides what needs doing and when. He is part of the telephone-company team that looks after those clients, and he is even encouraged to promote sales. The new appearance is meant to symbolize a change in the status of the blue-collar technician. "We want them to look and feel more professional," says Hugh Jacks, national director of AT&T business services.[9]

Glenn Watts, president of the Communications Workers of America, is considered one of the most thoughtful spokesmen for the future of unions and their proper role in a technology-intensive era. Generally, the labor-union movement in the United States is in decline. The CWA is one of the few large unions that is growing in membership. Watts recalls the immense labor changes that technology brought to the telephone business. Remember when millions of telephone operators handled each individual call? In the 1930s there was fear that, as telephone service expanded arithmetically, the number of operators would have to expand exponentially. Today, American telephone companies still employ large numbers of people—over one million in prederegulation days—but only a fraction of them are still operators. How to handle such massive, increasingly rapid changes in job skills?

Watts proposes that a goal of union-management cooperation should be to produce workers who have a "portfolio of skills," the generic opposite of specialization and fragmentation of job duties described at Blue Cross/Blue Shield. This will require substantial changes in the way work is organized. Probably the most important change is to think of job tasks in terms of teamwork. Small teams of people, each with individual skills, should take responsibility for a whole range of tasks. They should be viewed not as a cost center but as a profit center. Their responsibility should not be the repetitive performance of a single task but the handling of a "family of tasks" to satisfy a client's total service needs.

We have already cited examples at Ætna, but Citibank, the largest and most profitable financial institution in the United States, is also experimenting with such teamwork approaches. The traditional way to organize work in a commercial bank is to have large rooms filled with officers, assistants, and clerks specializing in a single function—for example, providing letters of credit. Foreign exchange is another function, another room, another set of people. When information was kept on paper in bulky file cabinets, it seemed natural to organize according to specialized function.

At one of Citibank's major offices, the work has been organized into what is called the "Paradise" concept. We visited one such team, "Paradise Five," which consists of about twenty people who work in their own office space handling letters of credit, foreign exchange, and all the other functions typically performed by a large multinational bank. They have thirty clients assigned to them, and are responsible as a team for providing for all their clients' needs. Each member of the team may retain a specialty, but each member also develops a portfolio of skills. As job requirements change, the portfolio of skills also changes. Citibank has an ambitious program of providing clients with personal computers (PCs) to access their accounts. Eventually, each member of Paradise Five will become familiar with the use of PCs as their clients acquire them.

What is especially interesting about the Citibank case is that it was the introduction of extensive communications and computer technology that allowed Paradise Five to come into existence. Networking the computers from one department to another, and building an interconnected distributed data processing system, is at the heart of making Paradise Five work.

Hand in hand with this immense technological push, Citibank has instituted a massive education program to train all its personnel in the use of the new technology. Lowell Grumman is one of the people in charge of technology education in the booming Asia region covered by Citibank. "The best planners are the doers. We're an action oriented company. This applies to education as well. We have to touch thousands and thousands of people." James Collins, a senior Citibank officer responsible for the bank's North Asia operations outside of Japan, said that a goal of all the training was to promote a company-wide sense of participation. "We needed to erase the traditional view that people were mono-functioning clerks who had no responsibility for service but were just adhering to the rules in an impersonal environment. Now they view themselves as people who can decide, as a member of a group, how to best serve clients."

Citibank plans to expand the Paradise concept by clustering the operating groups into actual integrated units. These will become "virtual banks" and will be almost fully self-sustained. According to top officers, the company will reach the "virtual bank" stage in mid-1984.

AT&T and Citibank—one unionized, the other not—illustrate the beginning steps toward an important new concept of work. Technology is being used to create teamwork and to integrate different tasks and requirements. This integration function is probably one of the most important pieces in the puzzle of how to ensure that jobs are not deskilled. At Citibank, people talk, for example, about integrating the marketing and technology functions. Marketing personnel need expertise in their own field and "literacy" in technology. Operations people responsible for installing and maintaining technology need technical expertise and literacy in marketing.[10]

To get integration and teamwork will require changing the way jobs are designed. Technology has traditionally been seen as requiring great expertise. Designing jobs that use technology has often been left to technical experts alone. The technology, however, is changing; and as it does, job design needs to be done with the participation of several groups in a new partnership. Those groups include the users of the technology, the management, and those responsible for the technology as well.

What does history tell us about the impact of new technology on jobs? H. H. Rosenbrock, professor at the University of Manchester in England, gives an insight into the historic impact of new technology on job design.[11] He shows the importance of the *intention* of the inventor or the implementor. When James Hargreaves invented the "spinning jenny" in 1764 and Samuel Crompton created the "spinning mule" in 1779, both machines were regarded as highly developed tools that extended the skills of the user. Both inventors knew the textile trade and intended their inventions for their own use. Their machines were subject to the users' control and necessitated the continued use of human skill.

Later inventions, however, had different intentions. Richard Roberts invented the "self-acting mule" in 1830. His goal was to replace the skill of workers in order to pay lower wages and to reduce their power. According to Andrew Ure, a social historian writing in 1836, "the only, or at any rate the principal benefit anticipated, was the saving of the high wages paid to the hand spinner, and a release from the domination which he had for so long a period exercised over his employers and his fellow work-people."

The contrast between the Hargreaves and Crompton inventions and the Roberts machine is instructive. The first ones amplified muscle power while retaining human skills. The second removed human guidance and skill. Roberts's machine, the self-acting mule, paced and controlled the worker, who no longer needed to go through the apprenticeship system or to acquire any special knowledge and skill. According to Rosenbrock, "the work that remained was fragmented, and required not skill but only dexterity, while its pace was largely controlled by that of the machine. This could no longer be considered a tool of the user, complementing his skill. Rather, the workers who remained were the servants of the machine. All of these were in fact the consequences desired by the inventor."

The question of how technology will be used is an old one. There have always been fears that new technologies will both eliminate jobs and, even worse, dehumanize the ones that are left; indeed, there is potential for both. Yet it is not the technology that makes the difference but the engineers who design machines and the managers who deploy them. It is the prevailing value system and its regard for the skills and potentials of workers that ultimately determines whether technology will be integrated with a worker's skill or deployed to destroy it.

In the last industrial revolution, conventional wisdom came to regard factory work as a lower form of life where mental abilities were eliminated and manual skills were fragmented. This laid the basis for Frederick Taylor's *Principles of Scientific Management,* which, while no longer the bible of management theory and practice, still influences our industrial system to the present day. The way his principles were interpreted was that all judgment about how work is performed should be taken from the worker and vested in management. Workers were paid to do, not to think. The role of management was to decide how to organize work for best results. As Taylor put it: "Under our system the workman is told minutely just what he is to do and how he is to do it; and any improvement which he makes upon the orders given to him is fatal to success."[12]

The appeal of Taylorism was that, by breaking work down into limited functions, quality, uniformity, and efficiency were improved in the short run. Of course, another benefit that appealed to management was that one worker was no different from the next and thus they could be pitted against one another to drive down the cost of labor.

From the present perspective, Taylor's scientific management is a bankrupt philosophy, although it has taken sixty years to fully uncover its faults. In the long run, it lost its punch, with regard to both efficiency and cost, primarily because it failed to take into account the human side of the equation—the fact that humans are capable of far more than routine tasks and ultimately will revolt when their skills are underutilized and their jobs are boring. When workers are demotivated by the nature of their work, efficiency drops, quality erodes, and costs escalate. Taylorism is equivalent to requiring workers to bowl on an alley where a curtain blocks the view of where the ball goes. When the curtain is lifted and pins are set at the far end of the alley, an otherwise boring task becomes a game of skill and excitement that people will pay to play. Management is gradually coming to learn the simple truth that people want to understand the game they play. When they do, there is an incredible reservoir of skill and motivation that is drawn into the work process.

Unions were quick to learn that worker boredom and exploitation could be mobilized to defeat Taylor's management game. The net result was a legacy of a costly adversarial union-management system. Union rates for routine and unskilled jobs rose well above those for even skilled workers, and job specialization was used against management to exert control over how work was organized. For some fifty years, both management and labor persisted with ill-conceived notions about the true potential of workers. With self-serving contracts that resulted in job fragmentation, they fought their own battle. In the meantime, costs rose while productivity, quality, and international competitiveness declined to the crisis state we face today.

Surely this experience teaches how not to use the new technology, but have we learned the lesson? Even today, attitudes toward workers in industry are still largely influenced by Taylor's thinking. The endless chatter about the dehumanizing effects of robots and computers once again misses the point. It is not the technology that matters; it is how the technology is used. To circumvent another costly round of mistakes, we have to put an end to Tayloristic thinking and adopt new attitudes toward the capability and intelligence of workers.

Whether the future economy will provide more or fewer jobs, fulfilling or dead-end jobs, high- or low-paying jobs, will continue to haunt planners, politicians, labor unions, managers, and the public at large. Many of the calls for reindustrialization fail to recognize that we have embarked upon an economy whose most important product is knowledge and whose most important tool is high technology. Labor, in the traditional sense of highly specialized tasks on the production line, is losing its old meaning and taking on a new one. Work today means having a portfolio of skills. Changing knowledge is an increasingly vital ingredient of jobs.

The intellectual twists and turns in the jobs maze defy even the best analysis. To get a better feel for the realities in this transition, we decided to study three state economies. The first is Massachusetts, probably the only state in America that has gone through the full cycle from a traditional industrial-based economy strong in textiles and shoes to an information economy based on high technology and services, especially retail and banking. Unlike Massachusetts, other high-tech states like California, Minnesota, and Texas "started fresh." They did not have to go through the sometimes painful, often humiliating experience of virtually shutting down one economy to make room for another. Thus while Massachusetts is in many ways unique, it is nonetheless instructive. It may give some clues as to what other states will need to make the shift and what they may want to avoid in terms of the cost of a transition.

The second state we profile is Michigan. Hardest hit by international competition, the auto industry centered in Detroit and all the associated industries sited in the industrial heartland of America are now in the process of adjustment. Whether they will make it is still an open question. The auto industry, for example, shrunk by 30 percent in employment between 1978 and 1983 as a result of import competition and the recession, may not bounce back even if sales of U.S.-manufactured cars take off again. Plant automation may leave little room for extensive job creation. Thus it is not even sure what "making it" might mean in Michigan. We think it means revitalization of basic industries to be up-to-date with the technologies and revamping management practice to draw on the full potential and motivation of workers. It also, in our opinion, means the creation of new jobs and new economic bases through the development of a set of high technologies appropriate to the state. These are likely to be different from those around Route 128 in Massachusetts. Presently Michigan is experimenting with an unprecedented partnership in two new institutes—one focused on robotics, another on biotechnology to exploit the state's huge agricultural base and northern forest reserves. But Michigan is a late starter. The jury is still out on whether it can succeed, and succeed before the social pressures become too great.

Finally, we take a look at some surprising developments in Mississippi, one of the poorest states in the union. A new educational push has been initiated by the governor, putting Mississippi among the first to reverse the decline in a sector more strategic than ever to the future. The hope is that new economic development will be stimulated.

8

Textiles to Micros

Twenty years ago, few would have suspected that a region with an economic base as antiquated as New England's could ever pull itself together again. New England's landscape was littered with communities stripped of jobs in textile, leather, and related industries. As the Pacific Coast and Sunbelt beckoned, the New England economy atrophied. In Massachusetts, largest of the six New England states, towns like Lowell, Lawrence, Haverhill, Holyoke, Springfield, Adams, and Fall River, once world-renowned in an earlier industrial era, had for all practical purposes died. Their old-fashioned three-decker immigrant homes epitomized an American dream that had failed.

Today, for reasons as much fortuitous as deliberate, many of the same towns are undergoing a metamorphosis. Take Lowell, for example. This once-exhausted old mill town has recently revived into a thriving urban community. While its rebuilding was initiated by the public sector, which devised a coherent and well-thought-out reconstruction plan, the successful implementation of that plan was due to a partnership with Wang Laboratories and its founder, Dr. An Wang. No public policies or grand plans created Wang Laboratories; nor was its transformative effect on the town part of a grand strategy. But the success of one has led to the revitalization of the other.

The New England and especially the Massachusetts success story is important because it represents a rare case—unique in the United States and exceptional worldwide—of a rapid transition from traditional labor-intensive industries to today's technology-intensive industries. New England has gone through the full cycle. Unlike California, Texas, or many other technology-intensive states, it started with an old industrial base which it had to shed in order to move into the new era. While our analysis of why this change occurred will highlight a convergence of unique factors, we believe that the case contains lessons for many other states. Something remarkable has happened in sleepy, accented, old New England; now the rush is on to clone a feat which may prove difficult to duplicate.

Old New England can still be found in the scenic Merrimack Valley running through northern Massachusetts. The Merrimack River links a chain of one-time water-powered industrial centers like Haverhill, Lawrence, and Lowell with those farther north in New Hampshire like Nashua and Manchester, once the site of one of the world's largest turn-of-the-century textile mills. Francis Cabot Lowell, from whom the town derived its name, was the first to tap the river's waterpower when he built a textile mill on the Merrimack in 1821.

From visits to England Lowell brought to Massachusetts the latest technology for cotton spinning and weaving. He was an innovator—not an inventor. In a way reminiscent of contemporary perceptions of Japan, he adapted and refined British ideas by amalgamating their technologies into one continuous process from raw cotton to woven fabric. Such production-line innovations by Lowell and other textile entrepreneurs enabled New England companies to compete with British manufacturers. By 1900, Massachusetts was the world's largest producer of woven fabrics. Eighty years later, much of that activity had dispersed, first to the South and later to Asia. In Lawrence, some textile production survives, although a vast stretch of brick mills containing a million square feet of unused space is about to be re-marketed to high-tech tenants at low rents. Malden Mills, founded at the turn of the century, still employs 1,200 people, specialists in the making of imitation furs, fleece, and sweatshirt materials. The firm filed for bankruptcy protection in 1981 but successfully recuperated and now has annual sales of $160 million.

In another mill town, Maynard, on the Assabet tributary of the Concord and Merrimack rivers, the Digital Equipment Corporation (DEC) started in an immense, abandoned wood-beamed mill building. Rent was cheap. For years DEC computers were manufactured in plastic tents to prevent century-old warehouse walls and ceilings from shedding dust on intricate electronic components. The firm's founder and president, Kenneth Olsen, still insists on maintaining his corporate headquarters there. Today, the Merrimack Valley is home for industries that make guided missiles, jet engines, semiconductors, computers, solar-energy products, and telephone equipment. Visitors unfamiliar with this eastern portion of Massachusetts might mistakenly think the mill economy was still humming—the new technology firms have fit perfectly into the traditional New England towns with their industrial-revolution architecture and wooded landscapes.

Most of this transition from old to new occurred over a three-decade period spanning the late 1950s, the 1960s, and the 1970s. It can be explained in part by a number of deliberate decisions; but more significantly, fortuitous circumstances provided the region and the state with a unique competitive advantage over other parts of the country. Of these, the most important was the extraordinary concentration of higher-education institutions with a long tradition of excellence. These proved fundamental catalysts in the region's economic metamorphosis from shoes and textiles to chips and computers.

The employment effects were the most dramatic, often painful, aspects of this shift. From 1947 through 1979, New England's old textile and leather industries shrank by 77 percent and 49 percent respectively with a loss of 275,000 jobs. At the same time, the nonagricultural labor force increased by 62 percent. More than two million new jobs were added to reach a combined six-state labor pool of about six million people.

Contrary to popular belief, the absolute number of manufacturing jobs did not decrease. The manufacturing-job total stayed perfectly level at about 1.5 million. Jobs lost in the textile and leather industries were superseded by jobs in new manufacturing industries: electrical machinery, transportation equipment, instruments, and computers. Most of the new jobs occurred in small companies. Of the 2,358 New England firms classified as high-technology employers, almost three-quarters employed fewer than a hundred people. L. Thomas Bryan, head of high-technology lending at the Bank of Boston, says: "The Route 128 process has been largely driven by small companies bringing new products, processes, or software to market."[1]

Not all the high-technology action has been in high-tech firms. Recently, some of the old industries that did survive have been absorbing electronic technologies into their pre-postindustrial environments. United Shoe Machinery in Beverly, Massachusetts, is a case in point. A number of textile manufacturers could also be cited. Foxboro Corporation, a maker of measuring equipment, and Wyman-Gordon in metals are among the companies that made successful adaptations to state-of-the-art technologies. This absorption of new technology is producing a whole new generation of world-competitive companies, cushioning both the impact of recession and the effects of structural shifts in employment that New England, like other parts of the country, has experienced.

The most painful part of the transition is that high-technology industries are for the most part not able to directly absorb "old industry" labor. Boston University professor Bennett Harrison traced what happened over a seventeen-year period starting in 1958 to 674,000 people who left their jobs in traditional New England mills, either voluntarily or through layoffs. By 1975, only 18,000 had taken jobs in New England high-technology firms; 281,000 had retired, died, or were disabled; most of the rest found their way into service, trade, or government jobs; approximately 150,000 remained unemployed, or were working in jobs not covered by Social Security. The major point here is that people with skills built over a lifetime were left to their own devices. At that time, no one took seriously the need for massive retraining. In many cases, the sons and daughters of unemployed mill hands were precisely those who took up the modern high-tech jobs. U.S. Senator Paul Tsongas remembers the distress in his hometown, Lowell, which had not been prepared for changes of such magnitude. "We can't let it happen ever again," he says solemnly. "Education and retraining are critical."

Following a pattern common to the nation, immense growth in employment occurred in the nonmanufacturing sectors of the New England economy. Employment in government, finance, insurance, and real estate rose 275 percent to 2,287,000; jobs in retail trade almost doubled to 1,150,000. The labor force grew to six million. Two million *new* jobs had been created. There is no way to judge what would have happened if high-tech industry had not appeared in New England, but it is questionable whether such healthy rates of growth in services could have been achieved in the absence of a vibrant high-technology industry.

A recent study sheds light on the way high-technology manufacturing creates demand for services. Economist Lynn Browne of the Federal Reserve Bank of Boston observes that "high tech expansion has had a multiplier effect on local business services."[2] In advertising, for example, she reports a 30 to 40 percent employment increase in Massachusetts attributable to high-tech-company expenditures between 1975 and 1980. Even more rapid employment growth is evident in data processing and management consulting. Her analysis details nearly a one-to-one ratio nationwide between jobs created in computer hardware and jobs in computer services. For every computer manufacturing job, a computer-related service job is created. In addition, there is a closely related "management consulting and public relations industry that is about the same size as computer and data processing services."

Recent figures in New England's biggest state, Massachusetts, confirm these trends. Massachusetts weathered the recent recession with unemployment rates some two percentage points below the national average. Its long list of rapid-growth stories in high-technology electronics and computer firms has grown even longer. During the last half of the 1970s, its total employment base grew from 1,875,000 jobs to 2,165,000. The leaders in this

290,000 increase were the service sector (117,000 new jobs) and the manufacturing sector (94,000 new jobs). In the latter, almost one-third of the new jobs are in electronics and computers. By contrast, Michigan has only 8 percent of its workers in such firms, or about one-fourth the Massachusetts level. Massachusetts has now established a strong state economy based on the high-technology manufacturing sector. A state which in 1983 accounted for only 2.75 percent of America's total employed work force had 10 percent of computer-related employment and 9 percent of the employment in components and measuring and control equipment. Such ratios rank Massachusetts and the other New England states of Vermont, New Hampshire, and Connecticut as the leading high-technology employers. The Massachusetts High Technology Council (MHTC), with a membership of 137 firms with total annual sales above $11 billion, estimated in a survey prepared by Coopers & Lybrand that between 1981 and 1983 61,000 new jobs would be added among its members alone. About one-third of these would be for professionals and para-professionals.

Service jobs in Massachusetts have exploded—they now number nearly 1.5 million. Retail trade is presently the single largest service-employment category with 442,150 workers in 1980, or 17 percent of all people employed. Health services employ 230,000 and education an equal number, or about 7 percent each. By contrast, high-tech employment is much smaller. Even using a broad definition, high-tech firms employed only about 236,000 people in 1980, or about one-third the total manufacturing employment in the state. But this number dramatically understates their impact. For many people, technology was not only the best game in town, it was the only game. Computer manufacturers were employing twice as many people as six years earlier; communications and electronic components 40 percent more. Without that additional high-tech employment, Massachusetts would have looked a lot more like Michigan and other auto-dependent states plagued by unemployment rates in some hard-hit cities as high as 20 to 25 percent.

Change did not spread evenly to all parts of the state; some parts of Massachusetts did not adapt. Old textile towns like Fall River still have not experienced the economic revitalization generally felt elsewhere in the state. Worcester, on the other hand—the home of many old metal-processing and foundry industries—is now experiencing an economic rebirth after many tenuous years. Here, too, high technology, absorbed into old firms or applied to new ones, is a primary force in giving new life to the local economy. One example is the Wyman-Gordon Company, founded in 1883 to forge metal components for the region's textile-manufacturing industry. Today the company is the nation's leading producer of exotic high-alloy metals for aircraft, one facet of a wide array of high-technology metal products which generate half a billion dollars in sales annually. Company chairman Joseph Carter says, "We're the blacksmith for the stars," in reference to super-alloy metals he produces for spacecraft. This small city is also the home of ten colleges and universities, including Clark University and Worcester Polytechnic Institute, as well as a number of medical research centers. Worcester's educational resource was recently (1983) coupled to a business consortium in order to found a $100-million biomedical research and engineering park.[3] An estimated 3,000 related new jobs are anticipated in Worcester.

With more than thirty years of accumulated investment in a new economic infrastructure, Massachusetts is poised for a new round of growth. As this occurs, it is expected that other parts of the state will benefit from the expansion of high-tech companies looking for untapped labor markets close to their current centers of activity. Digital Equipment Corporation has purchased open acreage between Boston and Cape Cod in anticipation of expansion; and Wang Laboratories, after recentlly locating 1,000 new jobs in the abandoned old Springfield Armory, once the manufacturing site of the famed Springfield rifle, is buying property in the Connecticut Valley around old mill towns such as Holyoke with similar expectations of expansion in the state.

Three factors converged to make New England particularly well suited to the rapid growth of high-technology industries: a long history of excellence in private and public higher education;

a tradition of entrepreneurship and willingness to innovate; and the mixed role of defense- and space-related research, which helped launch high technology in the early years but now threatens to retard it.

With 260 colleges and universities concentrated in the six contiguous states, New England is unquestionably the most knowledge-intensive region in the world. In their March 1982 report, the New England Board of Higher Education, a congressionally authorized regional agency, calculated that the region of 12.5 million inhabitants had 800,000 students in colleges and universities. "This knowledge-intensity may be a key—if not the key—to the future prosperity of New England," observed the Board. Massachusetts contains both the most scientifically oriented universities, such as MIT, and the largest engineering schools, such as Northeastern University. In 1960–61, the state with only 2.6 percent of the national population produced 4.2 percent of all the bachelor's degrees granted that year in all disciplines, 6.3 percent of all the master's degrees, and 7.4 percent of all the doctorates. Twenty years later, Massachusetts still retained a lead despite rapid expansion of higher-education institutions nationwide. The ratios held at 4 percent, 4.5 percent and 6 percent respectively.

In sciences and engineering, Massachusetts had an even greater advantage in the 1950s and 1960s when high-tech firms were just starting to spring up. In electrical engineering, 5.6 percent of America's B.S. graduates came from the state, 10.7 percent of the M.S.'s, and 11.6 percent of the Ph.D.'s. By the late 1970s this numerical advantage had abated somewhat as other states added to their educational systems; yet New England still remained far above the national averages. Of 63,000 engineers receiving bachelor's degrees nationwide in 1982, 5,000 came from New England and of these 3,000 were Massachusetts graduates. These figures are critical to high-tech firms; about one-third of their employees are college graduates, of whom more than half have technical degrees in electrical engineering and computer sciences.

The excellence of its educational institutions acts like a magnet to draw top talent to New England. A student who graduates from a New England school is likely to continue living in the region. Lynn Browne, of the Federal Reserve Bank of Boston, writes that "almost all scientists and engineers living in New England received their last schooling there; conversely, very few of those living in the region were last educated somewhere else. Such a pattern makes a persuasive case that New England institutions of higher education play a vital role in attracting and retaining professional manpower." Other studies show that 94 percent of the engineers and scientists in Massachusetts were last educated in New England.

The Massachusetts Institute of Technology is a net importer of students to the region. Ninety percent of its students are from out-of-state; yet one-third remain in the region after graduation. Ten thousand of its graduates live in Massachusetts. Not only are many of these locally employed by commercial firms but a significant number are faculty members in other institutions, each of them strong in its own right: the University of Massachusetts, Northeastern University, Worcester Polytechnic Institute, Tufts University, Boston University, University of Lowell, and others.

Another factor that played a pivotal role is a tradition of entrepreneurship and a willingness to innovate. Just how strong the "spin-off spirit" has been in key universities is illustrated in a report by John Donovan, professor at MIT's Sloan School of Management. He studied 216 high-technology companies in the greater Boston area and found that 156 of these were born in MIT departments or laboratories. Thirty-eight of MHTC's member companies are run by MIT graduates. One of the largest and best known, Digital Equipment, was founded in 1957 by MIT graduate Kenneth Olsen.

The entrepreneurial drive is backed up by one of the world's highest concentrations of venture-capital firms. Nearly sixty venture-capital firms are in the Boston area, and large sums of investment support flow into the region from all parts of the nation and the world. Since capital obviously can flow freely from region to region, this close location of venture capital may at first glance seem unimportant. But for start-ups—for what is called the first round of financing—it is a big advantage to have financier and innovator in close proximity. High risk requires trust—and trust travels poorly over great distances.

A third important factor explaining the rapid growth of high-technology industries in Massachusetts has been one of mixed blessings—a high investment by the Department of Defense and the National Aeronautics and Space Administration in research facilities, both educational and corporate, such as Lincoln Labs and the Mitre Corporation, as well as a high concentration of government contracts in high-tech firms. During the industry's start-up phase in the late 1950s, almost half the high technology employment was Defense- or NASA-dependent. By 1965 the proportion had risen to about 60 percent. Research support from DARPA—the Defense Advanced Research Projects Agency—was instrumental in supporting key scientists early in their careers and new companies that spun off from research labs. Draper Laboratories, a recipient of large defense contracts, engaged in projects that spun off forty-eight new commercial ventures.

The negative effects of this dependence on Defense and NASA research funds were felt when many projects were terminated as the government began to withdraw funding from military and space programs in the early 1970s. This caused immense dislocation in the growth of high-technology industries locally. During the early 1970s many subsectors of the industry experienced flat growth or declines. In Massachusetts, of twenty sectors constituting the high-technology industry only three showed significant growth: computers, transportation equipment, and photographic equipment. The state's economy continued to experience uneven flows of federal funds throughout the 1970s.

By the 1980s, however, it became clear that Massachusetts had made the transition to a commercially driven economy and also that the gap between defense and commercial needs was widening. Overall, defense contracts now account for only 25 percent of high-technology-manufacturing employment in the state. The state is still the eighth-largest recipient of defense-related dollars in the nation, and MIT alone receives more than $100 million in defense-related research contracts annually. An advantage of the projects, especially those supported by DARPA, is that they are relatively long-term. But now a different problem is beginning to emerge. As commercial demand increases, concern is building that insufficient skilled resources will exist to serve both commercial and defense sectors.

During the remaining years of the 1980s, the state's demographic profile will continue to show declining numbers of young people. By 1990, the pool of high-school graduates nationwide is expected to decline by 20 percent.[4] In Massachusetts the decline will be almost double that, with approximately 35 percent fewer high-school graduates by 1990. This larger-than-average decline is due to a significant out-migration of child-bearing-age people to the Sunbelt as well as to a propensity toward later and smaller families.

Will excellent educational institutions continue to attract young people to the state? Because of rapidly rising costs of private education—and most of New England's schools are private—some reports are forecasting increased difficulty in attracting out-of-state students. Other reports such as a May 1983 study by the National Center for Education Statistics predict only slight enrollment declines as colleges and universities attract more and more adult students in special programs. And the *New York Times* recently reported that applications to Ivy League colleges are higher than ever, despite rising tuition. A study by MHTC demonstrated the importance of higher education to corporate growth. At sixty-one MHTC companies with combined sales of $7.8 billion in 1979–80, 75 percent of new technical employees had either college or advanced degrees. About one-third were hired directly from schools. Since locally educated students have in the past often opted for employment and residence in the state, a decrease in the attractiveness of the state could indirectly impact the economy. Whether school will prove more attractive than sun is anyone's guess. Lynn Browne at the Federal Reserve notes: "The entire history of the United States shows a tendency for people to seek milder climates and open spaces. The improvement in the economies of the South has reinforced their basic attraction."

For Massachusetts there are several options. One is to improve steadily its public-education infrastructure, which has long been neglected. A second is to invest higher amounts of money in job retraining for adult workers currently in unrelated fields. A third, especially to meet entry-level demand, is to draw more women and minorities into the economic mainstream. These are two groups that are still vastly underrepresented in the more highly skilled jobs in high-technology companies. All three options have cost and employment implications, and all three will require more investment in education.

The educational situation in Massachusetts also reflects a nationwide problem of declining competences in math and science in the public schools. In an analysis of Route 128 lower schools, Dr. Elizabeth Useem of the University of Massachusetts found that "a generation of younger teachers has been laid off, class sizes are increasing in some schools, and needs for new equipment, supplies and textbooks are going unmet." And she adds, "most critical is the probable dissolution of a cadre of highly qualified, experienced mathematics and science teachers to industry."[5] The older habit of skimming the cream will no longer be sufficient to meet the state's needs.

Having come so far from textiles to minicomputers, it would be ironic if New England were unable to capitalize on its new economic base because of a shortage of qualified people. During the transition period, the region failed to engage in vigorous retraining programs and paid a serious price in terms of joblessness. Now the times call again for retraining, but this time to capitalize on a base already in place—and one sought after by other regions in the country, most notably Texas, North Carolina, and other Sunbelt areas. This does not mean that Massachusetts should seek to freeze Route 128 in its present configuration. It is natural to expect that the mix of high-technology firms will change over time. Those that become more mature and routinized may move out; newer technologies that still require exceptional innovation may find a birthplace in New England.

Whatever the mix, education and retraining become the key success variables. Most of New England's higher education is private. Because of this, the state ranks fifty-first (counting the District of Columbia) in allocation of revenue to public higher education. More could and should be done by state government in this regard. But the key to educational success in New England is partnerships that include business and academia as well as state government. So far, many such partnerships are taking shape, but the rate of progress may be inadequate to meet the region's needs.

Government leaders, corporate executives, and university officials have decided to found a Massachusetts Technology Park. Legislation in 1982 authorized $20 million in state matching funds to finance a research and teaching microelectronics facility as its first endeavor. Eight universities and a number of major corporations are involved. The primary agenda will be to focus on the professional skills involved in the manufacturing of semiconductor chips—the very U.S. skill gap pinpointed in conversations with Japanese executives.

Most of the partnerships have been initiated by individual businesses or by their associations. MHTC has made education one of its main priorities. In conjunction with the American Electronics Association, it has established a target of providing 2 percent of its members' R&D budgets for education. The 2-percent solution has been successful. In 1982 member firms—who were expected under this arrangement to provide $15 million to education—allocated $40 million to higher-education projects. Numerous other programs have been initiated to provide career awareness and possible transitions to high-technology careers. Among the most ambitious academically are the Wang Institute of Graduate Studies, established as one of two institutions in the United States offering a professional degree in software engineering. Another Route 128 firm, Analogic, is founding a graduate studies program. Harold Goldberg, vice president of the firm, explained the reasons for creating a new institution. "When it comes to engineering education," he stated, "there is no emphasis at all on leadership. Our aim will be to carry the engineer through all phases of work from development through design and production in actual projects." Planned to admit its first class in

1985, the master's level graduate program will be housed in space donated by the firm's founder at the company headquarters site and in a mansion retreat on the Massachusetts coast.

A lesson to be learned from the Massachusetts experience is that a relatively small number of jobs in the manufacturing sector can have enormous leverage on the overall economy. Only about 26 percent of employment in Massachusetts is in manufacturing, and of these jobs only about a third are in high tech. But the impact of job growth in this sector has rippled through the region in many ways. While a small number of people will end up designing and manufacturing computers, a much larger number will sell, service, and use them. Education must be adequate to assure that workers in every segment can tap the productivity-enhancing potential of the new high-tech tools.

Now many other states and regions would like to duplicate, or even shortcut, the process that Massachusetts and New England went through. California's Silicon Valley is of course at least on a par with Route 128 and is also experiencing the same problem—induced in large part by unaffordable housing costs—of shortages of qualified labor. New York and New Jersey are headquarters for the two giants in modern technology, IBM and AT&T. Minnesota has a concentration of electronics firms, including big companies like Control Data and Honeywell. North Carolina has its Research Triangle Park. Texas is using its oil wealth to diversify and build up its capacities in high tech. All these states share a common characteristic—a high concentration of technical universities turning out large numbers of engineers relative to their populations. These regions are capitalizing on new technology by designing and building tools and related components that can be used by basic and service industries as well as exported abroad.

But what about other areas of the country? The critical issue, it seems to us, is not so much to attract high technology but to provide an environment where the new tools available from this industry can be brought to bear on already existing, perhaps declining, mature businesses—whether in manufacturing, services, or agriculture. Michigan offers a good case study. How Michigan fares in the shift from old industrial technologies to advanced technologies may have much to say about America's future.

9

A New Heartland?

An era of prosperity and wealth comparable to the post-war period will never happen again. In Michigan, we will have to live with lesser expectations. We just cannot expect a continuation of the same standard of living.
— Gerald Faverman, Michigan consultant

Michigan is struggling through a most difficult period in its history. High technology may hold the greatest promise to expand Michigan's economy. New initiatives to combine state government, university, business, labor, and private foundation resources for economic development will help establish Michigan as a center of excellence in selected areas. The timing is right for such an investment.
— Peter Ellis, Program Director, W. K. Kellogg Foundation

In Michigan economic growth is topic number one. How to achieve it is topic number two. Unemployment rates of 15 to 20 percent are common in the state's urban centers dominated by the auto industry. The current jobs gap is approximately 200,000 to 300,000. In Pontiac, employment in the auto industry declined by over 25 percent between 1970 and 1975. For more than a decade, the unemployment rate in this city has been 2½ times higher than the national average. A study by the United Auto Workers estimates that nearly half a million jobs will be lost between 1978 and 1985, some due to automation, some due to foreign competition and imports.

Four ingredients are commonly viewed by local strategists as necessary to generate new growth: the economy has to diversify beyond the auto industry in order to make up for huge, and probably permanent, job losses; high technology must be applied to existing industrial bases in order to preserve current jobs and to create new ones; an environment conducive to new business start-ups and entrepreneurship must be fostered; and finally capital—which is abundant in the state—must be redirected and reinvested in Michigan rather than exported to other regions. All of these carry with them immense agendas, not the least of which is a political one.

Michigan and its declining auto industry presents a situation not unlike that of Massachusetts and its earlier faltering mill-based economy. But there are major differences as well. Michigan, the pivot state to the five-state industrial heartland, is four times larger in population than New England. Its industrial base is far larger and more diverse, encompassing not only autos but manufacturing of refrigerators, washers, dryers, and farm machinery, plus food processing and forestry as well. It also has antagonisms and polarizations that go far beyond the experience of New England. To overcome Michigan's problems will be no easy task. It is a critical one, however, not only for Michigan but also for the entire national economy. The key to change in Michigan is the application of new technologies to already existing economic bases. The approach consists of an innovative partnership that is being led by state government and private foundations. Whether it will succeed, and how it will affect the quality and quantity of jobs, will depend in large measure on how management and labor respond.

One-fifth of the nation's citizens live in five contiguous old-industry heartland states—Michigan, Illinois, Indiana, Ohio, and Pennsylvania. The region is home to more than forty-eight million people and to great industrial-era success stories in steel, railroads, airplanes, and cars. Inventors in Ohio's Miami Valley such as the Wright brothers in aviation matured their ideas here. So did others, like Patterson in aeronautics and Kettering in the auto industry. Ford made economic history in Detroit, Carnegie in Pittsburgh, Kellogg in Battle Creek. Oil was produced in Pennsylvania long before Texas knew of the wealth below its soil. A chronicle of the region, much of it displayed in the Henry Ford Museum in Dearborn, shows spectacular success in innovation from the mid to late 1800s on into the present century. The history, however, also reveals deeply rooted ambiguities.

One Michigan that comes readily to mind is the home of the U.S. auto industry. This is the most visible of the state's manufacturing activities, which also include steel, metalworking, and chemicals. Another Michigan, less in the news, is the home of food processing, including companies well known for breakfast cereals and baby foods. Forestry products are also important to Michigan. Half the state is forested, and its state forest system is the fifth largest in the nation. The interests of the manufacturing-based and resource-based economies do not always coincide.

The first is built around the saga of the American automobile industry—a story that reached its peak in the mid-1960s. It is symbolized by the still-thriving Rouge plant—where ores and coal go in at one end and cars roll out at the other—a legacy of Henry Ford's early industrial genius. And it is symbolized, too, by the entrenched powers of American labor. The United Auto Workers are part of the American way, a product of exploitative and adversarial battles between employer and employee. One Michigan is this polarization between management and labor; the other Michigan is the tranquility of productive forest lands and farms. Companies with such household names as Kellogg and Gerber have also made economic history here. So have cities like Grand Rapids, which is home to a large furniture industry, and country resorts like those along Lake Michigan where tourism and vacation industries thrive. Both Michigans are at a moment of economic truth.

The first has fallen on hard times. Its recovery may, at best, bring brief economic benefit to much of the United States but may never restore all the jobs that have been lost. The other is suddenly flexing its political muscles to try and redress almost fifty years of economic dominance by the auto industry. Between the two there is the beginning of an understanding that together they might make future economic history. Turn Michigan around, they agree, and you will have found the key to unlocking the vitality of the midwestern manufacturing heartland—and thus quickening the pulse of the American economy. For both, the solutions are to be found partly in the new tools of high technology and partly in a new spirit of cooperation and partnership. There is a sense of urgency in this part of the country, a longing to bridge the chasms between city and suburb, rich and poor, management and labor.

At the core of downtown Detroit is Renaissance City, a forbidding high-rise fortress of glass and concrete overshadowing the shattered city around it. The rest of the downtown area is a vast stretch of vacant lots, boarded-up buildings, and architectural relics left like damaged boats on a storm-cluttered beach. It takes about twenty minutes to drive from downtown Detroit to suburban Dearborn, where the Ford Motor Company is headquartered. The contrast between the two is testimony to the centrifugal economic forces that scatter metropolitan wealth out to the suburbs.

Dearborn, a vast acreage of neatly tended lawns divided by two highways, is home to Ford's sleekly modern engineering and administrative offices. The world headquarters stand in solitary gleam, seemingly unconnected to the devastated urban landscape a few miles away. Across from it are a giant hotel complex and a new suburban mall standing in equal solitude as islands of suburban wealth—the two linked by a Ford-built automated bus skyway. The psychology is one that an urban planner and theorist, Christopher Alexander, once labeled the autonomy-withdrawal syndrome, characterized by a search for ever greater individual privacy and distance from the inner city. The single-family home, the car, the shopping mall are manifestations of this search.

The contrast between rich and poor is strikingly delineated at Detroit's Alter Road, a paved barrier marking the boundary between the poverty of Detroit and the wealth of Grosse Pointe. A local politician described the passage from one to the other as though one were entering Disneyland from war-shattered Beirut. On one side are the bombed-out, graffiti-scrawled shells of the black ghetto. On the other side, grotesquely juxtaposed, are a recently opened antique store, a BMW and Jensen car dealer, a fashionable restaurant, and the well-tended lawns and country clubs of the wealthy. This is the world of executives from Ford,

GM, Chrysler, and American Motors who together manage half the state's manufacturing economy. They still live well, though they produced only six million cars in 1982—three million less than five years before.

Another play is also being acted out. This one involves union and manager, antagonists who for several generations have grown up treating one another as natural enemies. At the rambling Rouge plant mentioned in chapter 2, visitors are shown the famous bridge at Entrance #4 where fifty years ago hundreds of union men were killed or wounded in a pitched battle with troops called into action by the Ford Company. It was in the aftermath of such industrial struggles that Walter Reuther built his union leadership. Today, unions are as pervasive in Detroit as silicon is in California's famed valley. UAW, AFL-CIO, IAM, USW—the initials are part of everyday language here. You belong or you don't.

To those unaccustomed to unions, as are many in the high-technology world, the union presence seems carved in stone and permanently committed to self-defeating economic stagnation. This is most clearly manifested in inordinately high wage rates, themselves matched by equally excessive executive salaries and bonuses—a legacy of spendthrift policies during the profitable postwar years—which have grown out of proportion not only to international realities but national ones as well. Michigan's average weekly paycheck in 1982 was $443; in Massachusetts, it was $300.[1] The Detroit area auto worker gets 25 percent more than the similarly rated worker in the Boston area; the unskilled worker, 40 percent more.[2] Such wage differences are further exacerbated by a cost-of-living index that is 20 percent higher in the Boston metropolitan area than in Detroit. For many, the union delivered the good life: a lakefront vacation home, a camper, a snowmobile, a large benefits package, and generous vacation time. Housing was cheap—Michigan leads all other states in rates of homeownership. These were largely the rewards of a management/labor system that for all too long bought an industrial ceasefire with high wages and salaries to workers and managers paid for by the consumer. The system worked as long as an oligopoly controlled the market. When international competition struck, the system unraveled for management and unions alike.

Something had to be done. In 1980, Republican governor William Milliken convened a High Technology Task Force to advise him on future economic-growth policy. Its primary mission was to identify industries which had significant growth potential and which had not yet been captured by other states. Robert Law, who directed the staff work of the task force, recalled one of its early conclusions: "High tech alone was never seen as able to solve our problem. Rather, we saw it as a way of upgrading and creating new jobs. We believed that high tech would stimulate an immense amount of entrepreneurial activity."

What Michigan, or at least its lower half south of Lake Huron, started with was an extraordinary base of machine-tool factories—primary suppliers to the auto industry. This was viewed as a unique base for creating an automated manufacturing environment. A factory-of-the-future concept made eminent economic sense for restoring vitality to this sector. What the balance of the state had, both in Upper and Lower Michigan, was an excellent agricultural foundation of farms and forests. The proper application of biotechnologies and new food-processing techniques could turn these natural assets into a more competitive economic resource. "Of the eight or ten industries we studied," said Law, "these had the largest potential for growth worldwide."

A decision by the governor to focus on the revitalization of manufacturing and of natural resources gave birth to two promising and potentially powerful new initiatives. One, a nonprofit venture named the Industrial Technology Institute (ITI), would act as an applied-research catalyst for building the factory of the future for automated manufacturing industries in Michigan. Seventeen and a half million dollars were allocated to it by the state to be paid over a six-year period. This was matched by $9 million in cash and a $4-million contingency commitment over three years by the Kellogg Foundation—with a promise to consider an additional infusion of $21 million if things went well. Another $10 million, over nine years, was committed by the Dow Foundation.

A second nonprofit organization, the Michigan Biotechnology Institute, was created to concentrate on applied research and on stimulating start-up ventures in wood- and farming-related businesses. Another $6 million was earmarked for it by the state, to be enhanced—eventually—by private-sector commitments. A goal of $80 million was targeted to cover operating expenses over a ten-year period. In both instances, the state's contributions came from a newly constituted Michigan Economic Development Authority, whose resources are derived from state oil revenues and the sale of public bonds.

ITI is located in Ann Arbor in close proximity to the University of Michigan and other educational facilities. Its first director is Jerome Smith, appointed in August 1983. Experienced in aerospace research, Smith sees the goal of his institute as "focusing on applied research and advanced engineering development. We should be working in those areas that are too high risk for industry yet too applied for the university laboratory." His focus on all the technologies that apply to the creating of an automated manufacturing environment will serve the needs not just of the 7,000 manufacturing firms he estimates are within fifty miles of his institute but of a far wider region. "My mission," he states, "will be to act as a stimulant for the adaptation of modern manufacturing techniques. We can show the way by taking the risk out of the development."

The mandate of ITI is to create the factory of the future. For many, this may sound like robots. But the Institute's program is far more ambitious than robotics. The real payoff is to develop what is termed a "flexible automated factory." Several examples, described in ITI documents, illustrate the concept.

A leading company recently regrouped some computer-controlled machines into a "manufacturing cell" where metal wine goblets are produced. Computers control the input of the metal, feeding it into the shaping machinery, loading the computer program into this machine's computer, changing tools when needed, unloading and relocating the semifinished part to another machine, changing tools on this machine as well as its computer program, and unloading the finished product. What is significant is not so much the automation but the flexibility. Changing one computer program could cause this manufacturing cell to make goblets one day and tractor parts the next.

The next step in complexity is to expand the cell to encompass an entire factory. A single cell can cost $3–$15 million, and a factory $100 million or more. So far, there are probably less than a hundred in the world. The ITI documentation describes two of them:

The Harris Corporation's flexible manufacturing system near Kennedale, Texas, is a flexible, highly automated, fully computerized machining line. Robots and moving pallets handle seven hundred different work pieces. The system took four years and eight million dollars to build, but it will pay for itself in just three years. For the second example, the Fanuc plant located in Fuji, Japan, has been described as the most advanced flexible manufacturing operation in the world. It is not a single-product, mass production plant; it produces a line of machine tools and robots. The third shift is under complete computer control with just one manager to oversee and handle the unexpected, should it occur. Whether "flexible manufacturing system" is the best terminology for something the size of Fanuc is arguable. Perhaps "flexible automated factory" might be more appropriate.

The image that such factories portray is one without people, but such an image is highly misleading. There will be employees, but few of them will be workers on the factory floor. Another example of factory automation comes from a new California venture announced in the San Jose news in Silicon Valley. The company will make revolutionary new computer chips by a process of "fab automation," where process equipment in a clean zone will keep "personnel intrusion" to a minimum. This accent on absolute cleanliness is critical to success. But does minimal personnel intrusion translate into no jobs? No. The company needs 200 employees to start up and projects 2,000 employees by 1986.

Working in concert with university leaders, the Institute is locating its facilities next to the University of Michigan's engineering complex. This coincides with an intention by the university's president, Harold Shapiro, to concentrate all of his engineering departments in the university's north campus. The proximity of 5,500 students—undergraduate and graduate—as well as faculty in a single geographic location will, it is believed, create a critical mass of intellectual activity from which entrepreneurs can emerge. As Lansing-based political consultant Gerald Faverman likes to say: "Create the right concentration and climate for brains and you're OK. After all it's one guy in a basement who'll do it."

ITI is intended to serve the many auto-related industries which on their own are too small to conduct their own research. Notably absent are any of the Big Three car companies. Unlike IBM or other big high-tech industries, GM, Ford, and Chrysler have not yet launched significant industry-university partnerships. Nonetheless, ITI has an impressive statewide education resource to tap. In 1980–81, the eight leading engineering colleges in Michigan graduated over 4,000 engineers, including 800 with master's and 90 with doctoral degrees. In addition, junior colleges enrolled more than 250,000 students in vocational courses.

While ITI and its companion organization, the Michigan Biotechnology Institute, were being formed, another support group was founded, although at more modest funding levels, to serve as a catalyst for entrepreneurial start-ups in the Detroit area. Called the Michigan Center for High Technology (MCHT), its job is to provide all the services necessary to help a new company through the first stages of its commercial life. Its proximity to the facilities and academic resources of Wayne State University adds to its strength.

All of these newly announced organizations were inherited as self-sufficient and independent operational groups by Milliken's Democratic successor, Governor James Blanchard. Michigan has had a century-old tradition of Republican leadership. The shift to the Democratic party in 1982, with a razor-thin majority in the senate, raised yet another question about the continuity of a new economic program that would need more than four years for completion.

Apart from timing, probably the greatest difference between the Massachusetts and Michigan transitions has been the role of the key actors. In Massachusetts, progress toward a new economy was essentially left to the marketplace and to chance. Chance often favors the wealthy, and Massachusetts has a rich heritage of education and venture capital. Michigan, too, is wealthy, but not in the human and financial resources required of a technology-intensive economy. The Big Three auto companies, which might have been a source of such wealth, were too besieged by Japanese competition to act effectively. Michigan state government, backed by several foundations, took the initiative and conscious intervention became a political priority of the 1980s.

One of the new governor's first steps, in 1983, was to announce the creation of what he termed a Michigan Strategic Fund to provide state capital for investment in selected industrial sectors. Governor Blanchard, to sustain the inherited momentum created by his predecessor's search for an economic-growth formula, announced the creation of a cabinet council including his key departmental directors. He also created a parallel advisory Commission on Jobs and Economic Development, a blue-ribbon group of state leaders. Their assignment was to detail opportunities for growth in four selected industries: auto-supplier firms, food processing, forestry, and R&D companies. Industry targeting that seems unworkable nationally seemed a natural and sensible response at the state level.

For very different reasons, some of Michigan's leading private foundations decided to join the state's efforts. The Kellogg Company, physically as distant from the state capital of Lansing as is Detroit, turned around in a short time from being primarily concerned about national domestic-policy issues to being almost fully focused on statewide economic growth. Part of this activism came in reaction to an effort by the legislature to hike unemployment benefits for auto workers. Unwilling to be penalized for Detroit's management blunders, Kellogg turned its energies to affecting Lansing politics—which it did successfully. By virtue of this one effort, a new axis of political interest was forged, the influence of the auto industry—both corporations and unions—now being balanced by other economic interests in the state. The Commission's staff director, Peter Eckstein, noted this new form of cooperation. On leave from his position as research director for the AFL-CIO, he said: "A whole new atmosphere has been created. You go into a meeting now to get something done . . . to work something out."

Outside of the government-foundation world, a renewed sense of common purpose is also in evidence. In 1981, auto and union leaders buried their differences and created the Economic Alliance for Michigan, the outgrowth of an effort to boost economic growth in Detroit. The Alliance is focused on a single overriding problem: how to improve the business climate in the whole state. A list of about twenty issues—all of which avoid any substantive matters related to the collective-bargaining process—are principal concerns of this group. Cochaired by Irving Bluestone, a UAW founder and ex-vice-president, and by Fred Secrest, an ex-vice-president of Ford, it sees its goal as "getting away from a narrow company or union perspective." Its staff director, Robert Wack, thinks that "the process these people are involved in may be far more important than the product." With a short timetable to make recommendations for state actions, the Alliance is, in its director's words, "a forum for involving opinion molders." And indeed, in Detroit, just the fact of getting union and corporate leaders to meet on equal terms is an achievement.

One of the Alliance's major substantive suggestions is aimed at building a strong venture-capital base in the state. It had discovered, much to its dismay, how little of the state's wealth was reinvested locally. The staff found, for example, that out of a private and public pension-fund pool of $33 billion in the state, almost all was invested outside Michigan. It found, also, that there were a mere three venture-capital funds of any significance in the state with a meager combined capitalization of $25 million. In contrast, Massachusetts, with half the population, had twenty times more firms with a capital pool forty times larger. The Alliance proposed raising $100 million in venture-capital funds and working alongside the governor's Strategic Fund to stimulate start-ups in the state.

But traditional powers in Michigan may counter the best of

intentions. GM, the big brother of the auto industry, has taken issue with the new governor's attempt to offer myriad auto-supplier companies a political forum at the state house. The Commission's efforts to rethink the future of the supplier sector and to have strong representation of small firms were resisted by GM. The big automaker, instead, wanted the agenda to stress "negative business climate" issues rather than to focus on ways of strengthening or organizing small supplier companies into a stronger economic resource.

Because hundreds of thousands of jobs are at stake, it is apparent that a successful effort to restore vitality to the auto industry would have immense political repercussions, not only in the state but nationwide. Win the battle of competitiveness versus employment here and you'll win it anywhere. Gerald Faverman, a one-time Bostonian transplanted to Michigan as an economic and political consultant, puts the political stakes into a context of Republican and Democratic cycles in and out of national power. With the ending of the New Deal era sometime in the 1960s, a door opened to a new vision of the economy and a new leadership to guide it. "We're at a political watershed in deciding which party will dominate national politics for the next generation," says Faverman. "The real test is in finding a solution to America's economic crisis. Solving Michigan's problem is the key to the whole puzzle. It remains far from evident who will determine that solution. It's up for grabs," he says. "I'll tell you this, if we figure out the answer, the man who does will be the next president of the United States."[3] This view explains, in part, the willingness to engage in nonpartisan cooperation in Michigan state politics. Democrat Blanchard readily extended Republican Milliken's initiatives for a new economic future in the state, primarily out of a realization that the situation was so desperate that even the unconventional was acceptable.

Similar political pressures explain, also, a new surge of energy in places like Austin, Texas, where another view of the American agenda is forming which may propel a different network of people and ideas into power. For Texas, the agenda is to accelerate a shifting axis of power by strengthening and expanding the human resources for a powerful center of high technology. At the same time, it must contend with immense pressures for immigration from Mexico and other countries south of the border. In Michigan, for quite different reasons, the stakes are also high and of national consequence. An economy hard hit by competition and the inertia of old industrial ideas is forced to reconsider its future. Where else to better test the still abstract concepts of industrial growth policies that seek to utilize the new technologies where the ultimate job outcome is still unsure? If the policies fail to work in Michigan, can they work better anywhere else? If they do not bring union and management together, whom do they serve? If the biggest firms do not extend the necessary goodwill and desire to seek the common good, can there be a coherent program? If the proper balance between old and new technologies cannot be found, can we call them strategies of truly national dimensions?

The Michigan story of turning adversity to advantage is just beginning. It is an uncertain gamble with unpredictable results. Can a state-government-and-foundation-initiated alliance transform the economy more quickly and less painfully than a natural market mechanism left to management and unions alone? The shifting of state power away from Detroit by virtue of Kellogg's involvement, the building of catalytic institutions linked to universities in Ann Arbor, Lansing, and Detroit, and the clear recognition that capital resources must be invested locally bear strong witness to the commitment toward fundamental change. Success, however, may be a generation away. To forge an economic-growth policy that will have to reassign statewide investment priorities in order to create 200,000 to 300,000 new jobs within a decade cannot be achieved in a single governor's four-year term or in a quick-fix approach to growth. It will be the leadership of nongovernmental interests—foundations, universities, management, and labor—that will have to sustain this drive to a new future. What is apparent, too, is that success in Michigan may have to do far less with anything currently labeled "national industrial policy" than it does with an enlightened regrouping of the state's natural assets—its people, its traditions, and its resources.

At least that's how it looks from Lansing, Battle Creek, and Detroit. Far to the south, another state also has a great legacy of traditions, resources, and people but with a different story. We turn now to recent events in Mississippi, where a governor has likewise taken bold new initiatives.

10

A Hundred-Year Legacy

A trained, educated citizenry—that's our ultimate defense. We can build all the battleships anybody can sell to the Defense Department and spend all kinds of money on military hardware, but if we don't have an educated citizenry, then I don't think we've accomplished anything.
> —Mississippi Governor William Winter

Public sentiment for improving education in Mississippi has never been higher . . . There comes a time when life gets hard, when politicians must do more than warm their seats . . . Sausage making is out . . . No district is untouched by the disease of ignorance which has infected Mississippi for far too long.
> —From editorials in the Pulitzer prize-winning series by the *Clarion-Ledger* in Jackson, Mississippi, November 28 to December 26, 1982

Something new is happening in Mississippi. In a conservative Deep South state, among the poorest in the union, there is a move to revitalize the link between education and economic opportunity. As the American agenda of priorities changes, the new concern taking hold is the regeneration of wealth. For Massachusetts that process, as we have seen, led through a cycle of pain as old industries withered and new ones came to replace them. In Michigan the process is in midstream as state leaders attempt to reduce continued reliance on the auto industry and look to a new generation of employment opportunities. In both cases, a strong awareness of the role education plays is evident. Yet to fully understand how fundamental its role, we went to look at what had been described as heretofore a worst case—Mississippi.

For all practical purposes this Southern state is richly endowed.

Its land is fertile, producing abundant crops and providing vast acreages of timberland. Soybeans and cotton are large revenue producers. So are chickens and cattle. These agricultural riches translate into high land values—30 percent higher per acre than the national average. The state is located advantageously with access to America's largest river system leading into the northern heartland and to the rest of the world from ports on the Gulf of Mexico. Like others of its Gulf state neighbors, it enjoys the bounty of offshore oil. Some of its contemporary leaders like to think that new opportunity lies ahead by bringing new technologies to the state. Yet between the reality of resource richness and the realization of new economic opportunity is still an immense gap.

The economic reality shocks. Despite the state's wealth in natural resources, a large part of its 2.5 million residents remain unproductive, dependent on state and federal welfare payments for their subsistence. Eighteen percent of Mississippi's personal income comes from transfer payments—the second largest source of income after manufacturing. About 20 percent of the population receives food stamps—a rate two or three times higher than in Massachusetts or Michigan. About 25 percent of the population falls below the federal poverty level. The depth of the problem becomes even more evident in a comparison of what each state contributes per capita in federal income and employment taxes. In Michigan in 1980 it was $2,347 per resident, in Massachusetts $1,894, in Mississippi $680. The state in 1980 was forty-ninth in median family income. Average per-capita income was $6,580 in Mississippi, $10,125 in Massachusetts, and $9,950 in Michigan. Hourly wages in 1980 averaged $5.44 in Mississippi, $6.51 in Massachusetts, and a national high (with the exception of Alaska) of $9.52 in Michigan as a result of auto-industry hourly-pay scales. Per-capita retail sales—a barometer of a region's economic health—were the lowest in the nation, about $2,600 compared to a national average of $3,342.

A major reason for this poor situation, rooted in a complex history and a profound legacy of racial bias, is an undereducated or unschooled populace. It was this concern for economic development that Governor William Winter brought to his newly won office in 1980. He had long believed he had to start at ground zero. The only solution was to rethink Mississippi's commitment to education as a vehicle for change. Convincing the state's population of this relationship would be one problem; finding the money to do anything about it would be another. Poverty made new investments next to impossible. The assessable property-tax base—the traditional source of money for public elementary education—was a sixth of that in Massachusetts or Michigan. Winter, understanding that increasing taxes on sales or incomes might be anathema, focused on an undertapped source: taxes on offshore oil. Winter knew it would be risky. Losing would mean the end of a political career.

December 1982. It happened in only two weeks. That the governor called the legislature into special session was hardly novel. Crises had often required special legislative action. But this was not a normal crisis. Instead, Governor William F. Winter was asking the legislature to raise state taxes higher than at any prior time. His purpose was to infuse new energy and purpose into the state's dismally poor education system. Without it there could never be hope of economic growth, he argued. But in Mississippi, tradition ruled the legislature, which showed little inclination to tamper with the education status quo. For a governor to make waves on so fundamental an issue was not looked upon favorably in the halls of the capitol. In the political backrooms few gave the governor any chance of success.

Yet within two weeks, historic change was achieved. The governor not only won his battle but he emerged with twice as many new tax authorizations as he had asked for. Legislators in opposition lost, in part because their activities had been laid bare by a spirited journalistic effort of the Jackson *Clarion-Ledger*. Six months of research under the guidance of a new editor, Charles Overby, culminated in twenty-four days of steady education coverage prior to and through the unfolding debate in the capitol. Fifty-one stories, twenty-seven editorials, and several imaginative cartoons appeared. Editorials often reported on last-minute negotiations, readying the readership for action the following morning. Legislators became living people whose daily votes, deals, and alliances made banner headlines. This unique effort at political coverage and issue advocacy won the Pulitzer Prize for the *Clarion-Ledger*. Its support for the governor's measures had been relentless.

To those not familiar with the state's educational situation, some of the realities are hard to believe. Until the special session late in 1982, elementary or high-school education was *not* compulsory in Mississippi. An estimated 5–6,000 children never even started school each year. Kindergarten education did not exist in most public schools. More than 15 percent of first graders repeated the grade. For every one hundred students graduating from high school, another forty-two dropped out—the highest rate in the United States. Per-capita expenditures for education were the lowest in the nation. Vocational-school enrollments were four for every one thousand students; the average rate for the United States was ninety-three per thousand.

To finance its public schools, Mississippi counted on 24 percent of its revenues coming from the federal government—three times more than the national average. That source, though, was declining rapidly under budgetary constraints mandated by the Reagan administration. Mississippi's Title I funds were reduced from $66 million to $62 million; Title II funds fell by one-half, from $11 million to $5.3 million—big amounts for a state with a total elementary and secondary education budget of $487 million. The free-lunch program, which had started in 1946, and the free-breakfast program, which had started in 1975, both experienced a 10 percent cutback in Mississippi.

"The problem goes back to the Civil War," commented Olan Ray, a keen supporter of the governor's initiative and the superintendent of schools in Biloxi on the Gulf Coast. "The state was devastated. For some reason from then on Mississippians shut the outside world out. Part of that included accepting an inferior role for education in their lives." And he added: "We're talking about a poverty so absolute—and a repressive attitude toward blacks—that helped to reinforce the closing of Mississippi." When the U.S. Supreme Court in 1954 declared segregated schools unconstitutional, the state's most talented people went to work to obstruct reform. The result was a populace so deprived that even the military services were turning away 35 percent of Mississippi applicants as "educationally deprived."

In the governor's mansion, William Winter likes to point to a small painting of a one-room log-cabin schoolhouse. "That picture there," he points out, "that's where I went to school. That was a six-grade school . . . only six grades. I was the only pupil in a long time to go on and finish high school."

Despite its abundant raw materials, rich soil, and navigable river, the governor explains, the state has remained last in per-capita income in the United States throughout the century. "You ask yourself the question: What is the problem? It is obviously a lack of productivity among the people of the state. In short there is an inadequate development of the human resources. That leads to a discussion of what we can do from the standpoint of education—both basic and technical."

The governor—limited by state law from succeeding himself—had only four years to fulfill a long-held personal and political commitment to change the state's education standards. For two years a program presented in pieces to the legislature failed again and again to emerge from the machinations of obstructive committees. But the issue was gaining public attention. By 1982, already more than two years into his term, the short January-to-April legislative session turned a corner with a favorable house vote on one piece of education reform, but its vote was killed by a parliamentary measure engineered by the speaker, Buddy Newman. His manipulations caught the attention of the "20/20" ABC-TV investigative team, which traced his opposition to racial bias and to backroom deals with oil and gas businessmen whose industry was to be the source of the tax revenues to finance education reform.

Sensing a shifting public mood in the strong reaction to this negative national exposure, Winter saw an opening and the makings of substantial support. Pushing forward aggressively, he engineered what he likes to term a "campaign much like one I would run for an election." Money was raised from a small core of business supporters who understood their basic "self-interest," as Winter puts it, in building a stronger economy by investing in education. These funds purchased media time. An extensive program of 500 small meetings—many organized by Elise Winter, the governor's wife—was established, and a series of nine large public forums addressed by the governor were promoted. These events—planned to run from May to November—were intended to culminate in a public referendum for a constitutional change in the structure of education in the state. As these events gained momentum, an unexpected event took place. On June 1, 1982, the Gannett newspaper chain purchased the state's most influential paper, the *Clarion-Ledger,* a conservative "don't-ruffle-the-waters" old-line institution. The same day, thirty-six-year-old Charles Overby became the executive editor. One of his first decisions was to make education the main theme of a new editorial policy. "I had decided to support the governor and to make it our goal to educate the public as thoroughly as we could," he recounted later.

Meanwhile the arduous task of affecting public opinion went "on the road." "Our job," said Mrs. Winter, "was in some cases as basic as overcoming the misconception that public schools were all black. Most people just didn't believe that 90 percent of all our state children were in public schools." One argument used again and again by the governor and his wife focused on the negative cost of not investing in education. "I just put the humanitarian argument aside and based my appeal on simple self-interest," said the governor. "I'd say to them, 'Do you want to pay in terms of increased welfare costs, correctional costs, or do you want to pay an investment in terms of education and let the people be self-sustaining.' I got their help, got their understanding." Pressing the point home was the simple reminder that the second-highest source of income in Mississippi was transfer payments. "These welfare checks of one kind or another," he said, "are the single largest source of income in thirty-four of our eighty-two counties. This is *non-productive income,* so to speak. This is the philosophical background of what we did to get this education program going."

By November a significant political shift had occurred. On the second day of the month, the public voted in favor of a constitutional amendment creating a nine-person lay board to oversee education policy in the state. Five members would be appointed by the governor, two by the lieutenant governor, and two by the speaker of the house for nine-year staggered terms. The measure took authority away from a three-man elected committee including the attorney general (a legacy of civil-rights obstructionism), the secretary of state, and the superintendent of education.

The signal of a new public mood was not lost on the governor. His supporters urged him to call a special legislative session to strike while the iron was hot. "I was right up in Jackson the day after the lay board vote," said Olan Ray. "I told him this was a fight worth taking on. I said I was ready to put the gloves on and go to it." The stakes were high: failure meant the end of a political career for Winter; success meant taking on and beating the legislature. "That's something you don't do too easily in Mississippi," said Olan Ray, the Biloxi school superintendent.

A special session was called two weeks before Christmas. The only subject would be education, and the challenge was a $45-million tax increase to finance a comprehensive forty-six-point package of reforms including compulsory attendance, kindergartens, and other teaching improvements. The proposed source of revenue for all this was an oil and gas severance-tax hike from 6 percent to 9 percent—still a low rate compared to the 12-percent tax in neighboring Louisiana. Pessimism abounded, however. The man who would emerge as the central opponent, Ellis Bodron, chairman of the senate finance committee, didn't think that the governor's program could be "handled maturely, thoroughly, and intelligently" in so brief a session. On December 4, the senate president pro tempore, W. B. Alexander, declared confidently: "I don't think at the special session there will be any increase in taxes."

During the ensuing days, the *Clarion-Ledger* went to work. Its daily stories cut through the secrecy of political maneuvers normally obscured by the complexities of busy legislative agendas and by lackluster political journalism. Its coverage supplied facts, badgered on issues, and hit hard on who was doing what in opposition to the education package. The newspaper was calling on the public to participate directly in a political event—and the public responded. Because of phone calls, votes were reversed overnight. The headlines mirrored the political volleys: "Kindergarten Funding on the Ropes," an early defeat that led the editorial page to single out five legislators for blame. Seven days later: "House Passes Education Bill—Kindergartens, Raises Included in Package." Then a setback: "Senate Panel Rejects Kindergartens—Sales Tax Spells Doubt in House." Once moved to the full senate floor, an education bill was passed with a substituted sales-tax hike by a 43–9 vote. Twelve special-session days had passed as the house and senate now went into conference with tax sources and kindergartens still stumbling blocks. And then, just four days before Christmas, the victory: "Historic Education Bill Passed." Bodron's committee maneuvers crumbled as the governor rejuggled his pieces into an education package that exceeded his most optimistic expectations. For a funding measure twice as large as proposed, he allowed his oil and gas severance tax to be replaced by increases in income and sales taxes. For immediate results he allowed phased-in programs. For a shot at long-term permanent reform, he allowed trial periods.

"One is cautious about using the word 'historic,'" wrote the *Clarion-Ledger*. "But no other word will serve to sum up what passage of the legislation means for Mississippi. Anyone who still does not realize the significance of this effort has to be living in a dream world."

James Campbell, president and owner of a school-supplies firm based in Jackson and the chairman of the U.S. Chamber of Commerce's education committee, was an early supporter of the governor. "It had become clear to the public," he said, "that jobs would be available only if people were trained. The problem facing Mississippi citizens had seized their attention because it could be quantified. The numbers spoke for themselves."

The effects on the state were immediate. "Our perception of ourselves was down. We just didn't think we could perform. That's changed as a result of the special session," said Annette

Luther, a teacher at D'Iberville High School near Biloxi and president of the Biloxi school system's trustees. A few months later, Ellis Bodron was defeated in local legislature elections. Two of the governor's young staff aides, whom Bodron had labeled the "Boys of Spring," are running for secretary of state and state auditor. The *Clarion-Ledger* won its Pulitzer Prize but promptly lost its star reporter to a Denver newspaper. Compulsory education to age fourteen was to be instituted in annual stages. Kindergartens would be established. Teachers would get pay raises and additional classroom help. And new accreditation standards would be applied based on school-performance measures—perhaps the most controversial substantive item in the list of reforms. Olan Ray would chair a seventeen-person committee whose mandate was to define performance standards in local schools as a basis for receiving state funding. "Since the session," he says, "the adrenalin has been flowing. I can see the possibilities for effecting change now. A few months before I couldn't." For a man raised in a family of subsistence farmers with little or no education, the memory of "so many who were never given a chance to see opportunity" is strong. It's part of what drives him on.

"A trained, educated citizenry," says Winter, "that's our ultimate defense. We can build all the battleships anybody can sell to the defense department and spend all kinds of money on military hardware, but if we don't have an educated citizenry then I don't think we've accomplished anything. Reagan makes a good speech on education. His words are good. But they're unaccompanied by any sort of national commitment to do anything about it. Instead he's saying, 'You fellas down there do it.' We're asking for a commensurate national commitment."

Ensuring continuity will be the ultimate determinant of Mississippi's break with its past. Elected in the fall of 1983, Governor William Allain brings to his new office a track record of lukewarm interest in education issues. As the state's attorney general, until his election to the governorship, he sat on the three-person board overseeing state education policy. The new legislative initiative changed that board into a nine-person lay group. Governor Allain inherited the right to appoint five of its members and thereby set the tone for the evolution of a farseeing education policy in the state. Commenting on Winter's legislative package, he said: "While it is now a dream put to paper, I'll see to it that it is put to reality. The major effort before us will be how best to fund it."

The case of Mississippi, with economic and social conditions in many of its counties matching those of the poorest Third World countries, is dramatic testimony to a new mood in America. There can be no economic vitality without building and sustaining an educational infrastructure. Education in Mississippi may not, and probably will not, bring a quick windfall of high-paying high-technology jobs. "High tech alone won't solve our problems," says Governor Winter. "Although, the legislature has designated certain technologies for emphasis such as polymers at the University of Southern Mississippi, electronics at Mississippi State, and pharmaceuticals at the University of Mississippi—you just can't develop a higher-technology industry without trained people coming out of elementary and secondary schools." Now Mississippians better understand the link between education and economic opportunity.

Mississippi was a worst case in that it had to overcome a century of lost time. Yet it was far from alone in recognizing the imperative of building a future on a solid education base. In states as disparate as New Jersey, Florida, and Virginia, new education initiatives were urged upon the electorate by concerned political leaders. In most cases they focused on the need to create new job opportunities. In Virginia, a governor's task force summed it up: "There are one hundred and forty-one programs in forty-eight states concerned with high-technology enterprise. In fourteen states in addition to Virginia there are task forces at work on the issue. By one estimate there are forty-five hundred local economic development agencies pursuing high-technology industry. . . . To meet this challenge, our schools and colleges must adapt to the changing needs of our citizens and of modern industry."

11

Taking Stock

Innovation is everything. When you're on the forefront, you can see what the next innovation needs to be. When you're behind, you have to spend your energy catching up.
      —Robert Noyce, Vice-Chairman, Intel Corporation

Patterns begin to emerge from this picture of America. The past is being replaced by a clear sense of the future. At Ford Motor Company, Emhart, and Ætna and in states like Massachusetts, Michigan, and even Mississippi, one can feel a quickening pulse. After a period of apparent dormancy, innovation is reasserting itself as a vital force in old industries and new, in manufacturing and services, and in diverse state economies. The transformation of knowledge into marketable new products and processes is beginning to accelerate.

What is causing this reawakening of creative energy? Part of it is the Japanese challenge. A 1982 report in the *Harvard Business Review* showed that "in the late 1950s, over 80 percent of the world's major innovations were introduced first in the United States. By 1965, this figure had declined to 55 percent."[1] Even now, the task facing many companies is immense. In one recent study, the sponsoring company was told it needed productivity increases on the order of 300 to 800 percent to survive the competition. In another, the air-conditioner industry was shown to have average production-line defect rates *seventy times higher* than those in Japan. But for the most part, the signs are there that the innovation process is beginning to be revived. If this continues, we should be grateful to the Japanese. They will have done our country an immeasurable favor by awakening us from a growing complacency. As a worthy competitor, their challenge has begun to rekindle a basic American strength: our inherent willingness as a culture to experiment and take on risks. It is this innovative spirit that may ultimately reverse our flagging productivity and declining competitiveness.

Innovation has long fascinated those who observe and analyze human behavior. The whole modern industrial era, the Renaissance in earlier centuries, even the reign of Alexander the Great in ancient times, are case studies in man's ability to perceive innovation as a life-generating process. Studies of those eras tell us, also, that as soon as the adventuresomeness and willingness to experiment waned, societies declined.

Elting Morison, who has written extensively on this historical phenomenon, suggests "that in studying innovation, we look further into the possibility that any group that exists for any purpose—the family, the factory, the educational institution—might begin by defining for itself its grand object and see to it that that grand object is communicated to every member of the group. Thus defined and communicated, it might serve as a unifying agent against the disruptive local allegiances of the inevitable smaller elements that compose any group. It may also serve as a means to increase the acceptability of any change that would assist in the more efficient achievement of the grand object."[2]

Because America is in the midst of a period of rapid change—much of it technologically driven—the need to stand back and rethink the "grand object" looms large. Central to this is the need to better understand this phenomenon we call innovation. The process of innovation itself may be changing. What used to be accomplished by Alexander Graham Bell or Thomas Edison—individual inventors working on a shoestring—now requires teams of scientists and engineers working on large budgetary allocations. This is because innovation has become more expensive and increasingly complex, which creates pressures to pool resources.

Many are coming to agree that the answer to our productivity, quality, and cost problems lies in accelerating the rate of innovation. Bob Noyce, vice-chairman of Intel and the inventor of the planar process by which microprocessors could be made economically, stresses the importance of bringing the ideas to market. "We've got to foster more innovation. At Intel we do everything possible. We use 'individual achievement awards,' 'skunk works,' 'strategic business segments'—anything to stimulate change." Bob Swiggett, president and CEO of the Kollmorgen Corporation, a highly decentralized high-tech conglomerate, says that "innovation is not desired, it's required."

But innovation is not always easy to get. It is more than just invention; it also includes the implementation, or commercialization, of new ideas. And it's more than new products, it is also new processes. For example, it's not only the availability of new, powerful computers which can help drive the economy. It's the application of computers to fundamentally alter the way work is done that makes the real difference. But even to reach this stage requires improvements in every step of the process. Developments in materials like silicon were a prerequisite to the successful manufacture of semiconductor integrated circuits (ICs). Improvements in ICs were a prerequisite to the introduction of modern-day computers. But it wasn't until computers were embedded in robots, word processors, or automobile-engine test stands that these new tools could increase productivity. The collective impact of these developments on the way work is performed defines the common ground between high technology and mature industries. One's product becomes the processes of the other.[3]

Dependence on innovation is not a new phenomenon for America. More than one hundred years ago, the French writer de Tocqueville carefully recorded the distinguishing features of American culture by noting that the true source of American economic strength is "a clear, free, original and inventive power of mind."[4]

But in Washington, D.C., innovation is just being rediscovered. President Reagan asked John Young, president of Hewlett-Packard, to chair a presidential task force on industrial competitiveness designed to increase our innovative capacity. Gary Hart, senator from Colorado, also singles out innovation as critical to American competitiveness. In his formulation, a closely knit relationship between technology and education will stimulate a natural bent for economic innovation. Ed Zschau, a successful young high-tech businessman from Silicon Valley and freshman congressman, says "We should not try to copy the Japanese, or anybody else. I happen to think that one of our strengths has been innovation and the willingness to try new ideas."[5] Instead of targeting industries, Congressman Zschau supports the notion that we should target the innovation process as the key to industrial success. He and Hart, among others, represent the more visible signs of a growing bipartisan awareness in Congress of the importance of this process.

But what lies behind all this talk about innovation? How can it be stimulated? These are not easy questions to answer. There is an enormous diversity of activities and actors that are critical in implementing change. There are not only many kinds of innovation—in products, in manufacturing processes, and in management-labor relations—but one finds change emanating from almost any, and often unexpected, sources—from collective genius on the shop floor, from talented individuals, from governors, corporate presidents, and educators. As Elting Morison likes to observe: "Serendipity, while recognizing the prepared mind, does tend to emphasize the role of chance in intellectual discovery." And he adds, "change and intellectual advance are the products of well-trained and well-stored inquisitive minds, minds that relieve us of [what historian of art Panofsky terms] 'the terrible burden of inert ideas by throwing them into a new combination.'"[6]

What is, for example, the proper role of the federal government in stimulating innovation? In many ways, government may prove more an obstacle than a catalyst to change. Because the serendipity that Morison says is the soul of innovative activity is so diffuse, it is next to impossible to legislate it into being. Let's review the cases we've presented to see where innovation came from. Let's also note that while state governments often had important roles to play, it is not immediately obvious what the federal government could do to help.

At Ford Motor Company, foreign competition sparked a radical change in worker attitudes and management commitment. A net result is the creation of one of the world's most advanced factories of the future. The key to making these innovations work is not just the impressive new technology and capital investments to acquire it but especially shop-floor-worker attitudes toward it. The big question will be whether the momentum can permanently alter entrenched and adversarial union-management relationships.

At Emhart we saw that even one of the oldest manufacturing industries could revive itself. Here, this was due to key individuals like Wally Abel, a far-sighted president like Mike Ford, and a well-conceived strategy for conversion to high tech that is being implemented by John Rydz. This management team was prodded by domestic competition and changing customer demands, and in response launched a "mild" revolution to bring the company into the modern-technology age. Initial results have been promising, but the process requires patience and persistence. Now more middle managers and large parts of the work force have to make the shift quickly to absorb the new thinking and job changes implicit in the new technologies.

In the service sector, where the majority of the American labor force works, Ætna Life and Casualty has made a dramatic response. The financial-services industry is undergoing a complete revolution as insurance companies, banks, and brokers all vie for one another's business. A key component of Ætna's innovation strategy is education, and the critical piece to making the strategy work is the company's commitment to upgrading the entire work force, 40,000 strong. The firm has introduced strong educational leadership into the mainstream of company life. The director of the new Ætna Institute, backed by top management and with the support of the work force, has become the focal point of change. To be successful, partnerships with local colleges and universities will be essential.

The same diversity has characterized the new awakening at the state level. In Massachusetts we saw how an economy was left to market forces to go through a full cycle, from manufacturing based on textiles to high technology based on human resources. Now the question for Massachusetts is whether it can continue to rely on this process in an environment of direct competition to its high-tech industry with Japan.

Michigan's state government made a conscious choice to intervene in its economic future. Two governors, one Republican and one Democrat, have gone into league with private foundations to set up two new institutes—the Industrial Technology Institute (ITI) and the Michigan Biotechnology Institute (MBI). The net result is that these initiatives are becoming a focal point for policy. How well they can do it will depend on their ability to forge coalitions between the business interests of the state and its educational institutions.

The reawakening is alive in even our poorest state. Mississippi, with the lowest per capita income and the poorest record in economic and educational results, became one of the first states in the union to reverse the declining support for its already meager and deteriorating educational system. While California and Massachusetts had cut taxes supporting their schools, Mississippi reversed the trend and raised its taxes for elementary and secondary education. Governor William Winter, in what is now considered a textbook case of political savvy, was able to launch the state upward toward new economic possibilities based on upgrading the education system.

From our research and case studies, we have found four main issues essential to understanding and stimulating innovation. First, there is substantial need for innovation in management style both to make our work force more productive and to create an environment where innovation will flourish. Unfortunately most American managers function under personal values and management principles that are considerably outdated. David Jaquith, one of the architects of the American Management Association's education programs, used to remind audiences: "Most people, at every level, know how to do their job better than they are permitted to by management. Consequently American workers perform at only a third or less of their full potential."[7] And in a recent survey by Daniel Yankelovich on the work ethic of

Americans, 75 percent of those surveyed indicated they are willing and anxious to work harder if encouraged or even permitted to do so.[8] A growing number of companies are breaking authoritarian bonds and practicing participative management which draws more fully on the potential of each employee. Quality improvement programs too are spreading as vehicles to engage the minds of workers and boost their productivity. The climate for innovation is also determined by management style. We have much to learn about how to involve professional knowledge workers in the management of firms. We need to turn them on, not off, and to move new knowledge more rapidly from the university to the development lab to the factory floor at a pace compatible with accelerating changes in technology. Greater management effectiveness may in fact turn out to be the dominant factor in revitalizing the innovation process.

A second issue is the strategic nature of education. People's skills set the upper limit on how fast we can innovate. Resources must be directed to enhance these skills and knowledge. This means strengthening the capacity of universities to both create new knowledge and accelerate its transfer to useful products and services. It means rethinking how best to prepare students in elementary and high schools to participate and adapt in an innovative society. Lastly, it requires massive reeducation and training of people already in the work force to build their own self-esteem and sense of worth as productive citizens and to continuously upgrade their knowledge and skills in an environment of accelerating change.

Third, continuing investment in basic and applied research is essential to keep the innovation process moving. Most long-term research is funded by the federal government. Too much of this effort is now weighted toward defense, space, health, and nuclear energy. Too little goes directly toward industrial innovation. Present levels of civilian research to spur economic development are too low to keep us ahead in the technology race. At the same time, the linkage between new knowledge and new products and processes is weak. Much of the knowledge is generated in universities, which have historically kept at arm's length from the corporations and organizations where implementation has to take place. What is needed are ways to bring industry and academia closer together to increase the transfer rate of knowledge.

Fourth, a competitive cost of capital and incentives to invest are critical to creating the flow of funds that support education, research and development, and new capital equipment. High cost of capital shortens the time horizon of managers and employees. Lowering the cost of capital encourages longer perspectives and riskier ventures with greater payoff potential. It also accelerates the renewal of our capital stock to provide new and better tools for workers in all segments of the economy.

To stimulate and support more innovation, it will be essential that government understand the process of innovation so that federal and state actions support rather than impede the process. For example, defense secrecy, export embargoes, and regulatory restrictions put a damper on innovation, as do the antitrust laws that inhibit research-and-development partnerships. These conflicting policies must be continuously reviewed and more appropriately balanced against the needs for economic development. An even greater task for government is to elevate innovation as a matter of national economic priority. Federal policies, through tax or other incentives, can be designed to encourage risk takers. Without such support the serendipity so often attributed to successful innovation cannot fully blossom.

One of our most innovative industries is of course the high-tech industry. Yet recently, there were signs that even in this highly sophisticated field, the Japanese had become competitive. In the early 1980s, Japanese companies like Hitachi, Fujitsu, and NEC Corporation captured first 40 percent of the 16K semiconductor market and then 70 percent of the next generation 64K market. How could this happen in an industry essentially invented and developed in the United States? A recent study of the rivalry shows that labor costs were not the fault—they were higher in the Japanese semiconductor industry than they were in the United States.[9] Nor was excessive middle management an acceptable explanation: American companies like Hewlett-Packard and Intel are considered lean and well-managed. Neither was it solely Japanese government subsidies of exports and research.[10] What had happened?

Americans, the inventors of transistors, integrated circuits, and semiconductors, were overtaken by more efficent production processes and better product quality. Having established the lead by creating, inventing, and designing semiconductors, we let the Japanese surpass us in automating the manufacture and racing to the market with a better product. We had won all the early battles and still lost the war. We had been highly creative but had not carried through. This experience was an eye-opener to many Americans.

What the semiconductor case points to is the need to join together and refocus our efforts on reaching higher rates of innovation. The real battle in ongoing semiconductor competition is not for incremental improvements, valuable and helpful though these may be. Rather, it is for bold new approaches in computer-aided design, processing equipment, and materials needed to stay ahead in the exotic world of wafer-level integration of computers and multimegabit memories. This will require not only talented inventors and designers but also a new management orientation to rethink the relationship of manufacturing to product quality. It will also require building new ties between firms and especially with technical universities. Many such partnerships are already underway, most notably the Semiconductor Research Cooperative (SRC) and the Microelectronics Technology and Computing Corporation (MCC), which are described later.

Catalyzing these efforts are some new developments in Japan. In the next chapter, we will show how the Japanese hope to reverse their image as imitator and compete directly with U.S. creativity. However, the dynamic is actually far more complex than that. The emerging technologies have touched off a movement that puts pressure on the whole global system to climb higher. It's not only Japan that has moved up but many other Asian countries too. Korea, Singapore, Taiwan, and Hong Kong are experiencing an incredible boom. Their future is no longer based on the old cheap-labor advantage, as many still falsely believe, but rests on a new strategy that employs skilled people using new technologies at world competitive wages and prices. While many of these people may work somewhat cheaper, what is making the difference is their ability to work harder and smarter than their counterparts in the "advanced" economies. The heat is on. Even Japan is running hard to keep ahead of Korea and Singapore, who in turn are pressured by countries like Malaysia and the Philippines, which still thrive on low-wage advantages. And these countries too are threatened by an almost imponderable pool of even cheaper labor resources in India and the People's Republic of China.

This multitiered international competition means that no part of the American economy can afford to become lax. There are too many in Asia ready to work for less, there are many also ready to work harder; and as we will see, there are worthy competitors ready to challenge us in originality and creativity as well. We turn now to an examination of this new competitive dynamic in Asia, starting with the Japanese aim to compete in creativity.

12

Competing in Creativity

An irony of history is that because Japanese universities have failed, the rest of society has been forced to compensate.
     —Professor Michio Nagai, former Minister of Education (1974-76)

Both the Japanese and the Americans love baseball. Listening to the running commentary of a sports announcer covering a Tokyo Giants game can be quite entertaining to a visiting American. Great floods of excited Japanese language pour forth, interspersed by English bits of "ball one" or "strike two."

No one, of course, likes to be beaten at their own game. In the economic game we may already have two strikes against us. The first was Japan in the 1950s when they were "working cheaper"— that is, low-wage-rate competition. The second strike could be considered Japan in the 1970s when they were "working harder"—that is, with longer hours and more innovative production-line techniques. Will the third strike be "working smarter" by the 1990s—that is, could Japanese creativity surpass Yankee ingenuity?

Japan created a formula for success that produced fantastically in the 1970s. Within the country, competition between companies is intense, more intense than in the United States. One result is a constant search for new products. Part of the winning scheme is thus to let the market dictate product needs. The company can then concentrate on quality, mass production, incremental gains, and, above all, high speed turnaround from market need to product availability. The Sharp Corporation, one of Japan's leading electronics companies, illustrates these ideas at work. There used to be fifty companies making calculators in Japan before the shakeout of the mid-1970s. Now there are only two of any consequence—Sharp and Casio. The other forty-eight companies either succumbed or abandoned the calculator field. What distinguished the two survivors was their ability to sense market needs and translate these into high-quality, low-cost products so quickly that the Japanese still refer to the shakeout blitz as caused by the "Sharp shock" and the "Casio shock."

While the traditional formula is still practiced, a new concept is now uppermost in the minds of Japan's top executives. It comes from the haunting notion that Japanese companies might be outgrowing Japan. Increased quotas on exports to the West, renewed concern over energy supplies, and American reluctance to cooperate in high technology (the United States pulled out of a joint coal-liquification project when Reagan was elected) caused many in Japan to realize that the traditional recipe for success might call for some new ingredients. What is missing, in short, is creativity; what sort of creativity was illustrated to us by a team of executives and engineers at the Sharp Corporation under the direction of Dr. Tadashi Sasaki, director of the company's engineering center in Nara.

In the executive conference room, we sat engrossed by the expressions in Japanese and English and the drawings that filled the blackboard before us. Seven managers had assembled to sketch out Sharp's success in calculators and what it meant for future products. They explained that corporate research and development was market-driven; market *needs* had defined corporate direction. The word was written in large letters to one side. The debate at present is whether the better strategy is to be technology-driven. Can the company survive on market-driven needs alone, or is the creation of new markets through new technologies the key to the firm's long-term survival? Koichi Hirose, Sharp's deputy general manager of the engineering center, summed it up with an apparent balancing act. "What Sharp has to do," he said, "is to balance market needs with technology *seeds.*" And the word "seeds" was carefully written on the opposite side of the blackboard. In translation, this means shifting to more long-term laboratory-based innovation. The company is shifting part of its research agenda to a ten-year time horizon in order to create what is needed for survival in tomorrow's economic environment. Hirose showed what he meant by filling out the blank space between the words "seeds versus needs" (see figure 2).

The *interface* between market-defined products (needs) and laboratory-defined possibilities (seeds) describes the company's present technological priorities. Sharp—and many other companies—are now trying to extend the interface upward, beyond a pure market-driven definition, to one that gives more weight to an agenda driven by its laboratories. Some executives worry that the change might compromise its traditional strength of filling market niches quickly. But of most concern is how to fill the research gap with an ingredient heretofore missing—scientific creativity.

At Sharp, and at other companies, this puts new emphasis on basic research as a key focus of corporate R&D. As Sharp's manager for advanced-technology planning expressed it, "More creativity will come from planting seeds than from reacting to market needs." Success in seeds is recognized as essential if Japanese companies are to enter a new period of homegrown technological innovation. Sharp's way was to create a corporate research center insulated from the short-term priorities within product groups.

Many other Japanese companies face the same pressures and use similar concepts. The NEC Corporation, formerly known as the Nippon Electric Company, is one of the most innovative in Japan. Its chairman and chief executive officer, Dr. Koji Kobayashi, is considered tops among Japanese executives capable of far-sighted, world-class vision of the future of technology. His strategy for NEC is called "C&C," for computers and communications. Critical to C&C's success is continuous progress in basic research. Dr. Yasuo Kato, head of the C&C research laboratory, also uses the seeds-needs concept. He explains it this way: "We have a technology-oriented organization rather than a target-oriented one." The company has now established Fundamen-

Figure 2. Seeds Vs. Needs
The Japanese corporate R&D debate

SEEDS: Refers to basic research that is science or technology driven.
NEEDS: Refers to product-related, or market driven, research.

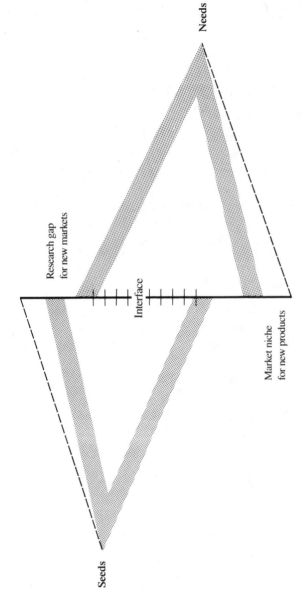

SOURCE: The Sharp Corporation, adapted by the authors

tal Research Labs to develop new technologies for markets that do not yet exist.

This move to competence in basic research is what the Japanese mean by the new creativity. In its *Vision of MITI Policies in the 1980s,* the Ministry for International Trade and Industry (MITI), in typically Japanese low-key expressive style, puts it this way:

Creativity should be brought into full play in developing software and systems technologies and in commercializing new technologies by utilizing Japanese characteristics. At the same time, it is necessary to attach importance to basic research, to take risks, and to pioneer in unexplored fields and thus become the world's [leading] innovator.[1]

To become the world's leading innovator is quite a goal. To achieve it, the country will have to go through a major metamorphosis. Among the obstacles is the image that the Japanese have of themselves.

Dr. Masaki Nakajima, president of the Mitsubishi Research Institute, expresses the still-predominant view in Japan when he laments the "lack of creative originality to be found among us Japanese. It is usually said that Japanese are very good at improvement but that they lack in creativity. This is clearly indicated by the very small number of Nobel prize winners from Japan compared to other OECD countries." He goes on to quote Dr. Esaki, one of the rare Nobel prize winners among the Japanese, who once said, "Japan is a country of soldiers with no generals; the United States is a country of generals with no soldiers." The reasons for this seem to be rooted in Japanese culture. Again Nakajima explains:

Japanese engineers usually work together and collaborate in a group, which is quite different from western people's way of invention. These engineers like to work in a group rather than in an individualistic way. Thanks to a high sense of curiosity, they collaborate very effectively in improving imported technology. They have thus become experts in technology improvement. The many suggestions made by blue collar workers in the plants verify this fact. That Americans have produced creative technology is demonstrated by the fact that they have produced the largest number of Nobel prize recipients. This must be the greatest property of the United States.[2]

It would be a mistake to infer from these statements, as many Americans still do, that Japan is a nation of imitators. It is true that they adopted and adapted ideas from abroad, first from China, then from England and France, and after the Franco-Prussian War of 1870–71, which coincided with the Meiji restoration, from Germany. The United States was the most recent source of new ideas, at least until the 1970s. But around that time, things began to change. "In 1955 when I was a young researcher," noted Dr. Kiyoshi Takahara, director of Nippon Telephone and Telegraph's Research and Development Bureau, "there were no Japanese-equipped research facilities. Now over half of our research equipment is made in Japan." In other words, Japan had begun to develop its own process equipment.

Bob Noyce, vice-chairman of Intel, is one of a growing number of Americans aware of the Japanese drive toward creativity and their difficulties in achieving it. His informed assessment: "The Japanese are superb at process innovation, but not basic or product innovation. Now at least they've gotten to the first stage of recognizing they have a problem. But how long will it be before the children stop wearing uniforms to school, or before Japanese graduates stop working for one corporation for life? I think it will take them a long time."

For Americans April 1 means one thing, to Japanese quite another. Throughout Japan, students recruited the prior year by corporations from colleges and universities begin their new jobs on that day. It is the start of a career and of a widely practiced business tradition that breeds total dedication to the needs of the company in its particular marketplace. Twenty-one-year-old Masao recalled the nervousness of his first day. "I got up very early and put on a blue suit—in Japan you cannot be different. And I went to the Fujitsu headquarters which was more than one and a half hours away from my home. There were about seven hundred and fifty of us standing in a large hall. I didn't take much of this very seriously. Around me many others shuffled feet or acted restless when people gave speeches."

In hall after hall of major companies throughout the country, ranks of standing new recruits listen nervously to speeches by executive leaders. In the following days, the company is introduced to them in a string of speeches. For most—if not all—a lifelong commitment is beginning.

Much of what the newcomers will do in subsequent months and years is planned in advance. For Masao, it meant a month of informal but comprehensive introductions to the company's philosophy. Two weeks of character-building and self-examination; two weeks of accounting, marketing, and product information; and two weeks of group sports: the firm takes an interest in the whole person. This attention would continue for Masao through five more months of working at various unskilled jobs and then a series of three-year training cycles carried during a full work schedule. "After a short time I began to understand my responsibility to the company," Masao recalled. "They were making a commitment to me and I owed the same back to them."

Many Japanese companies like Fujitsu, Toshiba, and Sharp have what they call the "forty-year company plan." After a newcomer's initial course, there is a second-to-fifth-year advancement course. This is followed by a fifth-to-eighth-year "middle" course, capped by the eighth-to-fifteenth-year course for project-leader trainees. During their training, many employees are encouraged to spend sabbaticals studying abroad. In most cases this means going to the United States, where they come into contact with state-of-the-art research in university laboratories—a form of American subsidy of Japanese corporate R&D. This education and specialization process will go on for about twenty years. Around age forty, the employee becomes a manager or a senior researcher whose major task is education of younger staff. By age fifty-five to sixty many are urged to retire. Often these "company graduates" become university teachers.

Some Japanese do not think of this extensive training as a system of lifelong learning. Dr. Kiyoshi Takahara, director of the Musashino Laboratories research bureau at Nippon Telephone and Telegraph (NTT), calls it a system of lifelong competition. Self-development and self-motivation are the key. Every season NTT hires 130 new recruits with electrical-engineering degrees. "What I look for in our new hires is not professional qualifications but human ability."

At NEC Corporation, it's the same story. Company education starts with self-motivation. Dr. Yukimatsu Takeda, head of NEC's Institute of Technology Education, bases his company's entire educational philosophy on self-development. And NEC is a significant pacesetter. Voted number one by 1982 engineering graduates—followed by Hitachi, Toshiba, Sony, Fujitsu, and Matsushita—NEC that year hired 800 new male recruits (of whom 630 were electrical engineers) and 100 new female engineers, fully 6 percent of the total graduating pool.

Masao's story at Fujitsu is corroborated by statistics at NEC. Corporate education is pervasive and massive. Like so many things in Japan, it is also paradoxical to Westerners. On the one hand, it relies on self-development and employee initiative. On the other, it is rigorously planned and relatively inflexible. Does it encourage creativity and innovation?

Japan's school system raises the same question. It produces the world's highest level of literacy, one of the world's top secondary-school achievement scores in mathematics and science, and great numbers of bachelor-level university graduates broadly versed in technical fields like electrical engineering and computer sciences that are critical to national success in high technology.

It is a well-known fact that Japan produces more than twice as many engineers on a per-capita basis than does the United States. In contrast, the United States produces about twenty times more lawyers. In all of Japan there are about 15,000 practicing lawyers. At present 606,000 practice in the United States, and there are 128,000 students in law schools. As one American high-tech executive put it, "If we can ever get the Japanese to compete in court we'll kill them." The tactic seemed to work when Mitsubishi Electric Corporation and Hitachi executives were taken to court after being caught red-handed surreptitiously acquiring IBM secrets in the United States.

What is less well known is that the engineering output at the graduate level at Japanese universities is dismal. In electrical engineering, the United States graduates more than twice as many masters and doctorates as the Japanese do. In computer sciences in 1980, only a handful of Ph.D.'s graduated from Japanese universities. Alan Newell, a professor at Carnegie-Mellon and considered a father of the field of artificial intelligence, notes that despite all the talk about the Japanese challenge the United States still dominates computer sciences. "If you don't believe it, ask British commissioners who reported on world computer research."

Dr. Michio Nagai, minister of education from 1974 to 1976, explains some of the weaknesses of Japanese education with a directness and frankness not often encountered in Tokyo. We went to meet him at the International House in Japan, a crossroads institute for scholars interested in Japanese affairs. We asked about creativity in Japan:

"Higher education is the most stagnant sector of Japanese society. The universities do not and cannot capably conduct basic research. It is inconceivable that the type of creative basic research which Japan now needs can be supported by private money alone. Yet 80 percent of Japanese higher education is private. Now that Japan's 'comparative advantage' of cheap labor, imitation from abroad, and absence of military expenditures has been fully exploited, this lack of basic research capacity is a serious stumbling block.

"The recent Japanese Nobel prize winner Esaki worked not at a university but at the Sony Research Institute," Dr. Nagai added. "The University of Tokyo—considered to be the Mount Fuji of the education system—is vastly overrated. You cannot cite any significant research results coming from there. Look at Japan's great innovators: Matsushita, Honda, and Ibuka, the founder of Sony. None graduated from the University of Tokyo. Ibuka graduated from Waseda University. But Waseda has also declined. As a speaker at Waseda's recent centennial, Ibuka put it brutally: 'The students we hire at Sony are poorly educated because Waseda and other universities have become so weak.

We won't waste time with universities anymore. We're setting up our own corporate training. As an alumnus, I am hoping that Waseda will regain its strength.'

"An irony of history is that because Japanese universities have failed in the area of technology, the rest of the society has been forced to compensate. Companies have been obliged to educate their work force. People are encouraged to take responsibility for their own lifelong learning.

"When I was Minister, we set up several basic-research laboratories. We did not dare locate them at the University of Tokyo or any other university which would have monopolized the money and never shared research results. Instead the Ministry of Education set up 'inter-university' centers wholly financed and administered by the Ministry of Education. The main ones are the molecular sciences lab at Okazaki, the accelerator at Tsukuba, and the plasma center. Another one concentrates on Japanese national literature."

In addition there are sixteen national laboratories administered by the Agency for Industrial Science and Technology. They employ about 4,000, many in a number of facilities located in Tsukuba, Japan's science center near Tokyo. High on their agenda of research is the identification of technologies with industrial potential.

At the most advanced levels of technological creativity, Japan has yet to show strength. Masanori Moritani, author of *Japanese Technology* and researcher at the highly respected Nomura Research Institute, appraises Japan's performance across five different levels of technological development. It's at the top level— Nobel prize-class discoveries and inventions of fifteen-year time horizon future technologies—where Japanese research efforts are thin. In the other areas—advanced technology such as robots, applied technologies such as calculators, and refinement activities for existing products and production processes—Japan has its real strength.

Moritani cites three reasons for the lack of success at the higher levels of creativity. First, Japanese do not work easily on projects with long time horizons. Products that would not mature until the 1990s or the twenty-first century are virtually ignored.

Second, projects that require a completely new approach and lack clear goals are seldom undertaken. For example, Japan, until recently was strong in steel, where it spends three times what the United States does in steel research and development, but it is far weaker in chemicals and energy, where biotechnology and solar research are fundamentally new. In these latter two areas, Japan spends only 22 and 12 percent of what the United States does.

And third, Moritani observes, the Japanese have no interest in research in specialized areas where the market potential is perceived to be limited. That is, if there's not a ready market in sight, there's probably no research budget available.

The net result? Risky ventures are taboo. This is reflected in the paucity of venture-capital firms. It is also reflected in the R&D system. In Japan, the government share of research was only one-third of industry's spending on research in 1981, whereas in the United States, the government spends almost as much as industry does on research.

Despite all that is said about the lack of creativity in Japan, we could not help but be impressed by the staggering numbers of executives, one after another, who reiterated their conviction of the need to achieve greater results in basic research, even if this meant revamping Japanese society itself. MITI's message calling for more creativity touched a raw nerve in Japanese society. Executives were quick to pick up the theme.

The president of Sumitomo Metal Industries, Yoshifumi Kumagai, says of his steel company: "Creativity is the key to success here, both in research and development of new equipment and processes in the labs and in the applied engineering resulting from *jishu kanri* (quality circle) activities by employees in the shops and mills."[3] One example of the intended results of this policy was the creation of a continuous annealing furnace line which does in one hour what it normally takes one or two weeks to achieve by normal methods.

While Sumitomo and other Japanese steel companies are investing heavily in R&D, the big integrated mills of the U.S. steel industry are doing just the reverse. U.S. Steel shut down its once-thriving Bain Laboratory for Fundamental Research. Its Monroeville research team was cut from 1,100 to 760 and further cuts are expected. Kawasaki Steel, on the other hand, has 944 researchers despite a production output half that of U.S. Steel. And at Carnegie-Mellon University in the heart of the industry, Professor Richard Fruehan has what he calls "the largest block of corporate steel research money of any North American professor." The amount: $120,000. As a result of such meager support of research and development, the American steel industry languishes in costly old-fashioned ways. In Japan, 70 percent of production in big integrated mills occurs in modern continuous casters; in the United States only 15 percent. Eight percent of American steel comes out of antiquated open-hearth furnaces, none in Japan.

Other industries and other corporations are on the move in Japan. Dr. Michiyuki Uenohara, executive vice-president and director of NEC's vast research enterprise, opened his conversation with us with the main question on his mind: how to create creativity. "In the past," he noted, "it would have been foolhardy for Japan to duplicate the research being done abroad. We did not need original research." What should rivet American attention now, however, is a fact that escapes most non-Japanese: The drive to creativity is fueled not only by external competition but equally by internal social needs. First and foremost are the unique qualities of the Japanese language. Dr. Uenohara's own excellent, fatherly English style added emphasis to his remarks: "The Japanese language is the most isolated in the world. Keyboards and computer input devices were designed for Westerners. To improve our productivity, we need Japanese word processors, Japanese computer languages, and, above all, voice-recognition systems. Speech is the most natural way to communicate with machines, and we have to perfect this interface."

In their quest for creativity, the Japanese are following varied paths, at least five of which were described to us. The first of these—forming a new company—is the most common pattern in America. While not so common in Japan, it happens nonetheless. Take Sord Computer, for example. In the late 1970s, several engineers, frustrated with bureaucratic slowness, broke away from one of the large computer companies to found Sord. Its first product, a small business computer in the $3,000 to $7,000 range, has been extremely successful. While there are not as many examples of such successful breakaways in Japan as in the United States, more and more are beginning to take place.

The Nippon Telephone and Telegraph Company (NTT) research division, modeled after Bell Laboratories, bets on proven geniuses. The company has five "named" research laboratories: the Mizushima, Furukawa, Ibuki, Nakagawa, and Kudo. The names are those of their five chief scientists, men largely in their fifties, who are supplied with five to ten assistants and have assured budgets for several years to conduct basic research. Some recent achievements: 1.3-micron optical fiber which can be used for long-distance communication, a 2,000-word speech-recognition unit, and commercially produceable 256K chips.

Sharp Electric Company has inaugurated a "two speciality, two generation" program for its engineers aged twenty-five to thirty-five. Each is expected to master more than one specialty and is periodically brought together with older engineers for systematic brainstorming. This double-faceted program is part of an ongoing controversy in Japan—whether creativity will come from younger people and whether it will come from specialization. Tsutomu Nakamura, a director of Sharp's semiconductor research labs, notes it is an assumption of company policy that engineering creativity comes early in the career and declines with age. "This means that we may need to change the boundaries of the 'forty-year plan' in order to give younger people more freedom early on."

Another approach is symbolized by an old Buddhist saying that "three heads lead to the greater wisdom." NEC Corporation practices this maxim by promoting creativity through group research. Dr. Uenohara's Fundamental Research Labs try to develop a group of engineers sensitive to human factors and social needs. What does he hope for an outcome? Computer languages appropriate to Japanese linguistics and voice-recognition systems, where NEC is already a leader.

And Yokogawa Electric Company has the most conventional Japanese program to foster creativity. It relies on "outside power to induce more creativity." Foreign professionals are hired to come to Japan to work with their Japanese counterparts. Presently they have researchers from the United States, the United Kingdom, and New Zealand.

The acid test of Japan's ability to be creative is the Fifth Generation Computer Project. When it was first announced by MITI in late 1981, many American observers dismissed it as blue-sky public relations and speculated whether this was not indeed the MITI intention—a great visionary document but no actual plan. Others in Japan suggested that its real intention was not scientific research but an informal cartel to combat IBM. Some thought the motive was to smooth the waters between competing firms. The competition among the Big Six computer companies in Japan had become so intense that the press referred to them as the "walking wounded." The new project was one way MITI could prevent them from destroying one another, they suggested.

Shortly after the formal announcement, MITI published the details of the project's funding, organization, and technical goals and specifications. It was clear a pressure point had been hit. An avalanche of interest landed on MITI's doorstep. The project captured the popular imagination as well as the attention of the world press. Everyone wanted to know more about the computer which was popularly described to have eyes and ears, to communicate through speech and pictures, to learn from experience, to translate languages, and to convert speech into print. It would even try to second-guess what the user wanted and present options to its slow-thinking but perhaps intelligent master.

Even if only a minor part of these capabilities could be realized, it is clear that a project like this could make Japan an unassailable leader in the next generation of computer technology. The country would have a running start on its competitors that might prove difficult to beat. Of course, many experts are not convinced. They say it is overambitious and underfunded, and they remind us that its overall concepts come from MIT and its individual components come from American research in artificial intelligence. But even the experts remain fascinated. Can anyone, especially the Japanese, put it all together? To do so will require extraordinary creativity.

The Fifth Generation Project has touched off a fantastic race of international proportions. By 1983, several countries had announced responses to the Japanese. The U.S. Department of Defense, through the Advanced Research Projects Agency, has announced its own Supercomputer Project for not one but for two machines—one "number cruncher" and another "knowledge processor." In the private sector, American electronics firms, largely in reaction to the Fifth Generation Project, are pooling research budgets to be the first to attain breakthroughs. IBM has its own agenda to meet the Japanese challenge. In Europe, a consortium under the name ESPRIT has been formed with company research staffs that in combination number over 2,000.

Who will be the first to achieve the Fifth will depend largely on creativity, but not necessarily on technological breakthroughs. Despite all the attention from the computer sciences, it may be the management of scientific inquiry that determines Japan's success or failure. How will Fifth Generation research be organized?

The Fifth Generation will be managed by ICOT—the Institute for New Generation Computer Technology. ICOT is a consortium of eight electronics corporations,[4] NTT (Nippon Telephone Telegraph), and MITI, which was the initiator. While its goals have been clearly described and MITI has committed almost $500 million of funding through 1990, its structure and potential for success are far more problematic. The reason is that the issue of who controls ICOT is unresolved. "The problem," says Professor Tohru Moto-Oka, chairman of ICOT's project-promoting committee, "is that companies are getting MITI money to do research but doing things their own way. This presents a problem of who controls. This is very important in understanding the internal competition."

In appropriate Japanese style, ICOT is organized to produce

consensus. Everyone is represented. The decision-making apparatus starts with MITI. The first surprise striking an outsider is to find that the MITI coordinating office is a modest team of bureaucrats whose primary job is to monitor the paperwork of ICOT's operations. The ten-to-twenty-member MITI staff is tucked away in a nondescript seventh-floor office piled high with paper as befits an overworked bureaucracy. In contrast, the president of ICOT, Takuma Yamamoto, is the chairman of Fujitsu. One discovers a balancing between MITI and corporate influence in the executive-director, an ex-MITI man, Tadashi Yoshioka. However, despite his title, he may have little power, being referred to as "a retired old-boy" from MITI. ICOT has a board of directors and a policy committee attached to it. This is a device intended to include representatives from many more interested parties, mostly academics, but the real power to decide research direction seems to lie elsewhere.

To an American, the formal organizational chart is clear and logical. It's what is unstated that leads to confusion. Two lines of authority funnel out of the executive-director box. One goes to a general-affairs office with ten members, chaired by Professor Tohru Moto-Oka of Tokyo University, who is recognized as one of the leading intellectuals in electronics research. His group, however, does not consist of academics but rather of MITI and company representatives. Its formal duty is to oversee and settle technical policy issues, the political battleground of any research program. It is important to note that there is no formal university representation here other than through the professor who chairs its meetings. As Dr. Moto-Oka puts it, "Industry does not expect leadership from professors."

The other line leads to Kazuhiro Fuchi, the director of the ICOT research center and former head of the information systems division of MITI's Electrotechnical Laboratory. Under him are three research laboratories with the dual assignment of doing their own basic research and of contracting with company laboratories for specified research. A group of about fifty researchers work at the center; most are under the age of thirty-five. This group is on loan from the corporate research labs of the eight participating companies; their term of stay is approximately three years before they return to home base. It would seem that this team of forty to fifty researchers would be the locus of original work, yet it is hard to see how three-year stints among a small group of researchers from competing companies can lead to the monumental results needed by the end of the decade. It is also unclear how a team made up of young researchers can exert personal authority over senior researchers assigned to work on ICOT projects in company laboratories.

Here the personal role of ICOT's research director, Kazuhiro Fuchi, becomes critically important in American eyes and perhaps controversial in Japan's. He is described as "ready to take risks, proud of Japanese native intelligence, and ready to take on a personal campaign to wipe out the uncreative stereotype that shadows the Japanese."[5] A highly respected research coordinator who brings with him the aura and power of MITI, he will be the one to keep the work on target and to protect unorthodox but promising ideas. Since one of his principal jobs is to define and delegate the contractual assignments to company members of the consortium, it will fall upon him to ensure that the appropriate level of pure research and coordination is carried out. His influence is made easier, at least during the first three years, because the budgets are funded solely by MITI. A fundamental problem arises in the subsequent years when the funding not only grows substantially but at least half the budgetary burden is taken on by the corporate members.

Dr. Moto-Oka puts the issue of sustaining an immense creative research effort into perspective. "The problem with a concentration of research in company labs," he says, "is that managers in Japan do not like basic research. It is too long-term. We don't have the experience of creative open-ended research. When you ask what kinds of people would be best on a research team, managers have no consensus on this."

Of course, American as well as European consortia that have formed in response to ICOT face many of the same issues. But organizing for creativity is not new to the United States. One advantage is immediately obvious in the American case. State-of-the-art research is rarely done directly in company labs but rather in universities or university-like places like Bell Labs. This provides a pool of long-term researchers whose personal careers advance with advances in technology. There is also a tradition in the United States of insulating new ideas from excessive criticism. Many funding agencies like the Office of Naval Research (ONR) are willing to fund a promising person, even if the ideas run the risk of turning out to be crackpot rather than genius.

Whether ICOT can manage to let creativity come through or not, there is little doubt among Americans and Japanese alike that the project will be critical in the race to build up trained human resources on the leading edge of pure research. Maybe the Fifth Generation Project will fail to fulfill its technological goals, but if it is successful as a learning device the Japanese will be that much closer to true creativity in technology and management the next time around.

Two decades ago, few Americans expected Japan to challenge us in production-line efficiency. After all, Americans saw themselves as the inventors of mass-production technology. Could we be caught sleeping again, this time in a challenge to compete in creativity? Most Americans doubt it.

Everything in American culture indicates a built-in advantage in terms of creativity and innovation. While all else may fail, tradition tells us that in a crunch "Yankee ingenuity" will prevail. The statistics bear out this faith. It is clear from the historical record that the United States is a leader in new-product creation. A National Science Foundation study showed that of the leading-edge technological innovations studied, 246 originated in the United States, 45 in the United Kingdom, and 26 in Japan. The United States has more registered patents, more Nobel prizes, more made-in-America inventions than any other country.

David Saxon, chairman of MIT and formerly president of the University of California, is in an excellent position to observe and assess the adaptive capacity of Americans. "We [Americans] have a great advantage over most other nations in our traditional willingness to experiment, to innovate, to take and accept risks in devising new organizational arrangements, such as the many experiments already going on between universities and industry. . . . This ingrained optimism of Americans, so often a puzzle to foreign visitors, will surely serve us well if it continues to encourage innovative arrangements."[6]

On occasion, Japanese managers like to refer to their business culture as a thoroughbred finely tuned to win the productivity game, and of the United States as a mongrel unbred to excel in so refined a competition. In time, however, the analogy may prove the exact reverse. The highly adaptive fighting strength of the mongrel could be more of an asset than is fully recognized.

But our ability to sustain this record is by no means a foregone conclusion. The experts in innovation are among the few calling attention to the fact that what has until now been a basic American strength is showing signs of weakness. Christopher Hill, a senior research associate at MIT and specialist in industrial innovation, notes that "in the last thirty years, concern has become widespread that the United States has lost its lead in technological innovation."[7] According to Burton Klein, professor of economics at the California Institute of Technology and previously head of economics at the Rand Corporation, "Since about 1965, the competitiveness of the U.S. economy with respect to both the newer and older technologies has steadily eroded."[8]

History is rich with examples of countries that were blinded by self-complacency. This happened in the past century with Britain. The British still claim to be on the forefront of *scientific* creativity, with more Nobel prizes *per capita* than any other nation. Yet in economic terms, the comparative advantage afforded by innovation clearly moved to the United States sometime during the last century.

While Americans maintain an image of the Japanese as imitators, this view is proving more illusory than real. Gene Gregory, an American professor in a Japanese university, notes in his article "The Japanese Propensity for Innovation" that "while Britain boasts ten times as many Nobel Prizes as Japan, Japanese universities are graduating ten times as many engineers as those of the United Kingdom . . ." Gregory goes on to challenge the West's misperception of Japan. The Japanese, he notes, who led the world in patent applications in 1928, did so again by 1977 when they were filing three times as many as West Germany and 50 to 60 percent more than the United States.[9]

The highly respected British news magazine the *Economist* sums up the English view concisely although perhaps a bit prematurely: "Japan's industries have caught up with the West's in technical innovation . . ."[10] Another look from abroad focuses on the innovation race between the United States and Japan. Christopher Freeman, head of the Science Policy Research Unit in Sussex, England, writes: "The problem of which country is best prepared to emerge as the new technological leader is of course a highly speculative question. Yet all the evidence seems to point toward either the old technological leader, the USA, or the major newcomer Japan. Why we believe that the latter might eventually emerge as the new technological leader is as much related to Japan's technological capabilities and general human skill endowments as to its capacity for rapid social organizational adaptations."[11]

What makes Japan run? Most Americans naturally assume that it's a catch-up game to compete with the United States. But from a Japanese perspective, something else is at work as well. Other countries in Asia, most notably South Korea at present, are running all-out to overtake the Japanese. Others besides Korea are doing the same, and in the background of course looms China. We turn now to this incredibly competitive dynamic that promises to transform not only Asia but the entire world economy.

13

Asia Boom

Koreans are the only people on earth who can make the Japanese look lazy.
          —Kim Dal Choong, Professor, Yonsei University, South Korea

Singapore is betting on its only resource: its people.
          —Juzar Motiwalla, Director, Institute of Systems Science, National University of Singapore

East Asia can easily be thought of as "one place." Yet the map of East Asia is dotted with large and small islands. Distances between them are great. A flight from Japan to Singapore takes about four hours; from Manila to Tokyo, another four. For many Americans, impressions of this region are a collage of memories of World War II battles and General MacArthur's island-hopping campaign; or of Philippine independence from the United States in 1946; the Korean War; Vietnam; the Japanese economic onslaught; the Aquino assassination at Manila airport. But there is another East Asia that extends far beyond these impressions.

To grasp the meaning of a new Asia in the making, one has to amend an old American vision of opportunity: "Go west, young man—far west to East Asia!" This twist reflects a growth story not well understood by many Americans: the Asia boom. A virtual explosion of economic activity not only extends far beyond Japan but it is beginning to eclipse the earlier European success story known as the "German economic miracle." American trade with East Asia now totals $125 billion a year, $10 billion more than our total trade with Europe. In recent years a number of East Asian countries have come to exert new muscle in the world economic arena. One group, the "newly industrializing countries" (NICs) of East Asia, grew at least three times faster than the United States and outpaced even Japan. Two of the most notable are South Korea and Singapore. In both cases, headlines in the local newspapers often report investments by the world's largest multinationals. Such announcements signal that something big is happening.

Early in 1983, for example, General Electric announced that it was moving its Asia Pacific division headquarters from New York City to Singapore—where it already employs 11,000 people. GE vice-president Frank D. Kittredge said that the choice of location was based on "the hard fact that Southeast Asia stands out as the growth leader." The Emhart Corporation profiled in an earlier chapter has a glassmaking-machinery operation in Singapore and is solicited by buyers from mainland China. The same firm's hardware division opened a sales office in November 1983—the reason: a burgeoning Singapore economy which grew even during the worst part of the world recession at a 6.3-percent annual rate. "It's unbelievable," says division president Fred M. Hollfelder, in reaction to the commercial tempo in Singapore. "We want to have a presence."

Foreign multinationals are doing the same, especially the Japanese, whose presence outnumbers all others. Matsushita recently announced the building of a fully automated integrated-circuit (IC) production plant in Singapore. Neither the high cost of living nor high wage rates was a deterrent. To the same island country, a host of companies are coming from Europe. Italy's SGS–ATES is opening a sophisticated wafer-fabrication plant for ICs as well as a design center staffed by Singapore engineers—a first for Southeast Asia. Nestlé opened a new central R&D facility, as did Varta, the battery-maker from Germany. Eight hundred major foreign firms are now active there. To put this into perspective one might ponder the meaning of 800 large companies coming into a U.S. state as small as Rhode Island over a short fifteen-year period. The economic implications are enormous.

Similarly in South Korea, AT&T and ITT are among a growing number of firms to have established substantial coventures.

AT&T chairman Charles Brown, in April 1983, said of his association with the Lucky-Gold Star group, "I expect Korea will become a world leader in the telecommunications industry, as it is
in other industries." This nation's steel, construction, and shipbuilding industries are now considered among the best and most
aggressive in the world. Its electrical-consumer-products manufacturers can outbid most others when it comes to such things as
televisions. It now has its eye on more sophisticated products
such as cars and computers. One is hard put to think of South
Korea as a down-and-out war-torn nation only three decades
ago, so active is its economy.

An entire Pacific Basin region roughly equal in population to
Europe is on the march. Just as West Europe was the magnet for
a tidal wave of U.S. corporate capital investments in the 1950s
and 1960s, East Asia offers an even wider range of possible opportunities in the 1980s and 1990s. Not counting China and India,
the East Asian or Pacific Basin region has a population of about
500 million, similar to Europe's not counting the Soviet Union,
and a GNP of $1,448 billion, approximately 53 percent of Eu-
rope's. A significant part of this population is edging into its own
era of middle-class consumerism.

Few generalizations fit the region. It can be most easily conceived as three tiers of countries flanked by two giants, China
and India. At the top of the tier, in a class by itself, is Japan,
which, as the MITI report *Vision of MITI Policies in the 1980s*
matter-of-factly states, "already measures up to the world's top
level in almost all spheres of industrial technology." At the bottom of the tier is a dwindling number of countries that can still
accurately be called LDCs (less developed countries)—Indonesia, the Philippines, Sri Lanka, and Thailand. In the middle
are another tier of countries—South Korea, Singapore, Taiwan,
Hong Kong, and Malaysia, internationally known as the NICs.
These countries are now playing their own version of a catch-up
game played decades earlier by Japan. The net effect of this
game is to ratchet up the levels of both international competition
and joint-venture cooperation, especially in the field of high tech.
As one Japanese commentator put it, "These are countries that

once were best at making products with no more than 5,000 parts; in Japan we do best making those with 5,000 to 50,000 parts; the United States is best at those things with more than 50,000 parts. But as others start making more and more sophisticated products it forces us either to move up into markets dominated by Americans or to automate on the lower end."

As the case of Singapore makes abundantly clear, Americans have something to gain by watching closely the success or failure of one of the boldest, most daring industrial policies yet devised. Outside of Japan, Singapore sees itself as an island economy whose future rests in large part on being Asia's principal automated-factory environment and technical consulting and services capital. It is leapfrogging from an underdeveloped, low-labor-rate economy toward a high-tech "regional brain center." It is doing in less than ten years what Japan took twenty-five or more to achieve. Progress just in the last three years is staggering, with computer software and flexible manufacturing systems surfacing from virtual obscurity only a short time earlier. Asia's first test-tube baby was conceived here, and delicate organ transplants are performed in the island's hospitals. Singapore's national strategy is a tightly interwoven collaboration between the government, private business, and the education sector. The latter, composed of a single national university, six international high-technology institutes, and a network of technical colleges and schools, is the kingpin of Singapore's policy. To some the experiment is free-market capitalism operating at its very best; to others it is brilliant planning implemented in a tightly run political fiefdom. Whatever the characterization, the goal is to multiply the supply of technologically sophisticated human resources by a factor of six in the short space of eight years. Indications are the target will be reached; the big question is whether it will pay off in the highly competitive Pacific Basin region.

South Korea tells a different story. The country is fast becoming what Japan was in the 1960s. It has a labor force still far cheaper than that of the United States, an unrelenting drive to compete, and government support and incentives that to conventional American thinking seem to go to extremes to promote

Korean economic success. American labor had better rethink how it wants to compete with the new Korea (we think it can, through advanced technology and training) and American management had better keep one step ahead in its thinking about the consequences of different forms of Korean–American collaboration for America's future market position. Korea needs U.S. technology in its drive to displace Japan from selected world markets, as it has already done in steel and shipbuilding and wants to do in some consumer sectors and in auto manufacturing. In the near term, this offers America access to a large domestic market and a stepping stone to China and other Asian buyers. In the longer term, Korean use of American technology may cause Japan to become even more competitive.

The Asian NICs represent both opportunity and threat at the same time. To the extent that American corporate strategies and U.S. competitive policies are well aimed, these countries can be more partners than challengers. All over Asia, much of the action centers on the high-technology electronics and computer industries. But unlike Japan, where a race for the Fifth Generation Computer is in full swing, Korea and Singapore have embarked upon other courses. Both have decided to import technology and to move ahead rapidly as manufacturers of sophisticated high-technology products, with electronics, communications, and computers as priority sectors; yet each is going about it quite differently. Korea is concentrating on technology transfer through licensing agreements; it recently signed a major agreement with AT&T for the joint production of 64K chips. Singapore is going for growth in new technologies through human-resource development; it recently signed a major agreement with IBM for support of a first-class research and training institute. The challenge here is not in basic research—which neither nation makes any pretense of competing in—but in the commercial production of sophisticated products in hardware, software, flexible manufacturing systems, and allied services.

What drives these countries to create new forms of competitive advantage? The answer is the obsolescence of cheap labor. Neither Singapore nor Korea can any longer compete as cheap-labor

manufacturing centers. Singapore's per-capita GNP rose from
$450 in 1965 to $5,120 in 1981—an amazing record. South Korea
jumped from $120 to $1,630. Japan, by comparison, grew from
$760 to $9,610, and the United States from $3,240 to $12,780
during the same period. In the case of Singapore, production and
manual workers earned about $300 per month in 1982 plus bene-
fits, twice as much as ten years before. What's more, it has managed to hold its inflation rate down. In 1982, it was held to 3.9
percent. Its diminutive population of only 2.5 million provides no
room for labor-intensive industrial growth. The island nation is
one of the few in the so-called Third World that has a labor
shortage. Singapore wants to avoid a large influx of immigrant
workers because of fears that it might destabilize the politics of a
complex ethnic balancing act carefully crafted by Prime Minister
Lee Kuan Yew. The island is already vulnerable enough: It imports all its raw materials and most of its food, including water
that is piped to the island from Malaysia.

In Korea, too, labor rates are rising fast, partly because national growth rates reached as high as 15 percent in 1976 and
about 10–12 percent for two or three years following. Now they
have leveled off at a still-respectable 6 percent. Technicians with
B.S. degrees in electronics assembly firms earn $500 per month
plus benefits, production workers $150 to $250 plus benefits. The
significance of changing employment and wage patterns was not
lost on policymakers. They saw the need for new strategies that
did not assume an advantage based on low wages. Korea is now
racing against time. Can the country develop its technological
competitive capacity and resultant growth fast enough to overtake Japan and still provide enough decent-paying jobs for its
rapidly growing population?

To a first-time visitor, Korea seems like an unlikely home for
electronics. The vast urban agglomeration of 8.5 million people
in Seoul—four times its size twenty years ago—has a dusty, un-
kempt veneer. Part of it is due to a steady tempo of construction,
and part to an arid, scruffy countryside. Yet throughout the nation an industrial revolution is humming in high gear. By the
early 1980s, electronics products were generating 10 percent of

Korea's export revenues. Sixty percent of these were sold to the United States and Japan. At present, most shipments consist of standard consumer products such as TV sets, which propelled Korea into tenth position in the world as an exporter of electronic goods. Government planners are aiming for a rise of Korea's ranking in exports to the United States from ninth to sixth place, hoping to displace France and the Netherlands along the way. To do so requires a change in Korea's strategy—a move beyond consumer electronics based on cheap labor toward more advanced technologies based on a well-trained work force.

National policymakers are guiding the nation's growth by formulating five-year plans. The new Fifth Five-Year Economic and Social Development Plan, which covers the period 1982–86, contains some bold initiatives. It shifts national attention away from heavy industry and chemicals to machinery, electronics, and shipbuilding. An important aim is to get into sophisticated high-technology products. "During the period," declares a background planning document, "the development of strategic high-technology products such as semiconductors, computers, and telecommunications systems will be emphasized."[1]

Behind these moves is the realization that Korea cannot continue much longer with an economy based on cheap labor. There are several reasons for this. One is the need to cover Korea's huge international debt, which in 1982 stood at $49 billion, the fourth largest in the world. A large defense budget, 5 to 6 percent of GNP, figures prominently here. Another is Korea's fast-growing labor force, increasing at more than 3 percent per year. Low-wage employment is under rising pressure from other countries, most notably India and China, which are starting to make consumer products of their own. Another reason is that the drive to overtake Japan has become a national passion and plays a significant role in setting the tempo of Korean economic achievement. A professor at Yonsei University, Kim Dal Choong, quipped that "Koreans are the only people on earth who can make the Japanese look lazy."

A comprehensive analysis of Korea's economic problems and alternatives was carried out at the influential Korea Institute for

Industrial Economics and Technology (KIET) by Jang Won Suh. His study of the domestic electronics industry shows that Korea buys most of its electronic components from abroad. More than 50 percent of the value of electronic products made at home in 1979 had to be imported in contrast to only about 11 percent for Japan in that year. He also found that "technology-intensive industrial products such as computers and telecommunication systems have been almost totally imported." In addition, at the start of the 1980s, more than nine out of ten electronics companies were so small that competition in foreign markets was closed to them—despite the successes of a few, very large electronics firms.

Equally revealing was a study released by the prestigious Nomura Research Institute in Tokyo. It showed that the capital invested in equipment and machines per worker in Korea's electronics industry was only a tenth that in Japan—indicating the same reliance on cheap labor that Japan had used, and discarded, in the 1950s.

To set the new course, Korea's president Chun Doo Hwan established a science and technology council composed of government and industry leaders. Its purpose is to set priorities and to ensure active business and government collaboration. First on the agenda is to emphasize the human resource, a familiar refrain from Korean planners. Kim Kiwhan, newly appointed vice-minister of commerce and industry, says: "We have no natural resources to speak of other than our people. Technology is imbedded in them; our task then is to develop it." One of the council's first decisions is to raise the nation's investment in R&D from 0.8 percent of GNP to 2 percent.

One of the principal recipients of research funds will be the Korea Advanced Institute of Science and Technology (KAIST)—presently the nation's only graduate-level institute for scientific research. Its activities are being directed to collaborative research with direct utility to industry. One example is a recently announced ceramics diesel-engine project financed by the Sangyong industrial group. Its goal is to bring state-of-the-art ceramics technology to Korea in anticipation of an immense new automotive and truck market which Japan and to a lesser extent the United States are rushing to tap. "Once we decide what we need to do," says MIT-trained Linsu Kim, an associate professor at KAIST, "we get to it fast. We are action oriented."

The key challenge for Korea's new strategy is how quickly it can develop a qualified work force. With a still relatively undeveloped education system, the country does not start with any advantages. Education is compulsory for only six years, compared to nine in Japan. A modest 3.6 percent of the GNP is devoted to education. In Japan the figure is 5.7 percent, and in the United States 6.9 percent. Korea's universities concentrate on undergraduates and lack the graduate engineers and scientists critical to high-tech industry. At present, of the approximately 250,000 people employed in high tech, only about 4.7 percent are considered technicians. This dearth of highly trained people represents one of the country's biggest hurdles in its goal of tapping new technologies as a basis for competitive advantage.

One way to fill the gap while preparing more graduates is to accelerate the transfer of knowledge from industrial countries. To achieve this goal, Korea is actively seeking and encouraging joint ventures. Offering access to Korea's large domestic market as a lever, the government is negotiating far more effectively than in the past. In April 1983 a landmark agreement was signed reflecting this approach. AT&T, represented by its chairman, Charles L. Brown, announced with unusual fanfare its willingness to "virtually transfer all its technologies to Korea." Said Brown in regard to one of his firm's principal products, an electronic switching system labeled the No. 1A ESS: "Although [these] machines have been installed throughout other countries, Korea is the only non-U.S. location that has [successfully] transferred the technology and established in-country manufacturing for this high technology item."[2]

Critical to the successful absorption of AT&T's production techniques and design talents is the extensive training program that accompanies the agreement. AT&T's local partner, Gold Star Semiconductor, is a division of the Lucky-Gold Star Group. Its operation is already up and running with a partially automated semiconductor operation. The technology and production-line techniques are supplied by AT&T's manufacturing arm, Western Electric, now absorbed into its reorganized corporate structure. To make up for local training deficiencies, Gold Star is sending 1,800 technicians a year to the United States for training at several industrial sites.

This major agreement stakes out positions for both AT&T and Korea in their rivalry with Japan. All are competing to be suppliers of sophisticated equipment to the anticipated China market and to the blossoming East Asia markets. From AT&T's perspective, this move provides a potential technological end run around Japanese competitors such as NEC Corporation and NTT in positioning for future market growth. For Korea it provides its own home base in the emotionally charged game of catch-up with its cultural competitor, Japan.

Korea's recent efforts to build a long-term position for itself in the world market for electronics is most tangibly illustrated by a visit to Gumi, a tidy small town of 100,000 south of Seoul on the main road and rail line to Pusan on the coast. A three-and-a-half-hour train ride through rolling hills and picturesque farmland brings a visitor to a railroad station facing a quaint and bustling main street lined with diminutive stores. Another few miles of car travel south and one reaches a surprisingly modern complex of apartment blocks and high-tech electronics firms in a widening river plain. This is one of Korea's biggest gambles to play a major role as a producer of sophisticated electronics technology.

Twenty thousand people are employed in this beautiful, serene rural setting. One side of the wide valley is dominated by a ragged mountain chain, the other by a flat-topped mountain with horizontal layers of geologically deposited material. The locals, with a sense of humor, call it Silicon Mountain. The natural beauty, however, does not satisfy everyone. A common complaint from many skilled workers transferred here is that it's too far from Seoul's urban life.

A centerpiece of Gumi's growing industrial park is the Korea Institute of Electronics and Technology (KIET—the initials are the same as those of the economics institute in Seoul). The strategy here is straightforward. Rather than rely on universities to create a new human-resource base, Korea has opted for special applied-research institutes, of which KIET is one. Founded in 1976 and in active operation five years later, it is supported half by government funds and half by industry contracts. The World Bank loaned it money in 1979. Finding the initial staff was no easy matter. The Institute had to undertake a recruitment campaign of Korean electrical- and computer-science nationals abroad. This proved to be successful. There is now a staff of 350, most of whom (60 percent) are in the semiconductor division; 20 percent are assigned to the systems division; and the balance are in administration.

The Institute's work is focused on applied technology in cooperation with local industries. KIET provides an R&D service that few Korean companies could afford to support on their own. Now two years in full operation, it already counts fourteen in-house projects of which six are cosponsored by industry. Within a short period the institute has brought together a critical mass of technical manpower closely linked to a sophisticated grouping of industries nearby. This collaborative industrial research/training arrangement is a distinct novelty for Korean business. The big question is whether this strategy will pay off, or whether, as a number of Korean critics fear, "the government will have to intervene before long to straighten out the traffic and perhaps subject these firms to another round of 'readjustment' and 're-structuring.'"[3]

The need for sophisticated manpower is graphically illustrated by the AT&T-Gold Star joint venture located adjacent to the Institute. There are actually two operations at work facing one another inside the company's two-story building—one an old cheap-labor assembly line and the other a new automated production line. One produces electronic switching systems and the other makes semiconductors but with different manufacturing methods. In one section, manually operated work stations are occupied by young girls, who work twelve- to fourteen-hour days looking through microscopes to solder wire leads to minute microchips. This is the conventional "cheap labor" method. Next to them is a brand-new automated wire-and-die-board manufacturing room equipped with the latest U.S. and Japanese production machines. State-of-the-art computer-aided design equipment, bought from U.S. manufacturers Calma and Applicon, fills several rooms. In total, there are almost 1,000 workers and engineers employed. Two hundred and twenty of the total are college graduates trained in electrical engineering, computer sciences, and mechanical engineering. Gold Star will need the maximum talent it can get. By 1984, it expects to be producing 64K RAM chips in commercial quantities for use in domestically produced hardware.

Gumi's training effort focuses on a number of different age groups. Within walking distance of the plant is Korea's first national residential high school for exceptional students in mathematics and science—an institutional experiment with strong similarities to North Carolina's residential public school for gifted students. A little farther, across a wide river, is a recently opened engineering college that will soon graduate its first class of bachelors. These institutions, if successful, should help to meet manpower needs in Gumi.

One company that settled here early was Korea Telecommunications—a division of the multibillion-dollar Samsung conglomerate. In 1977 it built a manufacturing and research plant in Gumi in a coventure with ITT. Six years later, a semiconductor operation was attached to it and the new entity with 1,200 employees was renamed Samsung Semiconductor and Telecommunications. Forty percent of its work force have B.S. degrees; another 20 percent are graduates of technical programs, many of them completed "on the job."

Joo-Hyung Lee, director of the telecommunications laboratory at Samsung, suggested that his research agenda and his growth potential will be achieved "only by the availability of qualified people." As a result, one of his major tasks is to ensure that advanced training is available to his engineers through in-house graduate courses. Lectures are offered in five fields, such as circuit design, four times per week in each. These are taught by university professors invited to Gumi for short stints. "We have to train our own people," said Lee. "We started our program only two years ago and now I can say it runs quite smoothly." The manufacturing and testing floor for telecommunications equipment, a vast covered space encompassing 440,000 square feet (reputedly the largest of its kind in Asia), equals those to be seen in Japan in terms of cleanliness, layout, and production flow. One of the primary products is the Bell Telephone of Belgium's M10CN electronic switching system. "We are the strongest outside Japan," said Lee. "Not even Taiwan can compete."

For the time being, the road ahead is marked by a clearer and more pragmatic policy than ever before. Decentralization of planning plus recent denationalization of the banking system are viewed as essential stimulants to much-needed infusions of private entrepreneurship and foreign investment. The key to success, however, rests in the nation's ability to educate wider and wider circles of technologists. In Gumi, at least, the potential of rising into the front ranks of electronics competition in the world seems real. By the end of 1983, the American electronics press was heralding the arrival of new Korean products. Peripherals and personal computers would be used to make inroads. At Gold Star, eight-bit PCs are being produced at a rate of 5,000 a month; 2,000 of these are earmarked for Japan and the United States. By 1984, sixteen-bit PCs were in production.

Whether Korea will ultimately be successful in implementing its new high-tech strategy is far from assured. To date, development has occurred at a spectacular rate. Growth, as mentioned earlier, led world rates for several years in a row during the 1970s. The changes are immense. In the last ten years alone, rural population has dropped 34 percent. This leaves only one out of four people living on farms. This has produced great pressures on the employment situation, as well as simply on urban centers. Urban development is phenomenal not just for its spectacular rate of growth—Seoul expanded from two to eight million in twenty years—but for its administrators' ability to supply adequate housing and huge new complexes of offices. Whether this kind of development can be maintained would seem doubtful for most countries.

But determination is intense in Korea. Even a short tour confirms a single-minded determination to grow rapidly as a supplier of more and more technologically sophisticated goods and services and to avoid the economic problems presently experienced by countries such as Brazil and Mexico. As one departs from Korea, the intense activity at Seoul's international airport seems to epitomize the fast but wearing pace of the modern Korean economy. Many passengers, returning workers, are loaded with bundles and makeshift packages. Tourists, businessmen, and homecoming citizens undergo lengthy and detailed inspections that produce long, slow lines and cartloads of confiscated goods. The presence of heavily armed soldiers is a reminder of South Korea's continued concern with internal tensions and with the ever-present North Korean threat.

A visit to Singapore is a walk into the future. First impressions are telling, and the contrast with Seoul is striking. Few airports in the world are as modern or well-run as Singapore's. The architecture is subtle and beautiful, fountains abound, and customs checks are cursory. The ride into town offers a panorama of stylish, modern apartment blocks and sleekly designed high-rise office buildings. Streets and sidewalks are spotlessly clean. A sense of Western efficiency seems to coexist with Eastern circumspection and dignity in a population that is more than 70 percent Chinese in origin.

Modernity has so crept into the Singapore landscape that many now criticize its sterility and loss of cultural identity, which is a mixture of Chinese, Malay, Indian, and European left by the British, who founded Singapore as a trading post in 1819. Its small size (2.5 million inhabitants), its enforced Confucian brand of puritanism, its role as a mature regional banking center, its cleanliness and order, and its industriousness have led some to label Singapore the "Switzerland of Asia."

But unlike Switzerland, Singapore is the leanest of all in terms of natural resources. Other than its people and their energy, this small city-state has *no* natural resources whatsoever. The only significant natural endowment is a strategic location where 300 international shipping lines must squeeze into the Straits of Singapore on their way to and from Europe, the Middle East, and Japan. Most stop for refueling, repairs, and trade. In 1982, 54,000 vessels were cleared through its port, more than half of large tonnage. The ninety-six million tons of cargo handled on its docks make this port the second busiest in the world after Rotterdam in the Netherlands. During the first months of 1983, it reached first place. But once-lucrative oil refining and tanker traffic are substantially down. This decline and a rapidly changing comparative advantage vis-à-vis its neighbors have given an added impetus and urgency to Singapore's economic leaders to look for ways to diversify and modernize their economy.

During the last few years some of the government's most talented thinkers and doers, many of them young graduates of America's and Europe's best universities, saw Singapore's vulnerability to rising wage rates and fundamental shifts in the world economy. For instance, the oil crisis of the early 1970s caused profound and unexpected changes by eliminating several old labor-intensive industries dependent on low transport costs. Further, industries like textile exports did not generate enough revenue to pay enormous oil-import bills. With Prime Minister Lee Kuan Yew's blessing and political muscle, the nation embarked on a crash program. The goal was to modernize its infrastructure and diversify the economy into new production and communications technologies. This put Singapore in direct competition with the growing economies of Korea, Taiwan, and Hong Kong and clearly distinguished it as a regional leader among the other Southeast Asian countries of Indonesia, Malaysia, Thailand, and the Philippines. While Singapore is predominantly Chinese, it shows none of the central-planning ideology of the People's Republic. "They shoot planners here," says the director of the Institute of Southeast Asian Studies, Dr. K. S. Sandhu, jokingly. "The total emphasis is on results."

The creation of a supportive infrastructure—the roads, schools, services—necessary to support high-technology industries is an overriding economic priority. Symbolizing this commitment is a newly created 480-acre science park in a well-landscaped residential and university setting. It will house firms engaged in the latest research and development in fields as varied as biotechnology, electronics, process automation, and chemical products. Government grants and subsidies will help accelerate their installation. Behind this effort and numerous other signs of recent progress is the two-decades-old Economic Development Board (EDB), whose job it is to attract a broad cross section of foreign high-technology investments.

Understanding full well that a nation with no resources other than its people could not expect to blossom economically without a massive commitment to education, the Singapore government implemented far-reaching programs marked by economic and po-litical acumen. The goal is nothing less than a complete realign-ment of what education is all about. An excellent infrastructure of schools and a belief in universal education, left by the British, were used as vitally important building blocks for a system geared to high technology. Dr. Juzar Motiwalla, director of the Institute of Systems Science, sees "education as the key to eco-nomic growth. That's because Singapore is betting on its only resource: its people."

One adaptation resulted from the realization that practice-ori-ented engineers would be in far more demand than theoretically based academicians. To achieve this goal, a university formerly dominated by politically active island Chinese whose interests were at odds with those of the prime minister was dismantled and reconstituted as a technology institute. This not only defused po-tential political opposition but led to an annual output of 500 engineers per million people, or a rate twice that of Sweden and a quarter higher than in West Germany. The sole multidisciplin-ary university, the National University of Singapore, plans to ex-pand its capacity from 9,000 in 1980 to 15,000 by 1985. By 1990 the technologically sophisticated labor force will have grown by a factor of six. This will increase the number of high-tech engineers from approximately 1,200 to 7,000–9,000. On a per-capita basis, this means going from half the rate of the United States to more than three times the American proportion of engineers in the work force. Indeed, on a per-capita basis, Singapore will have the highest number of engineers of any country in the world—a target that is an officially stated objective. Once again, one has to ponder whether an equivalent policy could ever emerge in the United States. If not, at what cost to our competitive vitality?

A tactic for transferring the latest technological know-how to the island fell into place quite by trial and error but in retrospect it looks like a masterful stroke. This was the creation of a series of agreements with foreign governments and corporations to establish training institutes in areas fundamental to modern manufacturing technology. France in electrotechnology, Japan in computer and software technology; Germany in manufacturing production; Sweden's ASEA company in robotics; the American firm Computervision in computer-aided-design; and Philips of Holland, Tata of India, and Brown Boveri of Switzerland are all partners in creating lower-level technical schools.

Singapore discovered the link between education and an economy based on high technology quite by chance, say government officials. In 1972, a basic technical-skills training center had been established with the large Indian firm, Tata. Its success made it a model for several more centers for educating young people in basic technical skills. With almost 4,000 students graduated from these training centers over a decade, the benefits soon became clear. "It did not take long to notice that many of these people were becoming the next generation of entrepreneurs and technical supervisory talent," said Bok Inn Ooi, deputy director of the recently founded German-Singapore Institute.

The combined effect of these resources is not just the value of technology transfer but the creation of people skilled in managing and running fully automated manufacturing plants. Realizing that electronics would be pivotal in achieving this goal, the government created the National Computer Board (NCB) in 1981 to nurture the evolution of computer and software industries. The NCB quickly established three goals amazing in scope. The first is to increase sixfold the number of computer professionals (not engineers) from 1,200 in 1980 to 8,000 by 1990. The second is to fully computerize ten of the government's fourteen ministries over a period of five years. And the third is to build a competitive export-oriented computer-software-services industry. Such ambitious goals could be the envy of any region—small or large—thinking of leapfrogging its way into the mainstream of modern technological competition. How Singapore is doing it becomes, therefore, a lesson in how best to accomplish such desirable aims.

The first step was to conceive and implement an elaborate education and training infrastructure dedicated to a single-minded objective: creating computer professionals. This was done by expanding the resources and capacity of the university's computer science department. "Foreign companies are anxious to assist us," says Soon Tian Lyou, head of planning and development for manpower at the EDB. An example is the new wafer manufacturing facility in the electrical engineering department of the university. Completed in May 1983 and subsidized by a Japanese manufacturer, it is superior to most that exist in U.S. universities and would make even MIT, Carnegie-Mellon, or Stanford proud.

The more innovative step, however, was to enter into partnerships with three foreign entities, American, Japanese, and British. This led to the creation of three highly unique institutes able to produce 600–700 professionals yearly. This foreign partner provides technological know-how, equipment, and the training staff; Singapore provides operating expenses, facilities, and local staff. The agreement generally specifies a period of several years during which Singapore aims to become self-sufficient in teaching the new technologies.

One example is the Institute for Systems Sciences, with IBM as a generous cosponsor. Not only did the company donate a 3033 computer system to the university, but it also provided all its own proprietary in-house course materials. In addition, it made available four faculty members for four years to help teach and maintain the technology as well as to train the local teaching staff. The payoff for IBM is twofold. First, the use of its own equipment will familiarize an important cadre of local professionals with

IBM products. Second, IBM gains a foothold in terms of research and personnel in this important new regional center.

Singapore is likewise happy to pick up some of the expenses and to provide the physical facilities. First, they get state-of-the-art training in the management of computer systems both in the public and in the private sector. If a multinational company wants to set up a branch or even Asian headquarters as GE did, top management can be assured of finding a pool of middle managers able to implement, run, and maintain complex international data-processing centers. Citibank, for example, has a major branch office in Singapore and has had no problem in finding well-trained Singaporeans able to implement its highly advanced electronic-banking system.

The second benefit is training for entrepreneurs who, it is hoped, may create software companies or similar small service enterprises that would cater to larger multinationals, either in Singapore itself or in neighboring countries. There is, for example, a large network of independent dealers who sell and service personal computers in Singapore. Nearly every manufacturer is represented, from Commodore to Digital Equipment to Apple. Of course, since most of the training at ISS is on IBM equipment, or in the case of another institute on Japanese NEC personal computers, these coventurers get an advantage.

The IBM faculty are proud of their accomplishments at the National University. "This should be the best teaching environment for systems training anywhere," said IBM staffer Robert F. Verhotz, looking out with pride on the busy construction site he helped design high on a wooded hillside. To Lee Gilbert, an American recruited onto the full-time ISS staff, the IBM relationship has turned the university into "a computer with a campus wrapped around it. . . . This is a very fertile working environment, especially when you realize that the university must compete on the open market for practitioner-teachers. It's really dynamic. You don't find many places like this in the world."

To date the ISS has focused mainly on upgrading the skills of existing technicians and managers already in the work force.

Forty-three students divided into eight groups have followed a systems-analysis curriculum over a nine-month period; another three months of work internship is expected for a student to complete the course. When its facilities expand into its permanent space, the ISS expects to become an exporter of knowledge by opening its educational service to all ASEAN (Southeast Asia) countries.

Less than a mile away is another example, the Japan-Singapore Institute of Software Technology (JSIST), housed in a modern high-rise shopping and office complex along the harbor. The institute is equipped with a virtual "wish list" of NEC hardware. The amount of equipment, the state-of-the-art quality, and the well-designed setting probably exceed anything that might be currently available in a single site of any U.S. university. At JSIST, the fifty CRTs are available on a twenty-four-hour basis to an enrollment of only one hundred students—a luxury rarely found even in the most lavishly endowed U.S. university or college.

The JSIST coventure was negotiated government to government. A staff of twenty is being trained in small groups in Japan for six-month periods per person. Six Japanese software experts are promised for a period of five years. At the Institute three groups of fifty students are currently enrolled each year for a two-year course. They will emerge trained as analysts/programmers. For those entering with higher levels of experience, the latest EDP techniques and high-level software technology are taught. One aspect of Singapore's unique education strategy has a special "public" payoff of its own. Most students participating in these university and institute programs are "bonded." The term defines an obligation of the student to offer one year of government service for every year of full scholarship support received. The net effect is to bring into government services the very best young minds—minds that might otherwise be quickly attracted into industry or banking.

The IBM and Japan ventures, as well as a third institute founded in partnership with the British firm ICL and the British Council, provide Singapore with the very best in computer-programming education in the world today. One can only be startled by the effectiveness of those who translated a vision into a reality so fast and so well. The implications are far-reaching as graduates enter the work force and as Singapore begins to train many more in the East Asia basin. These programs, and others filtering down into the primary- and secondary-school systems, are costing the government $80 million a year just for public computer training and infrastructure creation. In addition, training subsidies are offered employers at a rate of $8 million per year.

Everyone seems to have gotten the word—"computerize the island"—and everyone seems to be pitching in to make it happen. "Computer mania is seen all over Singapore," says Sushil Chatterji of the NCB. "The level of awareness is high, aided by public media," he adds. The contrast to Europe, where the acceptance of new technologies is moving slowly, is striking. Soon Tian Lyou, head of planning and development for manpower at the EDBA, says: "Europe, you know, has the cultural problem of inertia. They let sentiment slow them down," he observes. "Even the Germans have this problem. They still believe in hand skills but cannot keep pace with such things as computer-controlled numerical machines. We are quickly moving ahead of our German teachers. The next step," said Mr. Lyou, "is to build a center—now in the planning stage—which will put Singapore at the leading edge of computerized manufacturing systems. We already have three international manufacturers in mind with whom we can do business."

When it comes to computerizing its ministries, a process started in its defense services, the enthusiasm is as great. A $50-million investment is being made to provide computer linkages between ten key ministries. "The only question," says one government official, "is whether it will work. If it does it will become a showpiece in Asia." The applications range from weather forecasting and air-traffic control to integrated health-care systems and coordinated command for police, fire, and ambulance services.

The eventual aim of this initiative is to build a strong export capability in software and services. "The strategy we envision is clear," says Sushil Chatterji of the NCB. "Build up the manpower, increase utilization of computers and open the doors to advanced software technology." To speed up the process, generous incentives are offered computer users. No duties are imposed on hardware imports. Equipment can be depreciated in one year. And subsidies are offered those who can prove significant employment *reduction* by introducing computers and automated equipment—exactly the policy that would bring apoplectic reactions from European unions and some American ones. The result: Computer users shot up from 400 in 1980 to 1,800 at the end of 1982. Another result: Most of the world's major and many minor hardware and software vendors are represented on the island. Another sign of local users' sophistication is a thorough personal-computer-buyer's handbook, produced by the NCB, which is as good as or better than most found in American bookstores.

Another of the government's aims is to become a "regional brain center" by exporting engineering and management services and software to other countries, especially those in the Asia Pacific area. Software and services, in this case, means both computers and telecommunications. It is working hard, too, to attract foreign firms by offering computer-based manufacturing resources such as computer-aided design (CAD) and computer-aided manufacturing (CAM), robotics, and flexible manufacturing devices able to perform multiple computer-controlled tasks. Equally important to multinational manufacturers, the telephone and international data links work exceptionally well, as any business traveler who picks up the phone and dials abroad pleasantly discovers. A second satellite communication station is being built and fiber optics will be installed islandwide by 1986, allowing information processing to be communicated digitally. These assets are major attractions to numerous banking enterprises that have chosen to center their activities here. Singapore counts more than 180 international banks and financial institutions on the island.

As one looks back on an island visit, a precise and clear sense of goals is striking. Build the educational establishment right, support it well, and the economy will run as fast as you allow it. Build it wrong and the alternative is to fall back again into an untenable cheap-labor syndrome. That the strategy may be correct is already evident in moves such as that of the Sanden Corporation, a producer of air conditioners for cars. In early 1983 it set up an automated plant to produce compressors. Parts are imported from Malaysia and Indonesia. A monthly volume of 12,000 units was reached with a work force of only fifty workers. The reported reason for locating in Singapore was "the infrastructure and administrative efficiency."

Korea and Singapore, along with Taiwan, Hong Kong, and to some extent Malaysia, are seeking to break the old low-wage-rate model. They can no longer compete with wage rates in the Philippines, Indonesia, Thailand, Sri Lanka, and especially India and China. Because of their strong work ethic and increasing level of education, American companies find it hard to resist the lure of establishing assembly operations in these countries. For the past decade, nearly every American semiconductor firm has set up assembly operations in Asia—among them Intel, National Semiconductor, Motorola, Zylog, Data General, Sprague, and others. We visited one in the Philippines, for instance, where young Filipino women were assembling and inspecting tiny computer chips. For them, the job was a step up from the otherwise chaotic and impoverished back streets of Manila. This particular integrated-circuit assembly plant included 125 production workers, usually young women who earned 40 cents per hour or $85 per month, eight clerks and secretaries who typically earned $133 per month, twelve technicians whose pay was $133, fourteen supervisors who earned $333, four engineers at $533 and perhaps five managers. The total labor cost for a plant of this size in the Philippines comes to $293,000 annually. This would be about one-tenth the equivalent cost of such a plant in the United States, assuming that Americans could be found who would do the tedious, eye-straining work that the 125 Filipino women performed.

Despite the obvious political risks, the Philippines has one of the largest populations of U.S. semiconductor plants. The reasons are partly historical. The island country is English-speaking (the third largest in the world), labor rates are low compared to Korea and Singapore, and literacy rates are the highest among the Asian less-developed countries, or "LDCs." By 1983, assembled semiconductor chips exceeded coconuts as the country's number one export product.

In addition, Filipinos seem motivated to move up the educational ladder and to keep pace with expanding developments in the assembly business. Some plants are installing automatic bonders and other semiautomated equipment which will require more highly skilled people to operate and repair. Next will be automatic testing equipment. Part of the challenge of companies working in the Philippines is how best to upgrade their educational system and work force. Industry can and should support learning centers to train the kind of skilled and professional workers needed.

At present, the Philippine education system is struggling to support the type of high-level engineering training needed for the design and manufacture of high-tech equipment. But for an LDC in an unstable political situation, the struggle is not easy. The computer science department of the University of the Philippines, for example, has only seven small Radio Shack TRS–80s computers for its students—three of them sit unused in a storage room. The dean of the graduate engineering program at the University of the Philippines (UP) noted wryly that "although UP is tops in electrical engineering and computer sciences, it ranks number five here." Asked who the first four were, he answered with a smile: "There is no 1 through 4 in the Philippines."

In 1982, there were 342 engineers enrolled in his graduate program, but only eleven graduated. The drop-out rate is high because of the need to earn a living. Economics works against professors. A top full professor, after many years of service, earns $5,100 per year, and it generally takes twenty-five years to attain the rank of full professor. An instructor earns only $1,700 per year. Yet at private companies in the Philippines, a good B.S. graduate can start at a salary equivalent to a full professor with twenty-five years of experience.

Recently, three people studied abroad for their B.S. degree in computer sciences in order to teach at UP. They would have started at 1,900 pesos per month. Along came a recruiter for a Philippine company who offered them 5,000–7,000 pesos per month. Soon thereafter, an employer from the Middle East came along, willing to offer 20,000–30,000 per month ($2,000–$3,000). It's hard to hold good faculty members.

Private universities are no better. FEATI, a large vocational school in downtown Manila, has a stated objective to train the lower class for jobs in the economic mainstream. Tuition is rock bottom—$120 per year. This is the school's only source of income, which is attested to by the decaying state of its physical plant. Half the main building has been demolished to make way for the Manila light-rail transit system, leaving classrooms exposed and desks and blackboards falling out toward the Parsig River. The present government does not allow the school to raise tuition rates to pay for modernization.

Two-thirds of the school's 24,000 students graduate after five years with B.S. degrees (the rest earn an associate degree after one to two years). Many of these are in "electrical engineering" or in "electronics and communications engineering." Yet virtually no one graduates with training directed toward the type of electronics associated with computers, semiconductors, integrated circuits, etc. Most are aiming to become master electricians, especially for the construction industry where installers of wiring in buildings are in great demand. The next largest demand is for radio and TV repairmen and for telegraph/radio operators for the telecom industry.

Another Philippine private university, De La Salle, is considered one of the "Big Three" in engineering education. Here the courses are more up-to-date. In 1981, De La Salle started a computer-science program, and now has a PDP 11/34, twenty-four Sanyo microcomputers, an Ampex, and nineteen DEC VT-100 terminals. DEC provided the equipment at half cost, and now Toshiba is donating some microchips for laboratory experimentation. Yet even here most "electrical engineering" is training for the power industry. The largest electrical-engineering laboratory is filled with power generators. Faculty salaries are relatively high by local standards—up to 5,500 pesos per month for a full professor, whose teaching load is only half that of his UP counterpart earning 4,300 pesos per month.

According to an official in the Ministry of Industry, "We give lip service to technical education. It's a joke. This is where we suffer a lot." The official noted that the Philippines is still at an early stage of exporting the products of low-cost labor. They do not yet export as much as South Korea, and have not established any foreign trading missions seeking to attract the electronics industry. Should they be more aggressive?

"We've talked about setting up an industrial park," said an official charged with overseeing foreign investments, "because the South Super Highway is getting too full of companies. But this is our next homework. The problem is lack of manpower, like electrical engineering and basic science. I have never checked into the output of the schools, but I know there is a big gap between universities and industry."

But the situation might change. According to the director of higher education at the Ministry of Education and Culture, "Filipinos want education. They will sell their carabao [water buffalo] to get it." There were reportedly 225,404 engineering students enrolled in the Philippines in 1981 at fifteen state universities and some 200 private ones. For an LDC, the country has a good educational base. It has a springboard to leap ahead, if and when political stability comes.

The Philippines seems to be following the new Asian cycle: start with low labor rates, and through education build up to a more sophisticated technological level. Malaysia and Thailand are presently on this course. They have already "shut their doors" to labor-intensive operations. In Malaysia, labor rates are going up and are already double those in the Philippines. And this island country will have to do the same to stay ahead of Sri Lanka, India, and China, who are now competing for yet-lower-cost labor.

The struggling Philippine education system reflects the low-wage-rate orientation of its semiconductor plants. Without an extensive upgrading of human resources, more sophisticated approaches to high technology or to other industries cannot be launched. The link between education and the manufacture and use of new technology is critical. This is the subject of the next chapter—the link between education and technology in the United States.

14

Education Stakes

*Just when knowledge has emerged as a basic strategic re-
source, we as a nation seem to have lost the will, or the way,
to invest in knowledge.*
> —David C. Knapp, President, University of
> Massachusetts

Nothing matters more than education.
> —Governor James B. Hunt, Jr., of North
> Carolina

After a decade of decline and confusion, education in America
took a turn for the better in the 1980s. Public-opinion polls taken
during the 1970s showed that education had hit an all-time low as
the social institution least responsive to, and most in need of,
change. The last time our schools, colleges, and universities had
received national attention and significant resources for upgrading was in the late 1950s during the aftermath of Sputnik, whose
lessons twenty-five years later have been all but forgotten. Leth-
argy had come to permeate the soul of our education system and
innovation was foreign to most educators. Even the "brainpower" excitement evident in Asian countries that fueled their
economic boom and sharpened their competitive edge was slow
to reach America.

Then, with startling rapidity, the public mood shifted. The
spotlight turned on the inadequate preparation young Americans
were receiving. A relationship between the low caliber of students coming out of America's 16,000 school systems and the lagging vitality of our economy became clearer to a large public.
During 1982 and 1983, ten major studies reported on the sad

state of education in our lower schools. Many received extensive national press coverage.

During this same period, higher education was virtually ignored by the national media. Yet in colleges and universities something new was emerging. New opportunities arose for collaboration with industry. But unlike past relations with industry when universities accepted financial donations but resisted corporate intrusion in university research, industry now became an active participant. One reason is an awareness by many corporations that new knowledge would be critical to their futures and that much of this knowledge resided in university or college laboratories and departments. Tapping it took on strategic importance.

A number of institutions, some nationally prominent, others better known regionally, have embarked on novel approaches to accelerate the transfer of knowledge from laboratory to student to workplace. We will describe three cases that illustrate such initiatives. One is Carnegie-Mellon University (CMU) in Pittsburgh, Pennsylvania, where relationships have been forged with large *Fortune* 500 companies. A second is Worcester Polytechnic Institute (WPI) in Worcester, Massachusetts, where both large- and middle-size companies were sought out as partners. And third, the Benjamin Franklin Centers were established at four Pennsylvania universities where their purpose is to serve the technological needs of both large and especially small companies. In all cases the aim is to innovate; the method is joint ventures with industry partners. To date the results are impressive. What they reaffirm is not only an intimate connection between education and national economic development but also the potential for schools, colleges, and universities to reinvigorate and sustain Yankee ingenuity twenty-first-century style.

Three institutions rank highest as leaders in computer science in the United States. Depending on which criteria you choose, the top spot is shared by Carnegie-Mellon, MIT, and Stanford. Each is very different from the other. At Carnegie-Mellon the university president wields more discretionary power than in the other two institutions and academic departments are far less cloistered from one another. Some say it excels at turning theory into practice rather than just publishing theoretical papers. This is one reason why it ranks third among the three institutions (and way down on the overall list) when it comes to papers published in scholarly journals. When it comes to grants from the largest computer-science funding source, the Defense Advanced Research Projects Agency (DARPA), Carnegie-Mellon gets about as much as MIT and Stanford. Administrative coordination sets it quite apart, however. DARPA computer science funds have been provided to CMU in a single contract. At MIT three major contracts are used to handle similar amounts. At Stanford it takes over a dozen contracts dispersed among faculty members.

Dr. Richard M. Cyert, president of Carnegie-Mellon since 1972, presides over a paradox. CMU sits in the heart of Pittsburgh's dying steel industry where mile after mile of silent and rusting mills line the banks of the Allegheny and Monongahela rivers. At the same time, new technologies research projects backed by financial support from major corporations like IBM and Westinghouse—and notably not U.S. Steel—have spawned an incredible number of new initiatives.[1] The 7,000-terminals project, a new robotics institute, a magnetics technology center, a new computer-aided-design (CAD) research operation, and optical data processing are some of the most recent and prominent at CMU. These come in addition to ongoing support of top-ranked departments in computer sciences and expanding basic research in electrical engineering. "This is the CMU niche," said President Cyert, "to be an innovator in higher education."

The most imaginative and far-reaching of these new ventures is the project sponsored by IBM to provide all incoming students with a personal computer capable of linking campus-wide to one another and to vast educational resources. "We plan to be the first fully computerized campus in the country," says Cyert. "It's an experiment in saturation," adds Alan Newell, professor of computer science who along with Nobel laureate Herbert Simon has kept Carnegie-Mellon at the forefront of basic computer research.

The implications of the 7,000-terminals project and the IBM partnership are revolutionary for education. The goal is to build an easy-to-use yet educationally sophisticated operating system designed for a university environment. The intention is to double or triple the productivity of students by providing unlimited access not just to engineering or scientific materials but to all the university departments and resources. One surprising forecast by Cyert is that the biggest users may be in the fine arts, humanities, and social sciences, which, like most CMU departments, are actively participating in the design of software for the systems. Within a few years students will be able to plug their portable personal computers into wall sockets throughout the campus— and most importantly to access the entire campus from their own dormitory rooms. Cyert contrasts this system's unlimited access with the "old time-sharing way that isolated the student in a system that was limited in accessibility and in response time." This project will make time-sharing obsolete. And the impact is expected to be immense. "It will be the greatest addition of capital per student in all the history of education," says Cyert.

Projects of this scope, long a dream of far-sighted educators, are now a reality thanks to IBM funding and a new spirit of industry-university cooperation. In 1982 IBM announced a $20-million agreement with Carnegie-Mellon which provided the university with hardware, optical cable lines, and working ties to IBM in a team made up of ten corporate people and twenty campus academics. An additional grant from the Carnegie Corporation of New York will allow a consortium of other schools to participate in the development of the required software, of which there will need to be a great deal. Nobel laureate Wassily Leontief estimates that "production of electronic educational courseware [will have to] grow in real terms at over 35 percent a year in the 1980s and over 10 percent in the 1990s."[2]

"It's fantastic," says Alden Dunham, program officer for the Carnegie Corporation who, along with Doug Van Houweling, CMU's vice-provost for computing, and Jill Larkin, associate professor of psychology, masterminded the program. "The educational potential is enormous," says Dunham. "A personal computer twenty times more powerful than anything that now exists will be created. And with our grant, we'll seed a whole new generation of educational software."

The software consortium, called the Interuniversity Consortium for Educational Computing (ICEC), has fifteen members. These include nationally known schools like Brown, Dartmouth, and Berkeley as well as community colleges such as Southwestern College in Chula Vista, California, and Iona College in New Rochelle, New York. Howard University will probably join, and several educational and library associations also will participate. What is of note is the leverage. One industry-university relationship—IBM and CMU—has spawned an extensive new network that draws in powerful educational forces from around the entire country. The process could not have been foreseen, planned, or orchestrated. It happened because an individual, Alden Dunham, became a catalyst for change, building on initiatives that themselves were new and innovative.

Initiating change in a university environment was no easy task. Faculty, staff, and students, at first lukewarm toward Cyert's vision, have now embraced it. The president has a management style unusually directive for a university yet carefully aimed to gain consensus. In his first year of leadership, in 1972, early successes in expense cutting and fund raising allowed him to turn around deficit-ridden budgets of the late 1960s. Despite a tight austerity program, an astute tactic was to grant faculty salary increases of 12–15 percent annually. The best professors stayed on campus, and he gained the trust of the university community by committing the school to projects that worked, such as a new robotics institute. When an opportunity to fund the 7,000-terminals project was presented, the groundwork was thus in place. The idea was initially developed by Cyert and his staff and then taken to the Digital Equipment Corporation (DEC) in the spring of 1981 for corporate sponsorship. DEC, however, was reluctant to develop a new operating system and the generation of technological changes to accompany it. They wanted instead to build a new network based on the company's DECNET, whereas Cyert wanted to have an entirely new network developed. He then approached Lew Branscomb, chief scientist for IBM, and found a ready audience. Within four months a feasibility study was completed and by October 1982 an agreement had been signed.

What is revolutionary in this relationship is not just the "computer in every dorm room," but the potential for shortening the study time for a B.A. degree, especially in electrical engineering where the half-life of knowledge is five years and the time required to earn a degree is 4.5 years. By making library resources available in student rooms, by having powerful interactive programs readily available, and by maximizing the linkages among students and faculty, students are expected to work faster and more effectively. In addition, the quality of interdisciplinary instruction should be enhanced. The dean of the engineering college, James Williams, says: "We will do interdisciplinary things better than anyone else thanks to Cyert's vision. We're now, for example, interconnecting the behavioral to the cognitive sciences in order to have an overlap with computer technology. I have no doubt that over the coming twenty years the most important and exciting problems facing us as a nation will be interdisciplinary." He adds that in addition the computer connection will stimulate access to basic research by those who want to be more applied. "In math, for example, this has already pushed us to move from pure to applied math," says Williams.

Cyert's imaginative project touched some competitive nerves. Shortly after the announcement of the CMU project, MIT came up with its own plan to interconnect large numbers of its students, faculty, and departmental resources. To become the first fully computerized campus in the United States, Carnegie-Mellon will have to outpace MIT's Project Athena. The MIT project links both IBM and DEC into a single consortium, backed by $50 million worth of equipment and staff time, while MIT is expected to raise $20 million to establish a fifteen-person research center. In addition to the educational goals, one aim here is to make equipment from both manufacturers fully compatible so that one's machine can talk to the other's. The emphasis is more on user software than networking technology. Thus in the best spirit of American innovation, the ante has been raised. Two imaginative projects have been launched. They both draw literally thousands of students and faculty into active cooperation in building a system together. If successful, the potential to democratize knowledge and to raise the level of talent for the nation could be revolutionary.

The theme of partnership with industry is being worked out in several other Carnegie-Mellon programs with different but equally important goals as the IBM project. One of the most significant is the new robotics institute. The purpose is to accelerate the transfer of knowledge from the laboratory to the marketplace in the critical field of flexible automated manufacturing. In 1979, a robotics institute was created in concert with a number of industry sponsors. The mission: to create "seeing, thinking, and sensing robots with increased capacity." Doing it is the task of fifteen campus-based laboratories involving about ninety scientists, engineers, and programmers, and a team of sixty graduate and undergraduate students. The labs work on an array of related research tasks, including subjects as basic as finding ways to prevent robots from bumping into one another, developing tactile sensing by computers, and creating computer languages for flexible manufacturing applications.

University provost Dr. Angel Jordan says that the new institute "will be pervasive throughout the whole university. It pushes the whole institution to a much higher level of interdepartmental collaboration." Its existence has brought together a grouping of client and supporting companies with a funding pool of $7 million. The primary supporters are not only the high-tech firms but also companies in more mature industries like construction and chemicals. One of the more unusual problems brought to the university to solve involves a contract signed with the Three Mile Island nuclear-power utility company. The need is obvious, the deadline urgent. The institute was asked to work on three robot applications: a robot to test interior radiation levels (easy); another to take samples of concrete walls to determine how deeply radiation has penetraed (a little harder); and a third to be able to drill away at massive concrete walls so that contaminated debris

can be carted away (very hard). This last step requires a sophisticated marriage between mechanical engineering and electronic
controls all packaged into a mobile unit.

The larger, more substantive agenda at the institute, however,
is to bring together the computer sciences and traditional engineering to address industrial needs. "We are creating the new
fundamentals of engineering science and automation by working
directly with corporate partners," says Jordan. "Our task is to
marry components of applications and basic science and evolve
new methodologies. This means having scientists who don't mind
doing technology. All of this creates new paradigms, theorems,
and conjectures. It advances the state of knowledge."

To Professor Robert Ayres, a social scientist associated with
the robotics institute, "what you see is the clustering of innovator
complexes. This is becoming an explicit role of the university. In
principle the goal is to develop a new production technology that
eliminates the conflict between production and innovation." The
Westinghouse relationship with the institute illustrates just how
far this change in orientation can go. Instead of confining itself to
research, the institute was asked to develop a completely automated unit to produce, in this case, turbine blades for a new
plant in Winston Salem, North Carolina. Normally, it would take
about eighteen years in a university environment to get from the
idea stage to a new product. Carnegie-Mellon did it in two and a
half. The principal investigator, Paul Wright of the department of
mechanical engineering, went beyond the heretofore normal call
of duty. He found himself loading the prototype unit from the
robotics lab into a rented truck and driving it down to North
Carolina himself. "He was willing to get his hands dirty," commented President Cyert. "He may not want to do this every time,
but it's indicative of the new cooperative spirit that's developing
here."

The 7,000-terminals project and the robotics institute, as well
as a number of other conceptually similar projects, indicate not
only a new direction for CMU but a potential new role for higher
education itself. Urgent national problems are being addressed
by university-industry consortia. The research agenda and the

means to implement it are being determined jointly. Yet in large measure it is the university which is being brought more centrally into the process and which in the final analysis holds the key to success. Cyert was the first to remark that the role he and Carnegie-Mellon had played in defining part of a new national agenda was similar to the policy guidance that MITI provides in Japan. In terms of functions like setting research agendas, testing pilot projects, brokering industries and bringing them into cooperation with one another, the university had de facto created policy with national implications.

To play this role more effectively, more clout and cash would probably be needed to strengthen the university role. At present, neither NSF (National Science Foundation), DARPA (Defense Advanced Research Projects Agency), or other public or private funding agencies have thought in terms of universities playing a major role in policy formulation. But the initial success at Carnegie-Mellon in building an effective response to pressing issues of national relevance is encouraging. At the same time, it is leading to significant improvements in the process of education by linking the student and faculty to needs in the society outside university boundaries.

Many may disagree with this new educational experiment. Whether industrial funding is dependable and whether it will continue over the long run are open questions. Many further question whether it should occur in the first place. They are concerned that the curriculum will become too industry-oriented and too short-term in its vision and goals. Some would argue that this leads to vocational training—a code word among many educators for inferior intellectual preparation. These are clear dangers. But to date, these fears have not been realized at Carnegie-Mellon. The innovation, if given time to work, might just be successful.

Nationally known universities like Carnegie-Mellon and MIT have neither a monopoly on innovation nor the sole voice in formulating and addressing new national priorities in education. Worcester Polytechnic Institute (WPI), fifty miles west of Boston, has developed and highlighted its own special niche in the education world. Like Carnegie-Mellon, it too has a robotics lab. But unlike CMU, where considerable emphasis remains on basic research, the Worcester Polytechnic lab is full of robots whirring and turning. Graduate students and company employees teach them specific tasks and operate them together. What they are doing is applying known technology to the needs of the factory floor. Down-to-earth details inherent in any application of new tools are being worked out in controlled conditions. The result is an excitement among students, faculty, and industrial participants that charges the atmosphere.

The president of Worcester Polytechnic, Edmund Cranch, puts it this way: "We're a hands-on institution. What we're doing is creating a whole new echelon of expertise, a series of teams that might include fifty undergraduates, six masters, one or two Ph.D.'s, together with their faculty members and engineers from industry." Cranch and his administrative staff and faculty have become front-runners in creating a highly innovative and successful hands-on program working directly on the national economic agenda.

WPI is typical of beautiful New England campuses which in fall are transformed into a blaze of color. On warm, sunny days students enjoy the neatly landscaped grounds. Frisbees and touch football are common pastimes. Close by, however, is an activity not so typical of everyday campus life. Inside a large ground-level industrial lab, heavy jointed metal arms are moving slowly in sweeping, narrowing arcs. Carefully a robot's hand grasps an object and flawlessly moves it in a predetermined pattern before depositing it on a narrow tray. Students and representatives of a robotics firm cheer. It might seem like a simple achievement, but in practice it means the successful completion of a complicated working application for a robot. With student help, the corporate sponsor will soon move its robot onto a shop floor—at costs far lower than normal, with benefits to a large class of future engineers and technicians, and in an industrial situation where creditors might otherwise have knocked on the door before the robots did.

As of 1983, eleven robots were busy working at WPI—eleven more than three years ago. The scale may look modest. To those who planned it, it is a major breakthrough. Students, faculty, and corporate teachers on loan to the school are collaborating in tasks that will lead these robots directly to work in companies throughout New England. The whole effort is known as the Manufacturing Engineering Applications Center (MEAC). What is going on is not basic research but, rather, the critical art of taking an existing technology and expanding it to perform new tasks. The goal is to apply new technology to old needs. "Our aim is to thrive on openness to what is happening outside," says WPI's President Cranch. "That we can learn from corporate partners makes for a different mindset than in the normal engineering school."

That fifty students are now enrolled in robotics projects is having an impact. "It has sensitized faculty to student interests," said Frank Lutz, associate dean for projects. "Faculty are actually having to change their curriculum to attract students. They are competing, in a sense, for student interest." The result is a flexible curriculum that is quickly learning to incorporate CAD/CAM, holographics, and a variety of other new technologies. "Had we appointed a faculty committee to attempt this," said Cranch, "we'd have taken much longer and the probable capital cost to get started would have been ten times larger."

Worcester Polytechnic's tradition of focusing on problems of the day-to-day industrial world traces its roots back to the school's founding in 1865. This makes WPI America's third-oldest science and engineering college. A Germanic motto still prevails: *Lehr and Kunst*—theory and practice. For a school located in Worcester, "practice" meant focusing on manufacturing and metal-forming businesses. As these declined by the late fifties, the school's operation had grown rusty and the sense of vitality began to erode. In many ways Worcester Polytechnic had come to mirror the dilemma of an outmoded America—old institutions caught in their own inertia.

In the late sixties, a turning point was reached. WPI could have continued without change and chipped away at its financial reserves and reputation. But instead it engaged in a thorough reevaluation of its goals. This led administrators, faculty, and students to completely revamp the school's purpose and curriculum. A primary change in the school's philosophy emerged during the ensuing decade. It is known as the "WPI Plan" and it stands out in the nation as an example of clear-sighted vision of what constitutes an educated engineer. Its purposes are to sensitize engineering students to the social impacts of their work, and to require students to design their own education programs and to demonstrate their competence through hands-on projects in the working world.

The WPI Plan was instituted in 1970. The intention was to create a curriculum that sought an exposure to cultural issues, that called for academic rigor in chosen fields, and that required the student to look beyond the campus for self-initiated experience. The key to the plan is a requirement that junior and senior students engage in two projects: a socially relevant project and a technically demanding one in their major field of study. A third of their time for each of two years is devoted to these projects. There are 1,300 such ongoing projects annually. About half of these are carried out with the cooperation of corporations and other off-campus organizations. The school maintains a permanent presence in Washington, D.C., allowing students to complete projects at U.S. government locations. Other permanent sites are maintained with Digital Equipment Corporation for computer studies, Mitre Corporation for a space-shuttle project, Norton Company for mechanical engineering and management, and at the hospitals of the University of Massachusetts and St. Vincent's in Worcester, where biomedical and biotechnology projects can be completed.

The WPI Plan requires students to complete a "humanities sufficiency," adding a strong cultural dimension to their education. This is accomplished by taking five thematically linked courses tied together by a sixth integrating one. To graduate from WPI, students must prove themselves in a competency exam in which a "real life" professional problem must be solved. This plan, coupled with all the necessary course work in one of four engineering fields, produces an unusually versatile graduate—one open to understanding of social issues and yet trained to understand the application of applied engineering skills.

With the flexibility that the WPI Plan afforded, a second significant development could take place almost a decade later. This is embodied in MEAC—the Manufacturing Engineering Applications Center referred to earlier. Its goals are to link the expertise of mechanical and electrical engineers with the world of computers and microprocessors, and to connect the school's engineering students with operational needs and expertise of the real-world workplace. Three individuals sparked the creation of MEAC: Wally Abel, the Emhart innovator described in Chapter 4; Arthur Gerstenfeld, professor of management at WPI; and Ray Bolz, vice-president and dean of faculty. Their new program was started in January 1981, and four major companies are now MEAC sponsors.

"They brought the opportunity to start MEAC to me," recalls President Cranch. "The decision to go ahead was an administrative one without the normal faculty review. We created MEAC alongside the normal mechanical engineering program hoping to challenge the department to take an active role." This was done not by long-drawn-out faculty discussions but by demonstration. Once programs like computer-aided design, holograph and laser technology, and computer-software design were in place, the interest on the part of the faculty to absorb the new developments was immediate, accelerating a commitment and awareness of the new technology and its applications. Now, under the direction of Donald Zwiep and David Asmus, MEAC has blossomed into an exemplary case of academia and industry cooperation where students, faculty, and full-time engineering staff work with company engineers to solve shop-floor application problems.

A lot of misgivings had to be overcome to get such an industry-university collaborative to work. From the academic perspective, Cranch noted that a change in attitude was evident. "In the past, whenever a company approached academe, the institution would look out from its parapet and quickly raise the drawbridge to the castle. We're in a different era now, one that stresses partnerships. I think the siege mentality is behind us."

Companies also had their doubts. "The more a company may need something like MEAC," says Bill Grogan, dean of undergraduate studies, "the more fearful they are of becoming involved. Robots can be terrible threats. This is particularly true of a company that has been doing things the same old way for as long as it can remember. But if the threshold of entry is small, they'll come along. Once there is even the most tenuous involvement, they are overwhelmed by what students can do. They're probably saying: 'My God, time has passed me by!'" Company members pay $50,000 per year to be part of MEAC and pay all project costs and expenses. Members are required to send a company engineer to MEAC for at least one day a week for the project's life, and a company officer is asked to sit on the MEAC board during the same period. Peter Bulger, the robotics welder from Emhart, was one of the MEAC trainees. His work is direct evidence of accelerating the smooth transition of knowledge onto the shop floor.

"MEAC is a system with no waste products," says Bill Grogan. It elicits the real support of industry and avoids the "not invented here" attitude since the problems studied are those of immediate concern to the companies. The training goes both ways: Industry people are trained, as well as an important number of students. Also, new equipment is made available that keeps the WPI laboratories up-to-date. Thus the MEAC arrangement is helping to increase the capacity of WPI and to solve shortage problems presently endemic to engineering education in America.

MEAC is receiving considerable attention of late, and not only from American educators and industrial engineers. Soon after the 1983 "Robotics VII" national convention in Chicago, participants had the option to go on a tour of various projects. Among them was WPI's robotics venture. Sixty visitors came to see it— fifty-five were Japanese.

The Benjamin Franklin Centers in Pennsylvania are a case

where the approach and philosophy have taken a very different course. State government broke new ground in 1981 at the initiative of a deputy secretary of commerce, Walter H. Plosila. His imagination coupled with the political activism of many others led to the creation of four advanced-technology centers throughout the state. First funded with $1 million in matching public monies in 1982–83, these were quickly met by private contributions from a statewide grouping of companies, foundations, labor unions, universities, colleges, and economic development group members. A year later, so successful was the program that the state portion was increased tenfold in matching funds. A principal purpose of this undertaking was to create statewide partnerships devoted to accelerating the flow of new technologies into the economic mainstream. A second important goal was to put the resources of the state's universities and colleges within reach of small companies otherwise cut off by virtue of their size from new technological breakthroughs.

Located at four different universities, the centers are focal points for seventy colleges and universities to channel their creative resources into the economy. Research and development programs in each center vary according to local strengths and needs. The 1983–84 roster of funded projects counted seventy-five large and small consortia activities. Some got all their support from the Benjamin Franklin program, others only a minor portion of the budgeted project costs. One example, at the Lehigh University Center, was a laboratory network for computer-aided testing. It had a $70,000 price tag of which $8,800 came from the state. Several corporate partners were interested in linking the mechanical engineering and mechanics laboratory with the computer-aided-design laboratory so that experimentally generated data could be visually displayed. At another center, based at the University of Pennsylvania, a $250,000 project to develop a microchip chemical sensor for dental research received one tenth of its budget from state funds.

The Benjamin Franklin Centers are exemplary not just for the numerous evident and spirited projects funded in a two-year period but, more important, for putting into center stage the economic importance of a multitude of university, industry, and government consortia. As a statewide program fully exploiting the intimate relationship between technology, education, and economic growth, it stands out as a model for a national undertaking. At its foundation lies an understanding of a very subtle principle: that innovation in and of itself cannot be legislated, it can only be encouraged. In today's world this means building opportunities for partnerships no matter how large or small the participants.

What the events at Carnegie-Mellon University, Worcester Polytechnic Institute, the Benjamin Franklin Centers, and many other schools tell us is that the new technologies are raising a host of new opportunities for education. Probably the single largest opportunity today is for the nation's 200 to 300 engineering schools to join with American industry to help them absorb the new technologies into old business environments. WPI's vice-president and dean of the faculty, Ray Bolz, puts it this way: "Imagine all the expertise sitting in 200 or 300 engineering departments throughout the country. If you could put it to use, you would bring to bear a massive amount of brainpower on the older low-technology companies." Collaboratives that focused on this issue would also help to solve another problem: the shortage of people who understand not only the new technologies like computers and electronics but also the more established fields like mechanics and materials. As technology spreads into more and more industries, the educational action should also spread beyond the leading schools and into virtually all centers of technology.

The new technologies are also posing a number of difficult problems for education. In our recent book, *Global Stakes: The Future of High Technology in America,* we covered many of these issues in depth, one of which goes under the unassuming name of the "capacity" issue—the difficulty the nation's engineering schools have in handling the increased demands in electrical engineering and computer sciences.

While the 1981–82 recession mitigated its effects somewhat, the capacity issue has become severe. Two-thirds of the country's

244 accredited engineering departments had capped or reduced enrollments. In twenty-nine of them, accreditation is being challenged because of overcrowding. In many others, qualified and eager students are turned away. At the University of California at Berkeley there were 3,786 qualified engineering applicants for 525 positions in the undergraduate class of 1982. At Purdue University the average class size in engineering doubled between 1971 and 1982 before a cap was put on enrollments. At one of the nation's wealthiest schools, the University of Texas in Austin, undergraduate engineering was reduced from 6,500 to 5,800 and graduate enrollment limited to 1,350. At the University of South Carolina, inflation-adjusted funding levels for engineering education were down 10 percent in ten years despite a student enrollment 40 percent higher. At the University of Illinois, faculty overloads in engineering were estimated in early 1983 at 40 percent by the department head. The students it admitted into engineering were in the ninety-eighth percentile of high-school rankings—the absolute cream. Thus while the very best were filtered in, many others of high quality were filtered out.

At a time when new knowledge-intensive technologies are central to the revitalization of America's economy, it is dismaying to see the disarray in our educational base. The problems are not only with student enrollment pressures but with faculty shortages as well. W. Edward Lear, executive director of the American Society for Engineering Education, calculated a shortfall of 6,700 teaching positions in engineering—about 1,500 unfilled current openings and another 5,000 to bring the faculty workload down to a normal level. And he remarked, "The situation is undoubtedly worse now than in 1980–1981 when the last basic data were gathered. Since that time, another 22,500 undergraduate students were added to the system in 1981–1982."[3] According to Joseph Hogan, dean emeritus of engineering at Notre Dame, national surveys show vacancies of 25 percent for entry-level engineering assistant professorships in most disciplines, civil and chemical engineering being notable exceptions. "Many qualified youngsters are being turned away," he told a Senate audience in April 1983.[4] According to the American Council on Education, in the

1980–81 scholastic year, 1,583 positions were vacant in the nation's 244 accredited departments of engineering.[5] The overall rate of unfilled positions is estimated between 10 and 15 percent of the total full-time faculty pool.

Existing faculty are working with overloaded student and class commitments. Inadequate funds are available for equipment and laboratory improvements. The problem is exacerbated by a low level of masters- and Ph.D.-level enrollments because of students moving to higher-paying industry jobs. Different branches of engineering experience the problem differently. In chemical engineering, for example, there is presently a surplus and many graduates are not getting job offers. But in computer sciences or electrical engineering, a graduate teaching assistant or assistant professor can earn more in industry—anywhere from 25 to 100 percent more—to compete with the status and prestige normally associated with academic life. For bright young professors in their thirties, the discrepancy can be even greater in fields like VLSI, running as high as 200 percent or even more when the alternative to teaching is the lure of founding a new company. The personal pressure on a young student to take the immediate high-paying job offer can be great—even though longer-term career opportunities might be diminished by not going for a higher degree. The individual student's dilemma was capsulized in an excellent booklet written by the College of Engineering staff at Colorado State University. It is addressed to the student making career decisions.

Right now you can't help wanting out. Mostly it's the money issue. You've worked during the summers, you have a small scholarship, and your folks are helping out some, when they can. But just the same, it's a barren kind of life, being an undergraduate engineering major. You drive a beat-up VW bug, with measurable compression in only two of the four cylinders. Your wardrobe consists of two pair of jeans, alternated weekly, and half-a-dozen T-shirts and sweatshirts. When you buy a friend a meal, it's buttered spaghetti or pizza by the slice. So graduation day looms up like the fabled pot of gold at the end of the rainbow. No more classes, no more books, no more tuition-and-fees. Instead an honest-to-God job, and a real paycheck coming in every month. And no small paycheck, either.

Market forces are polarizing salaries to such an extent that academe requires more and more emotional commitment and offers less and less financial reward. And the fewer faculty there are, the more onerous is the workload for those who remain behind to teach. Since student-to-faculty ratios are increasing, the average engineering department faculty member has a teaching burden 40 percent greater than ten years ago. The National Association of State Universities and Land Grant Colleges surveyed twenty-nine of its member institutions and found startling impacts on student-faculty ratios in engineering departments. From 1976 to 1981, the worst case, Pennsylvania State University, saw its ratio jump 93 percent, Michigan State 65 percent, Ohio State 63 percent. One campus, University of California at Davis, saw only a 1 percent increase. Overall, however, the average increase for this sampling was 35 percent.

All these conditions bring home the message that there is a capacity problem in some fields of higher education. This has direct bearing on the health of the economy.

It has been clear for several years that high-tech companies are dependent on a good supply of engineers. Now it seems that even in mature old-industry companies like Ford, Emhart, and Ætna transformation and growth could be impaired by a lack of human capital. This was evident at Ford, for example, where a small group of fifty to sixty electrical engineers and computer scientists based in Colorado can directly affect the fortunes and competitiveness of an entire product line and the fate of a work force several hundred thousand strong. Similarly, at the Ford Dearborn engine plant a handful of electrical engineers—seven out of a plant of 1,800—are critical to the functioning of the production line's 700 computer-controlled machines.

Henry M. Levin and Russell Rumberger of Stanford argue that the future will bring more low-skilled jobs than high. They propose there should be less and less emphasis on technological education.[6] Better education should be sought for its own sake, they state, not "because of the claims that [it is] required for a high technology future." All of our travel, visits, and case studies give us a somewhat different picture. While it may be true that not everyone needs sophisticated high-tech training, the technology is affecting many job categories not normally associated with high tech. To not train these people in the use of technology is to relegate them to potential domination by machines. Among the kitchen workers in the Ætna cafeteria, for example, training via computers or training on how to use a computer was not only one of the most popular courses but led to the greatest increase in self-esteem. The computer is a symbol of our age. To limit access to it only to those in high tech is to intensify social disparities rather than bridge them.

For the foreseeable future, the economy will be driven at the leading edge by the strengths or weaknesses of the nation's high-technology industries and by the ability of other industries to absorb new technologies. Both situations require a sustained infusion of resources into education of the young and reeducation of older workers. Knowledge of technology will be necessary for all employed Americans to participate in improving and perfecting their working effectiveness and productivity—in short, their earning power. Even in basic industries, we found corporate officers putting *strategic* emphasis on education as a key to their competitive futures. This emphasis is new. It has never happened this way before. Upgrading of skills for an age of computers is a priority concern at an increasing number of companies.

Why shouldn't the United States just wait for the educational system to readjust or for the society to be satisfied with a choice of education for "its own sake"? At least one factor in the present situation makes such a wait costly—global competition illustrated by Japan's achievements in world markets. Japan has already switched its priorities to a knowledge-intensive society in order to compete head-on with the United States and to stay ahead of South Korea, Singapore, and other Asian countries. Japan's education system and its relationship to the economy operates differently than does the U.S. education system. Japanese employers rely heavily on engineers at all levels of corporate life—in contrast to a propensity in the United States to rely far more heavily on lawyers and financial experts. In 1972 Japan's pool of working engineers and scientists stood at 198,000; by 1980 it had grown to 305,000 and continues upward. On a per-capita basis, both the pool and its rate of growth outstrip those in the United States.

The demands of new technology on education raise another worrisome phenomenon. The humanities and many of the liberal arts programs and leaders are largely silent in leading the society to a better understanding of its technological future. Academia should be able to play a much stronger and more influential role in helping guide the country forward. Often, however, historians, sociologists, philosophers, and other humanists more easily criticize the mechanistic view implied in a high-tech future rather than attempting to understand and help guide the evolution of the new technologies. High tech need be neither mechanistic nor mysterious; having more socially minded spokesmen who fully understand and speak out on these issues will help to avoid these undesirable traits. The Carnegie Corporation decried the low morale in evidence in many colleges and universities in a recent report. "They seem to be waiting for new cues from offstage," write the authors, "rather than setting their own objectives."[7]

In Washington, D.C., neither the strategic importance of education nor its close link to economic growth opportunities seems to be fully understood. As Governor William Winter of Mississippi put it, "Reagan makes a good speech on education." But he failed to translate it into a national commitment of resources and political will. This failing is allowed to continue despite clear evidence from polls that Americans want federal aid to education to be increased. In October 1983, a national poll carried out by Group Attitudes Corporation found two out of three people in a 1,300-person sample calling for higher levels of federal aid. Earlier in the year, the *New York Times* found 81 percent of 1,500 adults it polled agreeing to have taxes raised to pay for better education in lower schools.

Even more incongruous at the federal level is a steadfast commitment to a massive buildup of defense spending without any parallel effort to invest in expanding the pool of engineering talent as an integral part of the defense budget. For 1984, $270 billion defense dollars will be spent, and an astounding $320 billion is being allocated to Defense Secretary Caspar Weinberger for 1985. Studies by the U.S. Air Force predicted several years ago "shortages of at least 10–15 percent in military personnel with the most current scientific and engineering requirements."[8] Will the government's demand for scarce human resources crowd out private-sector needs in much the same way that government demand for financial capital has driven up the cost of capital to unprecedented levels? It is still far from clear that national leaders have understood the trade-offs.

Incongruities in present national policy, particularly with regard to the role of education, can in part be explained by the fact that the society, and especially those elected to represent it, has failed to grasp the full significance of the transformation that is now under way. We are moving from a capital-intensive, physical-resource-based economy of the first half of this century to a knowledge-intensive, human-resource-based economy in the last half. The formulas, policies, economic theories, and conventional wisdom that facilitated the earlier transition from an agrarian to an industrial society are no longer applicable to the transformation now in progress from an industrial society to an information society.

What will be critical for the future is the strengthening of continuing education and the creation of extensive facilities for retraining. Ernest Lynton in "The Missing Connection between Business and the Universities" shows how the student age profile is projected to change dramatically. By 1990, people over the age of twenty-five in institutions of higher education will outnumber students of traditional undergraduate age.[9] This will require a major emphasis—by educators, business, unions, and governments—on continuing education.

But the attitude of the federal government has been to minimize support for education, or to divert public attention by concentrating on prayer in the schools. If the government does not mobilize more financial support for education, we may all need more prayer in the schools! While one effect of declining federal support is an increase in industry support, in the total picture, the dollar impact remains small. Federal dollars pay for two-thirds of university-based research. Industry, which paid only 3 percent two years ago, has now raised that by two percentage points. The real impact is not just that they are providing more money, welcome though that is to beleaguered college coffers. They are bringing new ideas and new energy to university research centers.

We described how Richard Cyert at Carnegie-Mellon brought IBM into an innovative partnership program, followed by MIT's arrangement with IBM and the Digital Equipment Corporation in Project Athena. Shortly thereafter, Brown University in Providence announced a $15-million IBM grant to carry out yet another initiative in computerizing the campus. In terms of research and development, there are other collaborative efforts underway. Two of these, the Semiconductor Research Cooperative and the Microelectronics and Computer Technology Corporation, are described in the next chapter.

At Ætna, we described the Ætna Institute and its Joint Advisory Council which links twenty-two Connecticut colleges and universities together, first with Ætna and now with other companies. At Emhart, we watched Wally Abel help trigger MEAC, the Manufacturing Engineering Applications Center at Worcester Polytechnic Institute. In Michigan, we saw a variation on the theme. The Kellogg Foundation, along with the Dow Foundation and others, teamed up with the state government to create the Industrial Technology Institute (ITI) and the Michigan Biotechnology Institute (MBI). In Mississippi, new taxes and business support went into elementary and secondary education. In Massachusetts, a consortium of businesses and schools is creating the Massachusetts Technology Park Corporation, a $40-million microelectronics training and research center.

Many, many more of these partnerships could be described and categorized. Some apply not just to universities but to community colleges and to high schools. Community colleges in many cases are proving highly resilient to employment changes. Catering to adults attending night school and special industry-sponsored classes, they are a critical link in a long chain of education and industry partnerships. While their large number suggests that something important is happening, it is critical to understand what that something is. The industry-university partnership represents a novel way to inject the expertise of universities directly into the national economic agenda of the United States. What we see in the making is a trend that brings colleges and universities directly into the national industrial policy debates, but in a decentralized manner consistent with American cultural preferences. In short, industry-university partnerships make sense, work successfully, and can provide direction to a nation seeking to restore its vitality. Probably no other country has such a capacity to turn its intellectual and research-oriented resources to the service of national problems. One of the weaknesses of Japan, for example, is the lack of serious university research and the necessity to form, through government agencies, separate research facilities.

These joint industry-university programs have at least two important effects. One is to bring students out of the ivory tower and give more relevance to their work. They work on real rather than simulated problems. Ask any student at WPI or CMU whether this is productive and exciting. For many of them, it is the highlight of an academic experience.

A second effect is to strengthen the development side of the R&D formula. In our next chapter we will show what needs to be done to improve basic research in America; at the same time, a lot of present basic research fails to get translated into usable innovations. The Japanese Fifth Generation Project highlights this American dilemma. Americans at MIT and CMU were among the first to accomplish the initial research and to plan the future agenda. Where they fell short was in getting these ideas accepted by industry. The net effect of the new partnership model is precisely to overcome this problem—to pick up the most promising research and translate it quickly into useful new products and processes.

Time will tell whether the partnership idea will be a lasting one, or whether it is a temporary and short-lived phenomenon. It may be that if the economy gets worse, industry's willingness to invest more money in education may diminish. Or if the economy improves and American competitiveness is restored, industry may not feel the need to continue making such investments. As these partnerships increase in number and significance, one of the emerging issues will surely be how to institutionalize them and to make them longer-term and more dependable. For the present, however, they represent one of the most innovative and valuable responses to the present situation where education needs support and where its contribution is increasingly critical to the nation.

15

The R&D Race

When he assumed the presidency in 1963, Lyndon Johnson offered a new agenda to the American people. He asked that they support his civil rights initiatives, experiments in urban development, and a war on poverty. He got the needed support. Yet he would eventually lose all the public goodwill he gained by fighting an undeclared war in Vietnam that eventually cost countless lives, caused incalculable human pain, and produced a bill in excess of $430 billion. The effects were to divert investments that might otherwise have kept American industry strong and competitive and to trigger an inflationary spiral that disrupted the U.S. and world economies. Johnson wanted America to believe we could afford "guns and butter." He was wrong.

The same issue confronts President Ronald Reagan but in a different form. He came into office with an unabashed promise to dramatically increase the defense budget but again with the illusion that the nation could pay for this defense buildup from current revenues. "There will be no deficits by 1984," he declared. For whatever the reasons, he too was wrong. By the end of his first term, he will have accumulated deficits larger than the total of all prior presidents of the United States. The Reagan administration has miscalculated the nation's ability to afford what the press has come to label a "Star Wars" military fantasy of exotic weapons providing America with a supposedly foolproof defense against nuclear attack. This Hollywood vision promises to bring pain. Whatever its military impact, the effects will be felt first in the inability of the U.S. economy to achieve its fullest potential as it competes for resources with a ballooning defense budget. The stakes are most visible when one studies how quickly our competitors are accelerating their investments in civilian research and development.

The race to create "machine intelligence" may be the most important technological event of the remainder of the century. To the winner will go an immense competitive advantage in the world marketplace. So important are the stakes that national resources are being focused on a few key efforts worldwide such as Japan's Fifth Generation Project. Europeans are collaborating on the ESPRIT Project. In the United States the effort is divided between military and commercial initiatives. The Defense Department is underwriting a significant amount of research through an array of programs including those administered by DARPA—the Defense Advanced Research Projects Agency. DARPA's Strategic Computing Program, announced in the fall of 1983, is a more sophisticated version of Japan's well-publicized fifth generation computers. Two new private-sector consortia, the Semiconductor Research Corporation (SRC) and the Microelectronics and Computer Technology Corporation (MCC), are pooling research funds to achieve breakthroughs in supporting technologies. A number of other related initiatives are occurring in corporate and university laboratories. At present, the major goal is to produce a new generation of supercomputers and machine-intelligence technology—a race in which Japan and the United States are running neck and neck.

This race corroborates a generally accepted proposition. Investment in research and development is a fundamental driving force of contemporary innovation. Behind this conclusion lies a series of questions. What is an adequate level of R&D funding? How is one to measure this investment? How does it compare with the R&D spending of competitors? Who pays the bill? Who sets the agenda? How can the productivity and yield of R&D be increased? There are no easy answers. Yet the questions are central to America's competitive future.

If we look at R&D expenditures in absolute dollar terms, the

United States comes out as the unchallenged leader. It spent $72 billion in 1981, or 18 percent more than the combined total of Germany, Japan, the United Kingdom, and France.[1] In terms of percentages of the gross national product (GNP), it was one of the top, with 2.5 percent of GNP invested in R&D in 1981, compared to 2.7 in West Germany, 2.4 percent in Japan, 2.1 percent in the United Kingdom, and 2.0 percent in France.

If aggregate statistics were conclusive, the presentation could stop here. But where the aim is to focus on economic development and national competitiveness in a global economy, then the aggregate numbers are quite misleading. Stripped of defense-related R&D expenditures, the U.S. investment is outpaced as a percentage of GNP by both Japan at 2.3 percent and West Germany at 2.5 percent. U.S. civilian R&D falls to 1.7 percent, the United Kingdom's to 1.5 percent, and France's to 1.4 percent.

Olof Palme notes that "countries which spend heavily on military research, notably the U.S. and the U.K., have a large scientific base, as measured by the proportion of GNP dedicated to research and development. But the civilian research effort of these countries has grown less rapidly than that of other large OECD countries, and is now smaller relatively to GNP than in several other countries. From 1967 to 1979, total civilian R&D in the U.S. and U.K. and France remained constant or declined as a share of GNP while in West Germany and Japan, they increased almost 50 percent."[2]

More critical even than the narrow financial considerations, though, is the tug-of-war between military and civilian projects over a finite supply of human resources—especially engineers who are in the shortest supply. Most defense R&D programs are far more engineering-intensive than commercial ones. This is due in part to more exotic performance requirements of space-age weapons compared to commercial products. Already, 25 percent of our engineering work force is committed to military needs. And the problem promises to become even more acute when one considers the whopping 18-percent increase in military R&D expenditures from 1983 to 1984 and a total defense budget rising from about $205 billion in 1983 to a forecast $399 billion by 1989.

The effect will be to draw even larger numbers of engineers away from nonmilitary endeavors. The gain may be in defense technology; the loss may be in a weakened competitive posture. The crowding out of product development for industrial and commercial purposes may be the most alarming long-term result. It will, in effect, drain the economy of its wealth-generating capacity and divert it to nonproductive uses which do nothing to raise living standards.

Since World War II, conventional wisdom has argued that military expenditures are a spur to economic development. Jobs are created and new technologies developed for later application to commercial fields, the argument states. And indeed, during the 1950s and 1960s, the facts corroborated this view. A whole new semiconductor and computer technology was accelerated into being by the cold-war push for missile- and aircraft-navigation and early-warning-detection systems. During that period only the federal government could marshal the massive resources for the required advances in technology. At that time, there was little civilian competition for engineering resources. Defense and space R&D was the only show in town. What's more, it was spinning off generic technology applicable to widespread civilian uses in the form of semiconductors, computers, and communications technology. All this occurred in the absence of any competitive pressure from war-torn European and Asian countries struggling to rebuild their industrial foundations.

Things are different in the 1980s. Military and civilian programs are in direct competition for both human and financial resources. Engineers in fields such as electrical engineering are in short supply, and universities are being drained of faculty resources. International competitors have reached, and in some cases have exceeded, technological parity with the United States. In short, the United States is struggling on two fronts—one an economic battle, and the other a military one.

Another shift is more subtle and more open to misinterpretation. The common argument that high defense R&D expenditures will again bring direct benefit to the civilian marketplace is far from convincing. An overwhelming proportion of current military technology is applications-oriented—that is, focused on specific weapons and systems few of which have civilian use. The coming generation of new weapons are largely based on currently available technology—much of which is far more advanced than in the Soviet Union. Relatively little basic or pure research was included in the huge allocation of $25 billion to defense R&D in 1983. The amount for pure research was a mere 3 percent—or about $750 million. Weapons *development,* however, swallowed up 86 percent.[3]

Capital resources—always scarce—are also vulnerable to the military pull. Leaders on both ends of the political spectrum agree that the ballooning national deficit can in part be attributed to increased military spending. The damaging by-product, they also agree, is measured in high interest rates and a suppressed rate of investment in commercial equipment that is necessary to remain productive in the world market.

Few would deny that an investment in national security is necessary. How much investment and for what purposes is another matter. James Fallows has argued cogently at one extreme for a more effective but smaller investment in military hardware. Defense Secretary Caspar Weinberger argues for the highest possible level of investment—security at all costs. Whatever the merits of either position, it is highly spurious to argue that benefits of job creation and new technology will come from military expenditures. *Direct investment in economic development* will create more jobs, more relevant technology, and more penetration of global markets than will military spending. When viewed from this perspective—and in the light of intensified foreign competition—there is a strong question whether the planned buildup in military spending can be sustained without paying a very heavy price—the loss of industrial leadership. The risks of this exposure are so great, in our judgment, that they will justify stretching out the plans for renewal of our weapons arsenal.

While most military R&D expenditures contribute little to economic development and may, as we have argued, even detract from it, there are exceptions. We would be remiss if we did not highlight one outstanding exception in the Department of Defense. In the major research universities, one of the most respected and sought-after government research agencies is the Defense Advanced Research Projects Agency.

DARPA, sometimes referred to as ARPA, was born in the wake of the Sputnik shock. Dismayed at being caught flat-footed by the Russians, President Eisenhower asked how such a strategically important advance could fall through the cracks. The answer was partly organizational. No agency or service was accountable for such revolutionary long-term research projects. Thus DARPA was established to cut across the traditional jurisdictions of the armed services and to maintain a technological vigil to assure that the technology available for national security was second to none.

Initially DARPA spearheaded the space race. Shortly thereafter the National Aeronautics and Space Administration was established and selected DARPA personnel were transferred to the new agency, including the Saturn booster program. Today the work of DARPA, with a budget in federal fiscal year 1984 of approximately $877 million and a staff of 150, is divided among five offices. Of these, the Information Processing Technologies Office (IPTO) is particularly relevant to our discussion of the role of government in innovation and international competitiveness.

This small IPTO group, presently numbering twelve professionals with a 1984 budget of $120 million, has had a disproportionately high impact on the progress of computer science and information processing over the past twenty years. For example, through IPTO's funding of ARPANET, packet-switching technology was developed which now serves as a cornerstone of modern data-communications networks linking computers in a wide range of commercial and industrial as well as military applications. Time-sharing technology, developed by Project MAC at MIT and others, was largely funded by IPTO. The development of the grandfather of supercomputers, Illiac IV, was funded by IPTO, and while only one machine was ever built, few would deny that its underlying technology, parallel-processing architecture, and advances in memory laid the groundwork for modern supercomputers. Perhaps most significant, IPTO has been the major actor in sponsoring the development of artificial intelligence—the heart of today's fifth generation computer efforts.

The progress and innovation sparked by DARPA is truly impressive, especially in light of its relatively modest budget. What is so unique here? What has permitted a government agency such effectiveness, and can it be extended to other areas of government or industrial involvement? By far the most important element of DARPA's success has been the quality and leadership capabilities of its staff. It was not run by professional bureaucrats. Rather, IPTO has attracted world-class talent. Its directors included such scientists as J. C. R. Licklider, I. E. Sutherland, L. G. Roberts, and now Robert E. Kahn. Each is recognized internationally for significant technical contributions and all are held in highest respect by their peers in industry and universities. Bob Kahn, a former professor at MIT, masterminded the ARPANET development and steadfastly fostered packet-switching technology over the past sixteen years, most of which he spent at DARPA. He has been director of IPTO for the past twelve years, almost twice as long as any of his predecessors. It is no exaggeration to say that Kahn has played a truly significant national role in planning, funding, and directing a large portion of the U.S. research effort in artificial intelligence, mostly in universities but selectively in industry as well.

Another factor in DARPA's success is that its relatively small staff is largely unencumbered by bureaucratic processes. DARPA's philosophy is to select competent, proven staff professionals and then to delegate authority to make significant and far-reaching decisions. Innovation is ultimately a risky business, and any effort to mitigate this risk through committee action dulls the cutting edge of technological advance. To quote Kahn, "Our approach is to identify the most talented researchers to work on critical scientific and technological problems of interest to defense. In the final analysis, our investments are in key people working on first rate ideas."

A unique aspect of DARPA's strategy is its visionary focus on the potential results of research. For example, to put a man on the moon or to establish a worldwide network for secure computer communications is the kind of mission that inspires imagination, demands innovation, and pulls together a critical mass of related activities. The output of generic research which results from these mind-stretching goals is far greater than the limited results from military R&D aimed at designing and building weapons systems. A great deal of DARPA's innovative strength is derived from the fact that it is not directly accountable to the armed services as end users, nor is it beholden to a rigid schedule that would compromise research goals. It is also permissible for DARPA to fail on some of its projects, which allows it to take the high risks others might be determined to avoid.

While less than 10 percent of the overall DARPA budget is earmarked for university research, a unique aspect of IPTO is that more than half of its budget is invested in university research. The bias of DARPA toward quality over quantity is reflected in the concentration of its funding among a handful of major research universities. MIT, Carnegie-Mellon, Stanford, and more recently the University of California at Berkeley, the leading universities in computer science, owe much to DARPA for their prominence in this field. Not only has DARPA been a consistent and reliable source of long-term research funding for computer science, but it has provided a sense of direction and discipline to knit into a coherent pattern the overall effort on various campuses.

By concentrating its funding in a few centers of excellence, both in universities and in industry, DARPA managed to generate a sufficient mass of resources to take on complex and challenging research projects. There is no question that it has succeeded in raising America's research capabilities in computer science head and shoulders above those of international competitors. A major goal in concentrating on leading research universities has been not only to develop innovative ideas but also to develop the needed human resources—trained scientific personnel and leadership talent. In an emerging new field like artificial intelligence, it takes a decade or more of consistent funding to build up a network of people who are conversant with a new generation of knowledge. Thanks largely to DARPA, America is now ready to move in bold new directions in information processing.

Twenty-five years ago DARPA led the charge to restore our technical leadership in the space race against the Soviet Union. The pieces were there, but they had to be pulled together and focused on a mission. Now we are faced with another race—this time with the Japanese for leadership in information processing. It took Sputnik to jar us into action then. It took Japan's Fifth Generation Computer Project to reawaken our economic competitive spirit. Again, DARPA seized the initiative. Its strategic computing program with five-year funding of $600 million was recently submitted to the Congress. It lays out a multiyear research-and-development program to assure U.S. superiority in information processing. Funding for the first year was set by Congress at $50 million, with $95 million proposed by DARPA in fiscal year 1985 and $150 million the following year. The basis for this focused effort is national security, but the potential to strengthen our industrial base is also immense.

By default, we find ourselves dependent on our military machine to cover our economic flanks. Will it work this time? One issue of concern is whether DARPA can continue to attract and retain a staff of world-class caliber when salary differentials between government and private industry continue to diverge. Another concern is whether DARPA will be able to maintain its highly efficient, nonbureaucratic process for a program that will reach funding levels of $150 million per year by 1986. Further, will the strategic computing program meet military needs while at the same time providing transfers of the generic technology to commercial and industrial applications? And at a time when top computer talent is so thin, will this program only rob Peter to pay Paul? For example, if the budgetary trade-offs in DARPA to accommodate the strategic computing program result in a reduction in funding for a buildup of computer-science competence, the underpinnings of the program itself could be jeopardized and the long-term investment in university research severely eroded. It would be especially valuable to broaden the funding to include the so-called "second tier" universities, given that MIT, CMU, and Stanford are saturated and unable or unwilling to expand further in this field.

Notwithstanding these concerns, on balance it is comforting to see DARPA take the lead in providing a coordinated response to the Japanese challenge. At the same time, it is disturbing to know that the principal federal effort addressing our long-term economic security is from within the defense establishment.

In contrast to DARPA, the National Science Foundation (NSF) is one of the largest of the government's civilian research agencies. Its major focus is science departments of universities, to which it provides about $1 billion per year in grants. Its principal strategy is to disperse its resources among individual researchers or small groups, and its awards are based on proposals reviewed and approved by peers. This approach, because it is highly fragmented, lacks the solid, tightly concentrated focus of DARPA. Its strength on the other hand is in helping to sustain a broad base of scientific activity within the American research community.

A major criticism directed at NSF is that it is an organization of professors for professors—a self-perpetuating club. The peer-review system means that ideas come from within the club. To those on the outside, this means an inbred attitude that constrains useful research programs. Such systems can be wasteful. Rustum Roy, professor and director of the Materials Research Laboratory at Pennsylvania State University, estimates that "many research grants made on a request for a proposal basis actually cost the nation more in lost time of thirty proposal writers than the award provides to one winner."[4]

The engineering community is particularly critical of NSF. One reason is that only 10 percent of the foundation's funds are earmarked for research in engineering departments—in contrast to science departments, which get the bulk of funds. What rankles is that engineering enrollments are at an all-time high and demand for graduates is rising—at the same time that funding is desperately needed for equipment, fellowships, and research. On the other hand, NSF has recently inaugurated projects and support for several industry-university cooperative research centers.

Because of the congressional budgeting process, NSF cannot guarantee funds for more than one year at a time. As Rustum Roy says, "That is equivalent to planting an apple tree in the spring and cutting it down in the fall of the same year." A better way, some propose, would be to fund long-term research programs and then increase or decrease funding, renew or cancel, on the basis of actual performance and progress.

Roy has one of the strongest arguments for changing the status quo and restoring a better balance between scientific and engineering research. He argues against the belief that science is the principal stimulus of innovation. He challenges the conventional wisdom that new knowledge and discoveries originate from pure scientific inquiry detached from any product or application. Roy argues that in many instances technology precedes science. He cites the example of the science of thermodynamics, which owes more to the technology of the steam engine than vice versa. The inventer of the steam engine did not have a scientific understanding of how engines work. The application came first, the theory later.

Technology and science have lives of their own, according to Roy. One does not necessarily take precedence over the other. Rather, technology and science are natural sources of cross-fertilization that breeds new varieties of innovations. What this implies, he states emphatically, is far more support for applied research and technology—in contrast to basic or pure science—in order to redress a huge imbalance between the two. He states: "The comparative history of Japanese science/technology with British science/technology has dealt a death blow to the science theory of innovation. If you want science to work for you, you must design an active technology system to link into it, utilize it and put it to work. Without these linkages, science has no specific value to the nation."[5]

To achieve greater emphasis on applied research, Roy argues for university-industry consortia which emphasize industrial innovation in important areas such as materials, robotics, VLSI, CAD/CAM. Funding would come from industry matched by grants from federal and state sources. This is like the High Technology Morrill Act, based on the 1862 Land Grant College Act, proposed in our earlier work, *Global Stakes*.

The allocation of funds within the federal R&D budget is an additional problem. Research budgets for defense, health, and space are huge compared to support for economic development. This contrasts sharply with Japan. For example, in 1978—the last year for which comparative data were available with Japan—49 percent of U.S. government R&D expenditures were consumed by national defense, 12 percent by space, and 11 percent by health, while economic development received only 9 percent, and advancement of knowledge 4 percent. By 1984, planned expenditures for U.S. national defense will absorb an astounding 70 percent of the total federal R&D budget. For Japan, on the other hand, while the government's share of total R&D investments was only one-seventh the U.S. government's rate, the allocation of R&D expenditure was much different—only 2 percent was devoted to defense, 6 percent to space, 3 percent to health, but 22 percent to economic development and a striking 54 percent to what is labeled the advancement of knowledge.

Why such high expenditures in the United States for defense, space, and health? These after all are wealth absorbers as compared to economic development—a wealth generator. The question is particularly pertinent when one considers the critical implications of projects like the fifth-generation computer as a means for holding our own with Japan. One possible answer is simply neglect. Another is the lack of any consistent strategy. A closer look suggests a third answer. There is no effective arm of the U.S. government to argue for consistency in our economic development strategy or for its direct link to the generation of new technologies. Absent is a strong voice combining the roles expected of a secretary of commerce and an influential senior science and technology adviser or counsel to the executive.

In 1980, the total R&D budget for the Department of Commerce, which includes the impressively titled Institute for Computer Science and Technology under the National Bureau of Standards, was $355 million, of which only $43 million was earmarked to support university research. This compared to a $25-billion R&D budget for defense, $4.7 billion for NASA, and $3.5 billion for the Department of Health and Human Services. We spend five times as much to support R&D in commercial fishing as we do in the steel industry. Tax incentives subsidize timber, housing, tobacco, citrus, and beef. The Export-Import Bank supports airplanes, locomotives, and nuclear power plants. But electronic engineering and computers receive far less than these other concerns.[6] Even NSF plans to spend less on computers ($77.5 million in 1984) than it will on its Antarctic research program ($102.1 million).[7]

Should there not be some agency concerning itself in a meaningful way with job creation, with trade, with industrial productivity and competitiveness, and with the role of new technologies as catalysts for economic development? Where today would one look in the government for a civilian spokesman for an aggressive program, for example, in automated manufacturing? There is one in the Defense Department, but none on the civilian side. We can send rockets aloft with an ostensible civilian mandate in NASA, but we cannot find anyone pushing with urgency for America to produce a ceramic car engine.

Funding priorities in our democratic system depend on advocacy. It is hard to argue that there is a better way to debate the priorities—presuming, of course, that all parties are represented at the bargaining table. For the present, however, this is not the case. There is no focal point in the federal government to zero in on issues of trade and industry other than through the Byzantine machinations of a legislative process susceptible to special interests. There is, in short, no center of power from which to advocate more balanced trade-offs between investments for defense, space, health, and welfare on the one hand and investments for economic development on the other.

There is, of course, the broader question of whether government should play any significant role at all in funding R&D for economic development and growth. One argument would hold that this is best left to industry with the encouragement of legislated incentives such as R&D tax credits. This view depends, we think, on whether one is talking about the R or the D of R&D.

Development is distinct from research. It accounts for more than 60 percent of all R&D expenses. These monies are spent primarily on creating marketable products and services. For the most part, with the exception of defense, it is generally accepted that such development work should be financed and carried out by the private sector. As is evident in the highly competitive computer industry, open-market competition provides the best guide to short-term, product-oriented investment decisions. And indeed nearly 90 percent of all nondefense development work is funded and performed by industry.[8]

The more perplexing questions have to do with the R part of the formula. Who should support and perform basic and applied research? Together they account for 34 percent of all R&D—12 percent is basic research and 22 percent applied. Long lead times and uncertain results characterize basic research. As a result, the normal profit motive and market guides to investments do not alone provide reliable bases for determining priorities or allocating investments. In America, our policy has been to rely on government as the source of three-fourths of basic research monies—with almost two-thirds from the federal government. Most of this research is carried out in university and government laboratories and only 20 percent in industry-supported labs. The final piece, applied research, falls somewhere between basic research and development. About half this work is funded by government and slightly more by industry.

In Japan, basic research accounts for a much lower percentage of total R&D than in the United States. There is substantial evidence that Japan draws heavily on U.S. and European research findings through faculty sabbaticals and graduate-student enrollments in foreign universities and exploitation of published research. A significant difference in Japan's research activities is that a much higher proportion is carried out in industry—as we saw in our discussion of Japan in a prior chapter.

The American method of relying on universities as a research resource seems to produce far better results. Because university findings are widely and openly disseminated, costly research duplication can often be avoided. Also important is the absence of inordinate pressure from funding sources to achieve immediate results. These conditions—characteristic of most U.S. university research—have another vital dimension. Ongoing basic or applied research allows many graduate students with freshly minted degrees to become catalysts in the transfer of knowledge and technology as they move into industry.

This system has a distinct disadvantage. Its openness allows ideas to flow domestically and internationally with equal ease and speed. New ideas travel at the speed of jet aircraft and electronic mail. Moreover, many more foreign students come to our technical institutions than Americans go abroad. At present almost half the Ph.D. candidates in engineering departments are foreign. While many will undoubtedly stay in the United States as faculty or industry employees, many others will return home. On balance, however, the benefits of open communication and rivalry between university research teams is a unique spur to progress. Most importantly, it contributes strongly to America's most powerful competitive advantage—namely, a high rate of technical innovation.

How strong this competitive edge is, and how effective we are in strengthening it, is of major concern. The significant decline, profiled in the preceding chapter, in the absolute numbers of masters and Ph.D. graduates in engineering deserves urgent attention. It is more than troublesome to note that, while undergraduate engineering enrollments are surging upward to almost double the level of six or seven years ago, the number of Ph.D. candidates has dropped by half. This is a rapidly shrinking pool from which graduate teaching assistants are tapped and future faculty members developed.

If successful results of basic and applied research are the forerunners of new industries and of new technologies to revitalize mature industries, then the concern of national or state industrial policy should be how to target research—*not* industries. But who should set the research agenda? Should it be left to university faculties? Should it be set by industry? Should it be determined by civil servants or political appointees, or by the Department of Defense with its own technology requirements?

A popular recommendation, drawing upon the apparent success of Japan's MITI, is for a federal planning board that could draw together the key participants—industry, labor, academia, and government—to collectively determine new areas for research and investment. This suggestion generates considerable opposition from those wary of so much concentration of power and authority.

A closer look at the MITI phenomenon raises some interesting questions. Has it indeed made a long-term contribution to basic research—at least so far? Or has the research agenda really been set in America? Have MITI planners identified winners based on after-the-fact observations of American and European research findings? Given the meager size of the Japanese research budget and the considerable success of its industrial development, one should be very cautious in using MITI—or Japan—as a model for how best to set national research priorities. What is more likely is that MITI has been very effective in helping to coordinate and to mediate the business of setting development goals with industry. There is no firm evidence that Japan knows any better than anyone else how to set a national research agenda. Indeed, the real test case is looming in the Fifth Generation Project, described earlier. It calls for considerable basic and applied research to be carried out in *industry* labs. One flaw in Japan: A critical intellectual mass for such research does not exist in their universities.

We doubt that any centralized agency can set an effective research agenda. In a little-known paper published in 1945, "On the Nature of Progress,"[9] Professor H. P. Phillips of MIT started with these words:

The purpose of research is to promote progress; progress is going forward. Is it possible to know which way is forward? In physics there is a principle of relativity which asserts that it is not possible to know which way we are moving nor how fast. Is there a similar principle applicable to all progress? At any one time actions of many kinds are being suggested. The practical problem is to distinguish which of these are trivial and which are of epoch-making importance. Is this possible?

Phillips went on to conclude that it is not possible to predict the future implications of present and past events because history shows that the future is not determined solely or even predominately by the present and the past.

All human affairs are thus subject to an indetermination principle. What happens five minutes from now is pretty well determined, but as that period is gradually lengthened a larger and larger number of purely accidental occurrences are included. Ultimately a point is reached beyond which events are more than half determined by accidents which have not yet happened. Present planning loses significance when that point is reached.

So here lies the dilemma. How can we make progress when the forward direction is indeterminate beyond a relatively brief interval? Phillips draws on an analogy to the genetic model of evolution in nature as the best model for progress:

Translated into the realm of human affairs this means that progress is made by trial and error. In any process of trial and error the probability of a favorable result is proportional to the number of trials. If we would find the conditions most favorable to progress, the conditions under which the greatest number of things will be tried should be sought. Such advances will be most frequent when the number of independent thought centers will be the greatest and the number of thought centers will be the greatest when there is maximum individual liberty. Thus it appears that maximum liberty is the condition most favorable to progress.

If we apply Phillips's genetic model to basic research, we conclude that a centralist approach is exactly the wrong one. It limits, in varying degrees, freedom of choice and thus diversity. The aim, rather, should be to encourage many bright and curious minds to pursue independent experiments, while at the same time monitoring results through open communications. The university provides this setting and therefore is the right environment in which to pursue basic research. The American university's role in encouraging diversity and independence is a unique strength, not a weakness. Our seeming inability to reach a consensus on direction may be the very thing that keeps America ahead in the race for technical leadership.

Our conversations with various university and research leaders throughout the country uncovered a similar conclusion. A consensus is building for a dispersed foundation of centers of excellence—competitive or complementary—in various research fields. Richard Cyert, president of Carnegie-Mellon University, offered a unique interpretation of how this might be given a more concrete identity. "If we thought of each of these centers as a mini-MITI," he suggested, "we would find the university playing a very special role at the core of industry consortia."

Professor Michael Dertouzos, head of the Laboratory for Computer Science at MIT, highlights a special part of the R&D challenge. He says:

It's not a lack of research or good ideas that's our problem. It's that industry is lagging in turning these new ideas into products. The Fifth Generation Computer Project in Japan is predicated on the research results of American universities—many developed right here at M.I.T. The Japanese have made a serious commitment to turn new ideas like artificial intelligence and parallel processing into products, and soon. American industry has not. That's both frightening and maddening.[10]

When does industry break with the past and gamble huge resources on a completely new generation of computers? For industry, it is a financial question of weighing risk against rewards. What can be done to induce our larger corporations to become even more aggressive in exploiting new technology? George Hatsopoulos, president of Thermo Electron, in a widely reviewed report, "High Cost of Capital: Handicap of American Industry," claims that investment decisions in larger companies are largely an issue of the cost of capital. Investments in R&D are made today in order to generate a stream of profits in the future. Thus the cost of capital has an important bearing on the length of time and the amount of risk involved in prudent R&D investments. His major point: High cost of capital pushes R&D investment decisions toward shorter horizons and more proven technologies.[11]

Hatsopoulos argues that over the decade of the 1970s, the costs of capital in Japan and the United States diverged to a point where it is now three times greater here than there. Thus Japanese companies are financially justified in taking larger risks in experimenting with new technologies and reaching further into the future in making R&D investment decisions. More and more, they are beginning to do just that. The cost-of-capital issue is even further exacerbated by the fact that Japan has followed a public policy of subsidizing investments in narrowly targeted technologies like VLSI in the 1970s and now supercomputers in the 1980s.

What are American policy remedies? In an open-market environment, there is no way to assure that private corporations will stay competitive in new technologies when the costs of capital in competing countries are significantly out of balance. The federal government has a unique responsibility to keep the cost of investment capital in line with that of other nations. But the cost of capital is closely related to the problem of budget deficits. Budget deficits are just another way of stating the stark conflict in priorities between investments in defense, health, and space—wealth absorbers—on the one hand and in economic growth and wealth generation on the other. To the extent that we spend more on wealth absorbers than our present GNP can support, we shrink the availability of investment capital through higher interest rates caused by budget deficits or alternatively by higher tax rates required to reduce them. That is, we eat our own seed corn. No nation can subsist long on such a course without serious consequences.

Tax policy also affects the cost and availability of capital. Through tax breaks which either encourage or discourage savings and investments, the federal government in effect allocates capital between personal consumption and business investment. Unlike Japan, for example, America encourages consumption by allowing tax deductions on interest paid for personal borrowings for such expenditures as automobiles, housing, and credit-card payments. At the same time, America discourages savings by taxing interest earnings on personal savings accounts. Both at the government level and at the personal level, Americans are induced to consume much more than to invest.

The R&D tax credit enacted in 1981 was an important corrective measure. The effect of this tax credit is to reduce the cost of capital specifically for investments in R&D. The importance of tax credits to high-technology firms is underscored by the fact that the liberalization of R&D tax credits and making them permanent, as opposed to the cut-off now scheduled for 1985, is by far the highest legislative priority for high-technology companies. A recent study for the American Electronics Association by Boston-based Bain & Company substantiated the effect of the tax credit. Spending of the companies surveyed increased by 9 percent in the first year during which the tax credit was in effect. The study indicated that this would increase 20 or 25 percent if the tax credit were made permanent and expanded to include computer software.[12]

Another approach to increasing R&D investments is to lower risk, as a partial offset to the high cost of capital, by pooling long-term, high-risk R&D investment through industrial consortia. And indeed we are seeing today the rapid emergence of many such consortia specifically to address the Japanese competitive threat in the present investment environment. Historically, joint R&D projects between corporations were prohibited by antitrust laws. Bruce Merrifield, assistant secretary of commerce for productivity, technology, and innovation, has developed the idea of "limited R&D partnerships" to encourage joint research. "Where companies have to get together is not so much in the invention of new ideas, which represents only 10 percent of an innovation's cost. It's the translation and commercialization of an idea where 90 percent of the funds are needed. We're trying to get the antitrust laws amended, and to allow a 90 percent tax credit, to encourage joint research in this sector."[13]

Permanent alterations of antitrust provisions will encourage and solidify such joint R&D efforts. Two recent examples of significant initiatives in the electronics industry are the Semiconductor Research Corporation (SRC) and the Microelectronics and Computer Technology Corporation (MCC).

The Semiconductor Research Corporation, led by IBM and supported by nearly twenty electronics firms, is an innovative form of industry-university cooperation in research. Based at North Carolina's Research Triangle Park, SRC came into being not only in response to the Japanese challenge but primarily due to the erosion of funds available for research. In many ways it continues the tradition started by Bell Labs in the 1950s and the Defense Department in the 1960s in their support of semiconductors.

SRC has three goals. According to its director, Larry Sumney, a former director of the Defense Department's VHSIC program, the first is to create "new knowledge of semiconductor materials and phenomena." The second, "new design and manufacturing technologies for semiconductors." And third, "an increase in the number of scientists and engineers proficient in related research, development, and manufacturing." By November 1982, eight universities had been selected for grants out of sixty-three that submitted a total of 166 proposals. By June 1983, some thirty universities were SRC participants. The chief recipients—or "lead centers," as SRC calls them—were Cornell, Berkeley, Carnegie-Mellon, MIT, Illinois, and Stanford, which together received nearly $5 million in SRC's first year of operation. By 1986, SRC expects to channel about $20 million per year to U.S. universities. Although some of the projects are shorter term, most of the programs have five-to-ten-year time horizons, which are certainly long by usual industry yardsticks and long enough to do significant pure research.

About a year after the SRC was announced, another industrial consortium was formed. The Microelectronics and Computer

Technology Corporation, with its home base in Austin, Texas, has a different orientation. In this case, thirteen companies led by Control Data Corporation (CDC) have come together to pool funds to challenge the Japanese Fifth Generation Computer Project. The focus is less on pure than on applied research. Conceived by CDC's chairman William Norris, it is directed by Admiral "Bobby" Inman, a former deputy director of the CIA. "While we are structured to do long-range research, our ultimate purpose is to shorten the commercialization cycle," says Inman. Thus while SRC is a research cooperative that farms out its projects, MCC's mission is to itself conduct "applied research and advanced development."

MCC has a unique structure. Its thirteen supporters are shareholders who invest in one or more of the four main MCC projects. They then have the right to use any licenses free of charge. Although MCC is not officially connected to a university, unofficial connections were the determining factor in the research unit's decision to locate in Austin. The University of Texas agreed to increase its computer-science faculty by adding three new professorships, and will provide seventy-five fellowships for graduate students to work in tandem with MCC. The university will be one source of personnel, especially over the long term. At present, Inman is relying on scientists supplied by the member companies. He hired his chief scientist in the fall of 1983, a Department of Defense man who had been a deputy chief of research at the National Security Administration.

"This is the Texas decade," says Seattle-born George Kozmetsky, a founder of Teledyne and now a professor at the University of Texas. "The reason is simple. This is one of the very few places with resources. But what this country really demands is a minimum of *twenty* centers of excellence." Kozmetsky is intimately familiar with the MCC plan and enthusiastic about it. "Can you imagine the excitement? This is like the 1950s—people can't wait to get to work in the morning."

Inman is equally outspoken about the role of partnerships like MCC. "What this comes down to is that the United States must put together the best combination of research programs with a strong pool of talent in order to stay competitive. The problem is that this goes against our national culture." What in his opinion is the proper role of the federal government? "The role of the federal government should be to clear the antitrust barriers and stand back. They should determine their own long-term agenda, and support research where there is no commercial application. But they are in a poor position to determine the commercial research agenda."

While antitrust barriers are falling on the one hand to encourage joint R&D investments, this by no means signals a uniform trend. The breakup of AT&T, for example, will likely prove to be one of the most short-sighted federal actions in the last fifty years, at least as it relates to nourishing the innovation process in technology. Bell Labs has been a national treasure which almost single-handedly underwrote the nation's applied-research investments in several critical fields. These include semiconductors, communications, fiber optics, and other new technologies that are now seen as vital to American interests. As a regulated industry, these research results were widely disseminated throughout industry with only modest licensing fees. But now with the breakup of AT&T not only will Bell Labs research funds be reduced, but the results of their research will become captive to what is now an unregulated company. The combined R&D budgets of Western Electric and AT&T in 1983 were $1.4 billion. It will take a ton of joint R&D programs like SRC and MCC—whose combined budgets are presently twenty times smaller—to even begin to compensate for the loss of Bell's superb research programs to the public domain.

Another way of commercializing new technology is through start-up companies funded by venture capital in early stages and public equity capital later in their development. Small start-up companies are not only extremely innovative but also much more productive in getting new ideas to the market than larger firms. The fusing of venture capital with entrepreneurs in start-up companies is a particularly American strength not well duplicated in Japan. For example, in 1982 $1.4 billion of venture capital was invested in the United States as compared to a meager $5 million in Japan.[14]

The 1981–82 surge in start-up companies can be traced to significant reductions in the capital-gains tax, almost by a factor of two as a result of the 1978 Revenue Act and the 1981 Economic Recovery Tax Act. These tax reductions had the effect of lowering the cost of venture capital for start-up companies and the cost of equity capital for high-growth, high-tech companies. Another reason for so many new companies is that the rapid changes of technology create unfilled voids of market opportunity which new companies can more nimbly exploit, particularly given what for the moment appears to be a bottomless supply of venture funds.

Incentives to take risk—to travel new and unproven trails—have been important not only for an outpouring of financial capital but also for a flow of human resources to new enterprises. Entrepreneurs and founders of new businesses are attracted by the lure of capital gains at low tax rates. But how does a new company attract the experienced professional managers and technologists it needs from the security and comfort of high-paying jobs in established firms? Stock options are the conventional method. Congress seemed to reflect an understanding of this process when it liberalized the tax benefits of incentive stock options in 1981. But only a year later, Congress gutted the benefits of incentive stock options by introducing the alternative minimum tax, forcing newly established firms to scrap their ISOs and grasp for untested plans like "Junior Stock" to provide continuing incentives for key personnel. This on-again, off-again policy of the government destabilizes the innovation process by discouraging the growth of successful start-ups, which have proven to be valuable contributors to our competitive standing. What's needed is a reliable, dependable tax environment to continue the impressive progress in venture firms.

But as beneficial as new start-ups are to commercializing technology and to long-term economic development, it would be far too risky to depend on this source of investment alone as a way of maintaining global leadership in the technology race. The resources of large corporations are just too mammoth to ignore in the battle against industrial giants in competing nations. For example, the R&D budgets of Hewlett-Packard, Sperry Corporation, AT&T, Western Electric, and General Electric all exceed half a billion dollars. And while the venture-capital pool exceeds $6 billion in the United States, the aggregate of conventional debt and equity financing is over $2 trillion.[15]

Furthermore, to dominate and control immense and rapidly growing *worldwide* markets such as computers and communications takes the sustained infusion of resources and the vast network of distribution channels available only to the larger multinational corporations. We see what can happen, for example, when a corporation like IBM turns its attention to a market niche like personal computers previously dominated by small start-up companies. The effect of muscle-flexing by a giant like IBM is truly amazing. Lucky for us, it was IBM and not Fujitsu which made the move on personal computers. To be truly successful, then, both our small and large companies must bend their resources to the challenges appropriate to their size.

Innovation cuts across a broad range of activities, institutions, and time spans. If any part of the pipeline is broken or constricted, the flow of benefits is slowed. This is felt ultimately in lower productivity and lowered standards of living. In this sense, the cost of capital is crucial not only at the early stages of research and product development but also at the later stages when high-technology products are installed in production processes, in both manufacturing and service industries, as new tools to improve worker effectiveness. Ultimately new technology is embodied in machines of one type or the other, and these machines cost money. The aggressiveness or hesitancy of corporations to equip their workers with the most up-to-date tools is closely linked to the cost of capital.

In his cost-of-capital treatise, George Hatsopoulos says that the significant difference in productivity between Japanese and American auto workers is not culture nor work ethic nor quality circles. It's simply the amount of modern capital equipment backing up each worker. Hatsopoulos points out, in this regard, that the productivity of Japanese auto workers is surprisingly low when you compare the magnitude of invested capital in Japan versus that in America.

At a time when new technology and higher energy costs have made obsolete a significant fraction of the capital stock of American corporations, it is alarming to observe that the rate of capital investment in the United States has been declining as a percentage of GNP while the investment rate in competing countries has been on the rise. During the 1970s, Japan was investing at a rate three times that of the United States, while France and West Germany had rates nearly double ours. The sooner we get on with replacing our obsolete capital equipment, the sooner these obsolete tools are renewed, the sooner American workers will become competitive again in world markets. But taking full advantage of the benefits embodied in high-technology products is substantially impeded by the high cost of capital. Thus high-tech and mature industries share a common concern that investment decisions not be constrained.

Do we need a national policy for R&D? Clearly there is a need for major changes in the attitude and behavior of business managers and policymakers to accommodate and even accelerate the major transitions in technology that are under way. MIT's Professor Dertouzos is right. Business must find better ways to get new knowledge to the marketplace faster and into practice sooner. Nonetheless, there is considerable evidence, as documented in this book, that corporate America—in old and new industries—has gotten the message. If allowed to function properly, our free-market system is very efficient in communicating failure. We are optimistic that our inherited tradition of Yankee ingenuity has been rejuvenated and is hard at work in America. Given the right incentives, the right cost of capital, and a supportive infrastructure, we are optimistic that the right answers will emerge. If it were otherwise—if management were not rising to the challenge—it is far from clear what direct actions government, or any other institutions, might take to induce an industry response.

But still government has an important role to play in assuring that the innovation process is thriving and healthy. As already noted, this includes fiscal and monetary policy which determines the cost of capital and tax policy which provides incentives for taking risk. It also includes the much larger issue of balancing the allocation of federal resources among the country's various needs—defense, health, energy, welfare, economic development, and others. More specifically, the percentage of GNP devoted to civilian R&D over time cannot be ignored, especially in comparison to our major competitors. Already Japan is investing at 2.4 percent of GNP with the goal of increasing this to 3 percent. To raise U.S. civilian R&D from its current level of 1.7 percent to 2.3 percent translates into $20 billion. Part of this can come through incentives like R&D tax credits, reduced capital-gains tax, and increased incentive options, and we can expect a growing investment by private industry in R&D, especially if the cost of capital is substantially reduced.

Nonetheless, federal and state governments will have to make greater investments in civilian research with an emphasis on increasing the interplay between industry and centers of research excellence in our university system. Japan has excelled in technology development and application, what was termed "needs" in an earlier chapter. Now the Japanese are calling for a strenuous effort toward a "seeds" or research-driven strategy. By contrast, America is already strong in research but needs greater emphasis on getting new knowledge to market expeditiously. Innovation depends on a better balance of seeds and needs in both countries but in reverse ways.

Despite our economic hardships, we would argue that a billion dollars per year, comparable to funding for the National Science Foundation, be focused on strengthening our major research universities through encouraging and supporting partnerships with industry. As we will show in the next chapter, matching support from government and industry can form the basis of a decentralized national policy that makes sense for America's future.

16

Refocusing the Challenge

American history is a case study in creativity—of individuals and institutions constantly testing new ground and probing new ideas. This experimental spirit helped to craft a new concept of government embodied in our constitution, to revolutionize public higher education after the Civil War, to invent and improve the tools and machines that launched our agricultural and industrial development to unprecedented heights, and now to lead in the development of the electronic innovations that have spawned the information age. Unlike Europe, whose history much preferred to enshrine battlefield heroes and successions of monarchs, the United States chose to lift its innovators to prominence and fame—Benjamin Franklin, Thomas Jefferson, Thomas Edison, Alexander Graham Bell, the Wright brothers, Henry Ford, William Shockley, and many others.

Creativity, innovation, entrepreneurship, and a capacity to deliver are the means by which America ascended to world prominence. Yet future historians may look back on the 1970s and early 1980s as the period when Americans lost their edge, when productivity rates declined and competitors gained unexpected strength. Some people argue that, despite new computers and other high-tech breakthroughs, Americans are losing their creative spirit. We have lost that special edge that comes from getting ideas to the marketplace faster and better than anyone else. Much of this is reflected in a deteriorating trade picture. A $20-billion balance-of-payments deficit in 1980 had by the end of 1983 turned into a $70-billion deficit, despite sharp reductions in imported oil purchases. The largest import increases came not only in autos and apparel but more ominously in data-processing equipment, telecommunications, and electrical machinery. Part of the deepening deficit can be attributed to an overvalued dollar that was 30 percent higher than in 1980. However, a principal explanation is the weakening U.S. capacity to compete with better products and improved production processes abroad.

At the same time, overall federal deficits have skyrocketed, and the deficit in Washington threatens the economy with a sea of red ink. Too much of our national resources—now 35 percent of GNP—are consumed by local, state, and federal spending, eroding the capital and human resources needed for private industrial development. The biggest problem is that federal spending has been misdirected, with too little going to renew industrial technology and too much for national defense and other non-economic-development missions.

Some trace our losses to top-heavy and bureaucratic institutions. Bloated government, in this view, is inimical to America's innovative traditions. In a paraphrase of Elting Morison: "Intuitively and quite correctly the *bureaucratic* man feels that a change in ways portends a change in the arrangement of his society. . . . The mores and structure of the society are immediately placed in jeopardy."[1] Industry leadership, too, has settled into a caretaker syndrome as managers sit on past accomplishments with no strong incentive to question the viability of what appeared to be continuing success.

Other people have different explanations for the U.S. slippage. It's not that we are getting worse, they say, but that others are getting better and are now able to match us point for point in what had been an exclusively American game. It doesn't much matter which argument is correct. In either case, the response to today's competitive challenge should be the same now as it was throughout our history—to nurture the sources of creativity and innovation. The central question is how to do it best.

There is no single formula for success. Our studies—of Ford, Ætna, and Emhart; of Massachusetts, Michigan, and Mississippi;

of Carnegie-Mellon University, Worcester Polytechnic Institute and the Benjamin Franklin Centers; and of the Defense Advanced Research Projects Agency—indicate that no single group, public or private, can take sole responsibility for preserving, much less enhancing, a national heritage. The answer lies in inspiring the nation as a whole to meet the challenge and accelerate our innovation—or to paraphrase one politician's terminology, to "target the innovation process." Those apt words of Congressman Ed Zschau of California suggest a need for the government to rethink the sources of vitality and strength in our culture and economy.

We emphasize these points for a simple reason. The need for innovation comes at a time when opinion leaders are engaged in a much-touted "industrial policy" discussion. As Robert Reich has appropriately argued, the issue is not whether we should or should not have an industrial policy. The fact is that America, for at least eight presidential administrations, has had either a stated or a de facto industrial policy. As long as huge amounts of federal revenues are allocated to defense or welfare, and priorities are juggled through tax incentives or trade preferences, economic policy is being shaped by government. Neither is the issue an either/or choice of government intrusion versus laissez-faire. Experience tells us that the economy will remain a mixture of both. Defense budgets and agricultural subsidies will have as much influence on the direction of the economy as will the strategic plans of large and small corporations. The key for the future is to focus on the best mix of initiatives—public and private, corporate, governmental, and academic—needed to accelerate the innovation process.

Most of the recent industrial-policy proposals before us call for a centralized top-down approach in which the federal government shoulders much of the burden for national competitiveness. This cannot work. It runs too strongly against the American spirit. But apart from this cultural incongruity, the diversity and complexity that breathe life into the American economy are just too enormous to be masterminded by any single body, regardless of how well-intentioned or how powerful. No single policy can encompass the strong regional differences underscored by the differing characters of local industries, the uneven heritage and changing goals of each state's educational establishment, or the competing knowledge and skills of regional work forces. In this regard New England is as different from the heartland states as the two are from the Sunbelt. Each region's future calls for unique directions that can best be fashioned by those closest to the issues, by those having something to win or lose in the outcome.

In contrast to a narrowly focused industrial policy, we advocate a wide array of decentralized initiatives that boost the visibility of innovation in the economy. We make no pretense of offering a comprehensive blueprint; rather, our purpose is to refocus the debate away from industrial policy and toward the different but interrelated elements of the innovation process. While there are countless subtle aspects to innovation, for emphasis in this book we have identified and discussed four major ones—R&D, education, management, and capital. These are pictured in figure 3, showing that innovation starts with creativity but should result in productivity growth—the cornerstone for improvement in our standard of living and quality of life.

Even a cursory study of the diagram brings home the point that no single actor alone can control or legislate the innovation process. For example, government could double basic research budgets, but if corporate managers are unwilling or unable to commercialize the new ideas, the net result would be a huge waste of resources. Likewise, if corporate managers embrace new ideas but universities fail to produce human resources in sufficient quantity and quality to exploit the new technology, then again the innovation process is impeded.

The message is clear. What is postulated as industrial policy is not a job for the federal government alone. There are other important actors with equally significant roles to play—state government officials, corporate managers, educators, and production-line workers as well. That is why in prior chapters we have highlighted the individual but interrelated initiatives of Governor Winter in Mississippi, of Mike Ford and John Rydz at Emhart, or

Figure 3. The Four Components of Innovation

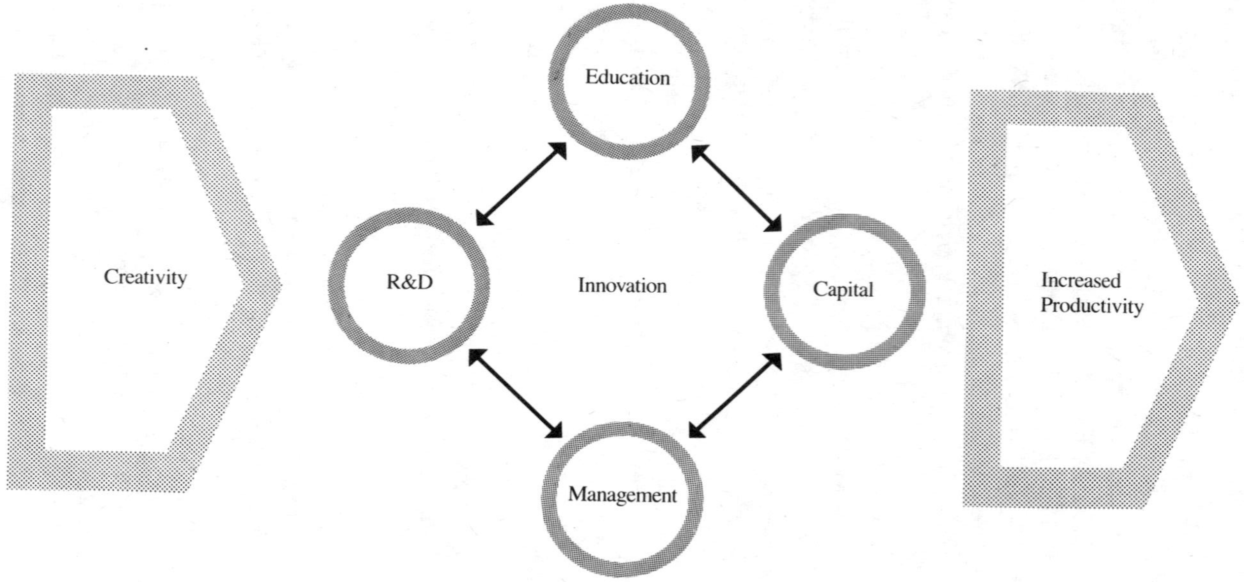

Richard Cyert at Carnegie-Mellon, and Thomas Maupin at Ford. Dampen the will to innovate by omitting any part of the loop and the process no longer works. The problem with many industrial-policy prescriptions is an implied cooption of initiative from precisely those whose cooperation is critical—an observation reinforced by unsuccessful European experiments with centrally directed industrial-policy prescriptions.

Nonetheless, the federal government does have important responsibilities. Among these is to assure that our cost of capital is competitive with that of other nations. Otherwise, private-sector investments in R&D and in capital equipment which embodies new technology will be restricted. R&D and investment tax credits, and reduced capital-gains tax are important ways to selectively lower the cost of capital for certain investments. But these measures are not satisfactory substitutes for sound fiscal policies and balanced budgets.

The present single-minded focus on defense spending and related security policies like export restrictions is excessive compared to industrial spending and economic policies designed to encourage a strong, competitive technological base. Peace and security are better achieved by an offensive strategy that builds a strong economy than by defensive strategies that consume our resources on nonproductive war machines. Nor is it possible for the United States to provide defense without the support of its allies. Even while we compete economically, we cannot continue policies that threaten the viability of the international economic system.

It has been a policy in America for the federal government to play a major role in funding university-based research—as much as 70 percent at the top fifty research universities. This high-leverage policy should be continued and strengthened. Yet it is state and local governments that carry the largest responsibility for funding public education, both at higher and lower levels, and for establishing educational priorities pertinent to their regional needs. This was clearly illustrated in Mississippi; it is evident in numerous other states. To support the innovation process, state and local governments can help guide the aims of education toward goals of regional development, for example, by more liberally funding university research or community-college and other programs that are relevant to the health of the regional economy.

But while we may turn to our political institutions for one set of needs, we must go elsewhere for others. A major burden for enhancing innovation falls not on government but on those closest to the process itself—that is, on business leaders and managers. We spoke earlier of outmoded production-line philosophies whose time has passed. It's time to end Taylorism, that old legacy of so-called "scientific management," whose result was to reinforce alienation between worker and manager. It's time to tap more fully the potential of workers and to involve them more in deciding the best ways to get the job done. Management must embrace a relatively new concept for American industry—that quality and cost are not trade-offs. Rather, quality improvement through better management of defect prevention actually lowers cost dramatically.

Joel Moses, head of MIT's department of electrical engineering and computer sciences, zeroes in on this management problem. Large American organizations lack the flexibility that large Japanese enterprises have mastered. Americans are not paying enough attention to the key U.S. problem—that organizational growth is spawning inflexibility and inhibiting innovation. The changes required are not structural. We don't need new boards or new departments. What is needed is a shift in management thinking. While the Japanese race to create innovation, American management has to step up to the starting block to infuse flexibility and creativity into large and unresponsive organizations. "The question is," asks Moses, "who is going to transform their society faster?"[2]

Managers have the challenge to deploy new technology in a way that motivates initiative and commitment as opposed to deskilling and dehumanizing jobs. They have a self-interest in accepting greater responsibility for continuous lifelong education and training of their work force. To ignore lifelong education will be tantamount to rendering employees obsolete and noncompetitive. In assigning a professional educator to its top management ranks, Ætna may be a forerunner of a coming change.

Finally, as our industries become more knowledge-intensive, managers must learn how to more fully assimilate professional knowledge workers, especially innovators, into a partnership of equals. Management has a key role to play in innovation not just in bringing life to new products and new technologies but also in changing the management process itself to empower workers at all levels to be more effective in reaching corporate and personal goals.

Glenn Watts, president of the Communications Workers of America, is one of the leaders meeting head-on the union problem of the future. His proposals for a "portfolio of skills" approach not only would achieve greater involvement and productivity in today's jobs but also would help anticipate a diversity of jobs along career paths of ascending contribution and responsibility. Union leaders too have a responsibility for keeping innovation alive. Flexibility in adapting to change, in acquiring new knowledge, in accommodating technology, and in adjusting to new management processes has become a central theme for both corporate and individual success, if not survival. If nothing more, the stagflation and recession of recent years has taught us that expending energy on union-management battles only weakens our strength against tougher international competitors. Management and labor must team up on the same side by crafting goals in which both have equal stakes. Improvements in a person's standard of living cannot be gained by simply negotiating redivisions of a shrinking pie. They are earned by enlarging the size of the pie or, in other words, through productivity growth.

And what expectations do we attach to education? The college class of 2000 just entered the first grade in September 1984. What will the class of 2000 need to know by the time it graduates in order to be competitive on an international scale? What caliber of teachers will it take to distill more and more knowledge into each year while still retaining its interrelatedness? How will we attract and retain quality educators in a profession that is underpaid and undervalued? Innovation must impact education as much as education impacts innovation. Educators have a central role to play in what is becoming an increasingly knowledge-intensive society.

In this regard, perhaps the greatest changes will occur in higher education. The question is not only what to teach but how to teach it. Four years of college are no longer adequate preparation for a lifetime of professional work, but the answer is not to extend the interval of full-time study. Instead, the wave of the future is cooperative work-study programs which formally extend university curricula to the work site to address continuing educational needs of people throughout their working lives. Such programs will require major innovations in the structure and financing of colleges and universities, as well as changes in the attitudes of educators toward their mission and the rewards associated with it. Also needed is a commitment by corporate managers to an aggressive renewal of human capital through continuous lifelong education as an integral part of their job.

A significant shift in the mix of higher education will have to occur. Engineering education is becoming a preferred background in many industries not only to staff the increasing number of technical jobs but also as background for management positions as well. Today only 7 percent of our annual one million bachelor degrees are in engineering. This is not enough to sustain the technology revolution, especially when compared to 20 percent in Japan. To increase the percentage in America will strain our colleges and universities at a time when the number of high-school students is shrinking.

But the largest educational challenge will be to renew and revitalize our faculty and curricula, especially in technology where the base of knowledge is changing so rapidly. The rate at which we can infuse new technology into our society will be determined largely by the rate that university faculty can renew their own bases of knowledge and codify new knowledge in the form of textbooks, videotapes, and computer-based instruction. By their very structures and traditions, universities have historically been slow to change. Innovation will be required to speed up their responsiveness to the needs of society and industry, which themselves are undergoing rapid transformation.

Beyond education is an equally vital agenda of research and development. How much R&D is enough and what kind? We have already mentioned that Japan is spending 2.3 percent of its gross national product on civilian R&D with the goal of reaching 3 percent. To raise our civilian R&D expenditure to a par with Japan's would entail additional investments of $20 billion. While this is a large increase, neither the government nor industry can afford to ignore these immense discrepancies in an area of such high leverage to the economy.

In R&D more than in most other areas, it's the results rather than the spending that count. You can't buy innovation by throwing money at the problem. Getting results from R&D depends on champions who have clear research goals and a burning desire to accomplish them. To fund a research program and then search for someone to do the work is a high-risk strategy. Instead we must develop technically talented people and provide an environment that is conducive to creative work. We must recognize and reward outstanding accomplishments and make it easy for those with proven records to pursue their dreams.

Because so many players—industry, academia, and government, both state and federal—are deeply involved in science and technology, this raises the question of who is or should be responsible for the outcome. What mechanisms can assure collaboration and cooperation among the parties?

Setting aside areas of special concern such as defense and health and focusing instead on industrial innovation for economic development, we would argue that business and academia should be the active players who set and jointly implement the R&D agenda while state and federal governments should be supportive players who accelerate the innovation process with resources and the needed infrastructure. We should not look for top-down direction from a single government board but rather for bottom-up evolution from a large number of separate experiments operating in a flexible and open environment. This is the lesson of the Phillips model of innovation discussed in an earlier chapter. It is corroborated by our own studies which show that, to a large extent, this kind of structure and philosophy is more closely attuned to American tradition and culture.

The missing link to date has been the proper mechanisms to foster and promote rewarding collaborative efforts among the players. Why the emphasis on collaboration? In an increasing number of instances, the scope and complexity of modern technology are so great that individual innovators or even large corporations working alone cannot make adequate progress. Furthermore, while some competition among research teams is beneficial, it would be a waste of human and financial resources to endlessly duplicate long-term basic research. Neither is it optimal for universities to perform basic research in isolation because they run the risk of becoming too disconnected from real-world needs. And even successful new ideas born in university laboratories with no industrial connections can take too long to be transformed into useful commercial products.

One of the most promising new responses to this dilemma is the recent emergence of "centers of innovation" at many U.S. universities. These are industry-university consortia organized to create new knowledge and to transfer it more effectively from universities and colleges to the commercial environment. These centers take many different forms and perform many different tasks. But one thing they have in common is their potential to revolutionize not only education but the economy as well. The rapid evolution of these centers has so far proceeded largely unnoticed by the public and by the architects of industrial policy. But it would be a mistake to ignore their potential to accelerate innovation and to prepare more Americans for a restructured, technology-intensive economy.

These consortia need not be just an industry initiative with narrow self-interest in mind. They can and should include foundations, federal agencies, and state governments. Unions could play a role as well, though few have done so to date. Some centers are based at a single university with many industrial partners (for example, the four Ben Franklin Centers recently founded in Pennsylvania). Others are groupings of universities with one or more industrial partners (like the Carnegie Corporation's Inter-university Consortium on Educational Computing). Some are state-initiated (such as the Industrial Technology Institute or its sister Michigan Biotechnology Institute) with major foundation support and informal university links.

Centers other than those few described in earlier chapters are already in operation. With the proper incentives, many more could emerge. One of the key points of these centers is that, without any of the rhetoric or politics of industrial policy, they bring all the key actors together to work on pieces of the national economic and educational agenda. To those who picture the university as an ivory tower, the idea of partnerships between business and academia may seem antithetical and ominous. But there are commonsense reasons why they are both needed and happening. Chief among these is the driving force for pooling money, knowledge, and human resources while providing a mechanism—namely, the university laboratory—to negotiate a research agenda that serves the various needs of society. Although research is the key goal, a vitally important by-product is education and training in emerging new technologies. Accelerating innovation and the rapid transfer of knowledge are the underlying themes in these centers of innovation.

Few leaders in government, industry, or academia have yet recognized these centers as the cores for high-leverage economic-development policy. The best way to understand their potential is to reexamine the American past. The historical precedents for present-day consortia date back to the Morrill Act of 1862, which led to the establishment of land-grant agricultural and engineering colleges, and to the Hatch Act of 1887, which created state agricultural experiment stations. These were landmarks in legislation for education and research that in time helped produce the world's best agricultural system and helped drive the industrial revolution in America by graduating generations of students in the "mechanical arts." Now, a hundred years later, the focus is on the new technologies of our present era and the new industries that have blossomed around them. They could again revolutionize and revitalize our agriculture, manufacturing, and service industries.

The linchpin for a national competitive strategy is already developing naturally in new university centers which promote cooperation between industry and academia. These centers offer a truly unique advantage for the American economy. They put the accent on what the Japanese would call a real "national treasure" of the United States—namely, world-class research universities which presently number some fifty to a hundred. The Japanese have nothing like this. Instead, they rely on the Ministry for International Trade and Industry—the famous MITI. What our centers of innovation are coming to represent are "mini-MITIs"—not one but many of them, each combining the collective wisdom of the education, business, and often government sectors.

Richard Cyert, president of Carnegie-Mellon University, first mentioned this "mini-MITI" concept. "If I were making science policy," he said, "I'd encourage the universities to act like MITI. This university has acted as if it were a little MITI. Come to think of it, American universities are like a whole series of 'mini-MITIs.'" In many ways, the growing number of cooperative industry-university consortia do act like miniature versions of Japan's MITI—except that they're much better. Their participants not only talk about new research but they do it. They are the new mediators between what in Japanese terminology are called "seeds and needs." The American method not only sets lofty visions but manifests them as well. And they get direct feedback from the marketplace as to what works and who has the competence and the motivation to make it work.

Like many things American, the scale or at least the potential scope for this approach is huge in the United States. We have at least fifty top research universities in America and another fifty in the making. On average, each research university could have two or three innovation centers. Some would focus on regional needs, adapting known technologies appropriate to local industries. Others could focus on the creation of new technology that might be national in scope and applicable in a range of industrial sectors.

Centers of innovation can be initiated in any number of ways. Companies with shared research goals, like the Semiconductor Research Cooperative described earlier, can pool their resources and encourage the formation of a center at one or more universities. Universities can on their own initiate a center and then seek industrial partners and government agencies for support, as was the case for Stanford's Center for Integrated Systems. State government can take the initiative in establishing a center of innovation to support or encourage industrial development, as North Carolina did in building the Microelectronics Center in Raleigh-Durham's Research Triangle Park. Foundations can play a central funding role, as the Kellogg Foundation did in supporting Michigan's state-created Industrial Technology Institute. The federal government can found similar centers of technological initiative as DARPA has done for military purposes in artificial intelligence.

Collaborative research efforts between industry and universities have been most successful when they have well-defined goals. They have worked best when both parties, the creators and the benefactors of innovation, perceive direct mutual benefit. As the research becomes longer-term and less specific in terms of applicable results, the question of who pays and who benefits becomes an issue. For this fundamental reason, we cannot depend on industry alone to fund basic research which will become property and useful in a broad range of applications and industries. Instead, industry should be viewed first and foremost as a source of seed money to validate the economic potential of research and to help shape its direction. Equally important, industrial partners can assure that new ideas will quickly find their way to the marketplace. But inevitably federal and state governments must play a major role in funding these emerging industry/university partnerships, preferably in a more passive than directive way.

Tax credit for industrial support of university-based research is one important way for government to encourage and support this process. But the leverage from this funding mechanism alone will not be adequate to underwrite centers of innovation on a large scale. To leverage industrial support will require matching grants with built-in multipliers. How large a multiplier? In our earlier book, *Global Stakes,* we recommended a multiplier where the government would match each industry dollar with several dollars—much as is done with federal monies in support of highway construction. Rustum Roy, professor at Pennsylvania State University and director of one of the nation's oldest and largest materials research laboratories, suggests that the multiplier should be from one to seven times the industrial contribution.

It is worthwhile to explore further the issue of who pays and who benefits from university research. Let's take information-processing science and technology as an example. Who benefits from university research in semiconductors and very-large-scale integrated (VLSI) circuits? Or in computer science and artificial intelligence? Or in robotics and machine vision? The quick response would be the high-technology toolmakers, companies like IBM, AT&T, Hewlett-Packard, Wang, Digital Equipment Corporation, Control Data Corporation, and others. But on further reflection, the most important benefactors are not the makers but the users of the tools—banks, insurance companies, automobile manufacturers, oil companies, and others in basic businesses. These are the ultimate users who depend increasingly on advances in information processing and communications to boost their productivity and competitiveness. In contrast to this group, the high-technology toolmakers today represent a very small fraction of the American economy—certainly less than 5 percent. It would be neither reasonable nor wise for our nation to gear itself to what the relatively small high-technology industry can afford to invest in university research. This is an issue that needs to be addressed by all segments of the nation—basic industries, mature service companies, and high-technology businesses as well as federal and state governments.

A special problem faces the nation in the field of information-processing science and technology. Anyone who has bought a new personal computer will know this problem well. So does every business that learns to live with one computer that cannot communicate with another. An IBM computer cannot "talk" to an Apple without expensive and time-consuming adjustments. Digital Equipment machines are incompatible with Wang Systems, and Wangs with Hewlett-Packards. It is much like countries building networks of railroads with different gauge tracks.

The issue of incompatibility is just a symptom of a larger problem. Despite all the talk of the "information age," we do not yet have a viable strategy for a nationwide electronics system equivalent to the railroads or the airways. We are rapidly approaching the time when such questions of national scope can no longer be postponed.

But what are the choices before us? How could a national effort for industrial innovation in computers and communications be launched? One historical precedent was the creation of AT&T with its Bell Laboratories—not a bad idea, were we not busy breaking up this heretofore public monopoly. Another is to create the equivalent of DARPA and locate it within a civilian rather than military federal agency. Are there any alternatives to forming another tax-supported government agency?

Robert Kahn, the director of DARPA's information processing technology office, has proposed an idea that would provide coherence to a chain of innovation centers, strengthening some existing university-based consortia as well as spawning some new ones. He proposes a U.S. Information Science and Technology Center whose purpose would be to foster cooperative research in information science and technology. The strategy is modeled in part on DARPA's impressive Strategic Computing Project described in an earlier chapter. The major difference would be that this one would focus on commercial and industrial rather than military applications. Kahn's vision is to develop the technology needed to interconnect a proliferation of presently incompatible computer networks. "A prospective user of such a network," he states, "is confronted by a bewildering choice of ill-understood and interdependent alternatives." The vision is to create a vast electronics highway so that every company could interconnect with every other company, so that products and services could be ordered and bills paid by electronic mail, so that teleconferencing would become a primary vehicle for business communications, and so that computers of all sizes and makes could routinely talk to each other. In time this would become an interconnected network permitting information to flow as easily as cars or trucks on interstate highways.

The Information Science and Technology Center would collect funds from widely disparate sources, users as well as makers of the tools. It would engage in its own research as well as channel funds to the country's best technologists working at various university and industry centers of innovation. An exceptional corps of researchers would craft an agenda of needed research into a coherent national information-processing strategy. The intention is "a different style of research activity," Kahn suggests, "in which basic efforts are cooperative and each research project involves two or more collaborating sites linked by networks."

Without such a coordinating center for advanced research in this area, the chances are small that the many isolated, independent research efforts will cause major changes in the way our business and society operates. Japan has already launched several such efforts. One of them, ICOT or the Fifth Generation Computer Project, was described earlier. Others like the INS national fiber-optics system is also under way. Projects such as these will provide Japanese companies an advanced infrastructure which, if successful, will amplify their productivity considerably. Can we allow challenges with such enormous potential to go unaddressed? Should we let such opportunities for economic development go unfulfilled because the federal government is too slow to respond to commercial and civilian needs?

While this program could start with modest resources, Kahn estimates that funding should reach $100 million per year in order to have an impact on problems of such scope. Who should pay the bill and how would the program be directed? A nonprofit, quasi-public institution would have more flexibility to carry out this complex mission than another government agency. For one thing, it is not at all clear where such an agency would fit into the federal bureaucracy. For another, it is doubtful that the talented people needed could or should be lured away from their present jobs and, even if they were, could be retained in the government to provide continuity over the long duration of such a program. And also, too much of their time and effort would inevitably be compromised by the need to cope with political issues.

Kahn's alternative is that seed money be provided by private corporations, foundations, and individuals to initiate the center and to formulate its strategy and objectives with guidance from a board of experts from industry and universities. Once the goals were established and supported by a broad coalition of industry and university leaders, the federal government would be approached for matching funds. For reasons already suggested, the high-technology industry alone could not afford or justify underwriting this investment, although computer and electronics companies would certainly be involved. The primary benefactors would be the users of information technology, chiefly basic manufacturing and service industries. Individual citizens and the government itself would also benefit from a standardization which would amply justify the participation and support of the federal government.

We have presented this proposal for a national technology center as an alternative to the idea that only federal agencies can fund and direct large-scale DARPA- or NASA-like research efforts of national significance. This privately initiated approach has the appeal of being entrepreneurial in nature. Its viability would depend on a champion stepping forth to provide vision and leadership and to coalesce support around an idea whose time has come. This approach would leverage already-existing resources and not create a large, cumbersome bureaucracy. And like other private institutions, the center could be terminated when and if it ceased to fulfill a useful purpose. Once proven viable, this approach might also be extended to other research programs, perhaps in biotechnology or materials science—wherever the scale of the initiative requires national centers of innovation beyond the scope of a single university.

In the spirit of addressing critical, well-defined needs, we advocate a significant increase in research expenditures for the nation. Part of this would come from private industry, not only to support university research but also to boost investments in corporate-specific R&D. Tax incentives to encourage these investments should be strengthened and continued. But also we advocate a significant increase in funding of research by the federal government. Specifically, we recommend a billion dollars per year, an amount comparable to the present funding for the National Science Foundation. We suggest that these funds be concentrated on industrial innovation, especially to encourage and support industry-university consortia and university-based centers of innovation. Some of these funds would come through increased tax credits for university research funded by industry. Some would go directly to universities in the form of matching grants. We would encourage experimentation with new organizational forms like the proposed Information Science and Technology Center that would pull together industry and universities to work cooperatively on well-defined problems of national scope.

We have emphasized that innovation is the key to progress and that the high-technology industry is not alone in its dependence on innovation. The facts are that high tech, basic industries, and services businesses need new technologies as sources of vitality and competitive strength. They share a common pool of resources—namely, our technical colleges and universities—for creating new technologies and educating and training a new generation of workers imbued with new knowledge.

The successful interplay of corporations and universities in creating and tapping this source of strength is critical to all American industry, either directly or indirectly. A challenge still before us is to enable industry and universities to work together as never before to learn how to adapt to new realities imposed by the accelerating change in knowledge and technology. The idea for centers of innovation offers a mechanism to accomplish these goals in a way appropriate to American culture and history. Assuring sufficient resources for this task should be a goal of highest national priority.

For two centuries since achieving its independence, the nation focused its energies on the business of generating wealth and raising the standard of living of its people—residents and immigrants alike. For two decades, though, through the 1960s and 1970s, that sense of drive has wavered. Japan propelled forward during the same period. By doing so it helped infuse new energy in America—where challenges are instinctively relished. Rediscovery of our creative energies is a task to which our innovators are well suited. It is their combined efforts, as businessmen, politicians, and educators, that will bring new vitality to the economic challenges ahead.

Acknowledgments

Much of our research and analysis was based on extensive travel and contact with numerous leaders in government, industry, labor, and academia, both in the United States and abroad. Some of these people are highlighted in chapters that focus on a single company or institution. These detailed studies could not have been completed without the generous and open cooperation of these public and private figures and their staffs. We are grateful to all of them.

A number of other individuals gave us detailed information and logistical and other practical assistance: at Ford Motor Company, Gerald terHorst in the firm's Washington office and Harlan L. Wendell at the Dearborn headquarters; at Emhart Corporation, Thomas Calhoun; at Ætna, Robert Nolan and David Rippey; in Michigan, Dr. Peter Ellis of the Kellogg Foundation, who offered his insights and statewide contacts; and in Mississippi, Andrew Mullins, a key aide to Governor William Winter on legislative issues. In Tokyo, we were helped in our visits to many corporations by Kozo Imai, who heads Analog Devices in Japan. His thoughtfulness and understanding are most appreciated. Hiroto Nakamura helped us immensely in Nara with our visits to Sharp Corporation. Dr. Juzar Motiwalla, at the University of Singapore, gave firsthand accounts of his country's development and introduced us to numerous individuals, as did Professor Kim Dalchoong of Yonsei University in Seoul, South Korea.

We'd like to give special thanks to Thomas Cummings, who

joined us during the project and was our lead researcher. He provided critical data and insight on jobs, R&D, industrial policy, and many other issues, for which we are grateful. Many others helped in this research. Helen Robinette at the International Center for Integrative Studies (ICIS) in New York City tracked down numerous information sources. ICIS also continued to provide invaluable administrative support, as it did for our previous work, which we appreciate greatly. We are grateful to Christopher Samuels, and to the Center for Strategy Research (CSR) in Cambridge for its ongoing research and administrative support. We are also indebted to Carol Franco, editor at Ballinger Publishing in Cambridge, who offered valuable professional advice.

The manuscript could not have been produced under the short deadlines required if it were not for the support of Dr. An Wang, who loaned word-processing equipment to the authors. Smooth and efficient completion of a manuscript would not have been possible without his assistance. We are also grateful to Robert Noyce at the Intel Corporation, whose timely support was greatly appreciated.

Particular thanks are due to the staff of Harper & Row for helping carry this book through the complex stages that led to final publication. In particular, Aaron Asher, executive editor, was especially helpful in offering experienced insights and encouragement in our attempt to craft a readable book.

As *The Innovators* goes to press, the Carnegie Corporation of New York announced its support to us for a year-long study of nationally prominent industry–university consortia. Stimulated by the conclusions in this book, the new study will detail the effectiveness of centers of technological excellence. From this analysis will come a deeper understanding of issues and opportunities for implementing a new national agenda.

Notes

INTRODUCTION

1. "Apple's Biggest Gamble," *Boston Globe,* January 24, 1984.
2. *Japan Commercial Gazette,* October 30, 1962.
3. For a useful overview of the industrial policy debates, see "The Industrial Policy Debate" by the U.S. Congressional Budget Office, December 1983.
4. From the *Wall Street Journal,* July 29, 1983, quoting Michel Alpert, an economist who authored a controversial, pessimistic report to the European parliament.

2. TRANSFORMATION

Note: The quotations and contents of this chapter are based on interviews with managers and workers at the Ford Motor Company over a four-month period during the latter half of 1983.
1. Henry Ford with Samuel Crowther, *My Life and Work* (New York: Doubleday, 1922), p. 83.
2. Proceedings of Business-Higher Education Forum, Dearborn, Michigan, June 23–25, 1983.
3. "Detroit's Merry-Go-Round," *Business Week,* September 12, 1983.
4. "Make or Break," *Forbes,* April 25, 1983.

3. HIGH-TECH TOOLS

1. "World Market Forecasts," *Electronics,* January 13, 1982.

2. "New From Silicon Valley: The Winchester Drive," *New York Times,* January 10, 1982.

3. Daniel Yankelovich and John Immerwahr, *Putting the Work Ethic to Work: A Public Agenda Report on Restoring America's Competitive Vitality* (New York: The Public Agenda Foundation, August 5, 1983).

4. John Bowles, "The Search for a New Engine of Growth," *Public Policy Analysis Report,* Washington, D.C., 1983.

5. Professor James Utterback, personal interview with the authors, Cambridge, Massachusetts, August 1983.

6. "The 'New' Capital Spending Cycle," *Morgan Stanley Economic Research,* July 13, 1983.

7. Richard Nolan, David Norton, et al., Nolan, Norton & Company, Lexington, Massachusetts. Figures taken from seminar presentations "Recharting DP: An Executive Perspective," May 1983.

8. Peter Drucker, "Demographics and American Economic Policy," in *Toward a New U.S. Industrial Policy* (Philadelphia: University of Pennsylvania Press, 1983).

9. Public Policy Analysis Service Fall Poll, as reported in Bowles, "The Search for a New Engine of Growth," op. cit.

10. "Inn and Out," *Harper's,* August 1983, p. 25.

11. "An Assessment of U.S. Competitiveness in High Technology Industries," *U.S. Department of Commerce,* Washington, D.C., February 1983.

4. A "MILD" REVOLUTION

Note: The quotations and contents of this chapter are based on interviews with management and workers at the Emhart Corporation during the latter half of 1983.

5. SYSTEMS, SYSTEMS, SYSTEMS

Note: The quotations and contents of this chapter are based on interviews with management and workers at the Ætna Life and Casualty Company during the latter half of 1983.

1. Wassily Leontief and Faye Duchin, "The Impacts of Automation on Employment, 1963–2000" (New York University: Institute for Economic Analysis, September 1983).

2. Bob Kuttner, "The Declining Middle," *The Atlantic,* July 1983.

6. JOBS: MORE OR LESS?

1. Yankelovich and Immerwahr, op. cit.

2. Henry M. Levin and Russell W. Rumberger, "The Education Implications of High Technology," manuscript (Stanford, Calif.: Stanford University, Institute for Research on Educational Finance and Governance, School of Education, February 1983).

3. Ronald E. Kutscher, remarks before a Labor Market Information Conference in Atlanta, Georgia, in June 1983, as reprinted in the *Monthly Labor Review,* November 1983.

4. "World Market Forecasts," *Electronics,* September 22, 1983.

5. The details, as reported in Juan Rada, "International Division of Labour and Technology," manuscript (September 1983), are as follows: 1970 (manual) Hong Kong cost is 0.0248 vs U.S. cost of 0.0753; 1980 (semiautomated) Hong Kong cost is 0.0183 vs U.S. cost of 0.0293; 1984 (automated) Hong Kong cost is 0.0163 vs U.S. cost of 0.0178.

6. Leontief and Duchin, op. cit.

7. "Robotics Extends a Helping Hand," *Iron Age,* March 19, 1982, p. 59.

8. H. Allan Hunt and Timothy L. Hunt, *Human Resource Implications of Robotics* (Kalamazoo, Michigan: Upjohn Institute for Employment Research, 1983).

9. Leontief and Duchin, op. cit.

7. JOBS: BETTER OR WORSE?

1. "High Tech Is No Panacea," *New York Times,* September 18, 1983.

2. Ellen Cassedy and Karen Nussbaum, *9 to 5* (New York: Penguin Books, 1983), p. 95.

3. Bob Kuttner, "The Declining Middle," *The Atlantic,* July 1983.

4. *Wall Street Journal,* May 6, 1983.

5. Leontief and Duchin, op. cit.

6. Dr. Louis Robinson, in a speech, "Technology Trends: Their Challenge to University-Industry Relations," to the NCHEMS National Assembly, Denver, Colorado, 1983.

7. *Ms,* January 1981, p. 56.

8. Reported by the International Ladies Garment Workers Union.

9. Jeremy Main, "Work Won't Be the Same Again (The Case of AT&T)," *Fortune,* June 28, 1982.

10. Presention by Thomas H. Johnson, director of research, Nolan, Norton & Company, Citibank Seminar, Manila, March 1983.

11. Quoted in H. H. Rosenbrock, "Automation and Society," speech to systems theorists, MIT, October 1982.

12. Ibid.

8. TEXTILES TO MICROS

1. "National Strategy Needed for U.S. Success," *Mass High Tech,* August 1–14, 1983, p. 2.

2. Lynn E. Browne, "High Technology and Business Success," *New England Economic Review,* July/August 1983, p. 5.

3. "Bio-Park for Worcester," *Mass High Tech,* April 25, 1983.

4. "High School Graduates: Projections for the Fifty States," Western Interstate Commission for Higher Education, Boulder, Colorado, 1979.

5. Elizabeth Useem, "Education in a High Technology World: The Route 128 Case," manuscript, June 1982.

9. A NEW HEARTLAND?

1. *INC,* October 1983, p. 140.

2. *Handbook of Labor Statistics,* Bulletin 2070, Table 107 (Washington, D.C.: U.S. Department of Labor, December 1980).

10. A HUNDRED-YEAR LEGACY

Note: Material quoted in this chapter is from interviews with named individuals and from published sources in the *Clarion-Ledger* or the governor's office.

11. TAKING STOCK

1. Robert Ronstadt and Robert J. Kramer, "Getting the Most Out of Innovation," *Harvard Business Review,* March-April 1982.

2. Elting Morison, "Gunfire at Sea: A Case Study in Innovation," in *Readings in the Management of Innovation,* Michael Tushman and William L. Moore, eds. (Boston: Pitman, 1982).

3. See for example, James Utterback, "The Dynamics of Innovation

in Industry," *Technological Innovation for a Dynamic Economy,* Christopher T. Hill and James M. Utterback, eds. (New York and Oxford: Pergamon Press, 1979), published in cooperation with the Center for Policy Alternatives, MIT. Utterback says: "What is a major product innovation for one firm may alter the production possibilities of other firms."

4. Cited in "The New Management Thinkers," *California Management Review,* Fall 1983.

5. *Congressional Quarterly,* August 20, 1983, p. 1685.

6. Morison, op. cit.

7. "Management Principles," management briefing to Analog Devices, Inc., September 13, 1977.

8. Yankelovich and Immerwahr, op. cit.

9. The source for this is Dataquest Inc., Cupertino, California.

10. Alan Wolf, "The Effect of Government Targeting on World Semiconductor Competition," Public Policies and Strategies for U.S. High Technology Industry, proceedings of the SIA Long-Range Planning Conference, Semiconductor Industry Association, in Monterey, California, November 22, 1982.

12. COMPETING IN CREATIVITY

Note: Unless otherwise noted, quoted sources or facts are from interviews by the authors with individuals in Japan and from sources supplied by these individuals.

1. "Technology Policy Seeks Creativity," *The Vision of MITI Policies in the 1980s* (Tokyo, March 1980), p. 153.

2. Quotes by Masaki Nakajima in "The Roots of High Productivity in Japan," reprint of address at Pepperdine University, California, October 6, 1981.

3. Sumitomo Company annual report #82.

4. Participating companies in ICOT are Fujitsu, Hitachi, NEC Corporation, Mitsubishi, Matsushita, Oki Electric, Sharp, and Toshiba.

5. Edward A. Feigenbaum and Pamela McCorduck, *The Fifth Generation* (Reading, Mass.: Addison-Wesley Publishing Company, 1983), p. 102.

6. Personal interviews with the authors.

7. Christopher T. Hill, "Technological Innovation: Agent of Growth and Change," in Hill and Utterback, op. cit.

8. Burton H. Klein, "The Slowdown in Productivity Advances: A Dynamic Explanation," in Hill and Utterback, op. cit.

9. Gene Gregory, "Japan: New Center of Innovation," in *Speaking of Japan,* Keizai Koho Center, Japan Institute for Social and Economic Affairs, Tokyo, Japan, June 1982.

10. "Japan Calls for Creative Thinkers," *The Economist,* August 6, 1983.

11. Christopher Freeman, John Clark, and Luc Soete, *Unemployment and Technical Innovation* (Westport, Conn.: Greenwood Press, 1982), p. 187.

13. ASIA BOOM

1. Jang Won Suh, *Policy Issues for the Electronics Industry in Korea,* Korea Institute for Industrial Economics and Technology, 1982.

2. *Korea Times,* April 2, 1983.

3. "Seoul's High Tech Dash," *Far Eastern Economic Review,* April 24, 1983.

14. EDUCATION STAKES

1. U.S. Steel does not specifically back any of the new technology projects. However, as pointed out by President Cyert, they pledged $2 million to the CMU fund drive that started in 1976.

2. Leontief and Duchin, op. cit.

3. "The State of Engineering Education," *Journal of Metals,* February 1983.

4. Testimony before the Committee on Labor and Human Resources, Washington, D.C., April 18, 1983.

5. "Survey Pegs Faculty Shortage at 10 Percent," *Engineering Education News,* January 1982.

6. Levin and Rumberger, "The Education Implications of High Technology," op. cit.

7. As reported in *The Chronicle for Higher Education,* November 25, 1981.

8. Special report of the U.S. Scientific Advisory Board Ad Hoc Committee on Scientific and Engineering Shortfalls within the Air Force, October 1979.

9. Ernest A. Lynton, "The Missing Connection between Business and the Universities," manuscript, July 1983, to be published by the American Council on Education and the Macmillan Publishing Company. For supporting evidence, Lynton cites *Projection of Education Statistics to 1990–91*, M. Frankel and D. Gerald, National Center for Education Statistics, Washington, D.C., 1982.

15. THE R&D RACE

1. *Science Indicators, 1982*, report of the National Science Board— 1983, National Science Foundation, Washington, D.C.; and updates from NSF sources contacted by the authors.

2. Olof Palme, Haruki Mori, and Shridath Ramphal,"Military Spending: The Economic and Social Consequences," *Challenge*, September– October 1982.

3. *Research and Development in Fiscal Year 1984*, United States Congress, Washington, D.C., 1983, p. 20. The remaining 10 percent is applied research.

4. Rustum Roy, testimony before the Subcommittee on Transportation, Aviation, and Materials of the Committee on Science, Technology, and Research, United States House of Representatives, Washington, D.C., May 19, 1983.

5. Ibid.

6. David Irons, "Inching toward a National Competitive Strategy," *Harvard Magazine*, November/December 1983.

7. Based on 1984 National Science Foundation budget requests.

8. The 1983 nondefense government development budget was $3.6 billion; industry development was $14.5 billion (in 1972 dollars) or $32.9 billion (in 1983 dollars). From *Science Indicators, 1982*, op. cit., and updates from NSF sources contacted by the authors.

9. H. P. Phillips, "On the Nature of Progress," *American Scientist*, vol. 133, No. 4, MIT, 1945.

10. Professor Michael Dertouzos of MIT, interview with the authors in Cambridge, Massachusetts, June 1983.

11. Dr. George N. Hatsopoulos, "High Cost of Capital: Handicap of American Industry," sponsored by the American Business Conference and Thermo Electron Corporation, Waltham, Massachusetts, April 1983.

12. "A 1983 AEA Membership Survey on International Competitiveness," conducted for the American Electronics Association by Bain

& Company, July 1983, and reported in the AEA Newsletter, September 14, 1983.

13. Personal interview with the authors. See also Bruce Merrifield, "Forces of Change Affecting High Technology Industries," *National Journal,* January 19, 1983.

14. *Venture Capital Journal,* July 1983, p. 9, as cited in *Technology Venturing,* The Institute for Constructive Capitalism, Austin, Texas, February 1984.

15. "International Competitiveness in Electronics," Office of Technology Assessment, Congress of the United States, Washington, D.C., November 1983, p. 270.

16. REFOCUSING THE CHALLENGE

1. Morison, "Gunfire at Sea," op. cit.

2. Joel Moses in private correspondence to the coauthors, April 24, 1984.

Index